FROM CIVILIAN POWER TO SUPERPOWER?

Also by Richard G. Whitman and from the same publishers

RETHINKING THE EUROPEAN UNION: Institutions, Interests and Identities (*edited with Alice Landau*)

From Civilian Power to Superpower?

The International Identity of the European Union

Richard G. Whitman
Lecturer in International Relations and Diplomacy
Jean Monnet Lecturer in European Union Studies
University of Westminster
London

First published in Great Britain 1998 by
MACMILLAN PRESS LTD
Houndmills, Basingstoke, Hampshire RG21 6XS and London
Companies and representatives throughout the world

A catalogue record for this book is available from the British Library.

ISBN 0–333–69477–5

First published in the United States of America 1998 by
ST. MARTIN'S PRESS, INC.,
Scholarly and Reference Division,
175 Fifth Avenue, New York, N.Y. 10010

ISBN 0–312–21030–2

Library of Congress Cataloging-in-Publication Data
Whitman, Richard.
From civilian power to superpower? : the international identity of the European Union / Richard G. Whitman.
p. cm.
Includes bibliographical references and index.
ISBN 0–312–21030–2 (cloth)
1. European Union. 2. European Union countries—Politics and government. 3. European Union countries—Foreign relations. 4. European Union countries—International status. I. Title.
KJE947.W46 1998
341.242'2—DC21 97–22740
CIP

---

10 9 8 7 6 5 4 3 2 1
07 06 05 04 03 02 01 00 99 98

Printed in Great Britain by
The Ipswich Book Company Ltd
Ipswich, Suffolk

Contents

List of Figures and Tables

FIGURES

TABLES

List of Abbreviations

ACP	African, Caribbean and Pacific states
ALA	Asia and Latin America countries
APEC	Asia-Pacific Economic Co-operation
ASEAN	Association of South-East Asian Nations
BIS	Bank of International Settlements
CAP	Common Agricultural Policy
CCP	Common Commercial Policy
CCT	Common Customs Tariff
CEDP	Common European Defence Policy
CET	Common External Tariff
CFSP	Common Foreign and Security Policy
CIS	Commonwealth of Independent States
CJTF	Combined Joint Task Forces
COMECON	Council for Mutual Economic Assistance
COREPER	Committee of the Permanent Representatives
CSCE	Conference on Security and Co-operation in Europe
DG	Directorate General
EAEC	European Atomic Energy Community
EBRD	European Bank for Reconstruction and Development
EC	European Community
ECJ	European Court of Justice
ECMM	European Community Monitoring Mission
ECSC	European Coal and Steel Community
ecu	European Currency Unit
EDC	European Defence Community
EDF	European Development Fund
EEA	European Economic Area
EEC	European Economic Community
EFTA	European Free Trade Association
EIB	European Investment Bank
EIM	European Institute for the Media
EMU	Economic and Monetary Union
EP	European Parliament
EPC	European Political Co-operation
EPU	European Payments Union
ERM	Exchange Rate Mechanism

ERP	European Recovery Programme
EU	European Union
EUR-OP	Office for Official Publications of the European Communities
FAWEU	Forces Answerable to Western European Union
FYROM	Former Yugoslav Republic of Macedonia
GATT	General Agreement on Tariffs and Trade
GCC	Gulf Co-operation Council
GDP	Gross Domestic Product
GDR	German Democratic Republic
IBRD	International Bank for Reconstruction and Development
IGC	Inter-governmental Conference
IGO	Inter-governmental Organisation
IMF	International Monetary Fund
IO	International organisation
JHA	Justice and Home Affairs
JPC	Joint Parliamentary Committees
LTA	Long Term Arrangement
MEP	Member of the European Parliament
MFA	Multi-Fibre Arrangement
MFN	Most-Favoured Nation
NAFTA	North American Free Trade Agreement
NATO	North Atlantic Treaty Organisation
NGO	Non-Governmental Organisation
NPT	Non-Proliferation Treaty
NTB	Non-Tariff Barriers
OAPEC	Organisation of Arab Petroleum Exporting Countries
OECD	Organisation for Economic Co-operation and Development
OEEC	Organisation for European Economic Co-operation
OSCE	Organisation for Security and Co-operation in Europe
OMA	Orderly Marketing Arrangements
PHARE	Poland and Hungary Assistance for Economic Restructuring programme
QMV	Qualified Majority Voting
SEA	Single European Act
TACIS	Technical Assistance for the CIS
TEC	Treaties establishing the European Communities
TEU	Treaty on European Union
VER	Voluntary Export Restraints
WEAG	Western European Armaments Group
WEU	Western European Union
WTO	World Trade Organisation

Acknowledgements

Sincere thanks are due in a number of directions for support and assistance during the writing of this text. Professor Margaret Blunden has provided the combination of intellectual insight, incisive criticism and chivvying that have guided both the development of this project and my own intellectual advancement. To Professor Blunden my heartfelt thanks for the certainty (to paraphrase T.S. Eliot) that 'my time future will always be contained in this time past'.

I also have a debt of thanks to offer to the staff of a number of libraries and institutions for their assistance in the accumulation of material for this study. The staff of the library of the University of Westminster at Riding House Street have faithfully processed my long lists of inter-library loan requests in a timely and efficient manner; similar service has been forthcoming from the libraries of the Royal Institute of International Affairs, the Offices of the European Commission in London, the London School of Economics and the British Library. The European Institute of Public Administration in Maastricht rendered considerable assistance during my stay and greatly assisted in gaining access to staff at the European Commission, Council of Ministers, and Permanent Representations of the Member States, who all gave generously of their time.

To no small degree my thanks must be extended to the trustees of the Quintin Hogg Scholarships and numerous other colleagues and friends at the University of Westminster. Finally, but foremost, my thanks to LKO for everything, and more.

1 Defining International Identity

> The Union shall set itself the following objectives ... to assert its identity on the international scene, in particular through the implementation of a common foreign and security policy including the eventual framing of a common defence policy, which might in time lead to a common defence.[1]

To Europe, a child was born on 1 November 1993: the European Union (EU). The Treaty on European Union had been subject to an arduous process of ratification that had taken in excess of twenty months to complete from the signing of the Treaty on European Union (TEU) on 7 February 1992 to the rejection of a legal challenge to the Treaty by the German Federal Constitutional Court in Karlsruhe on 12 October 1993. With the despatch of the German instrument of ratification to the archives of the Italian Republic in Rome on the same day, the ratification requirements of the Treaty were complete and, in accordance with the provisions of the Treaty, the birth date of the Union was set.[2]

The establishment of a European Union was not the herald of a transmogrification of the European Community; the elements contained within the Treaty had long been a part of the discourse on the future direction of the Community.[3] The European Community, and now the European Union, are *sui generis*. Indeterminacy as to what constitutes the final project for this entity have been apparent since the signing of the Treaty of Rome and remain unresolved under the TEU.[4] The goal articulated in the respective Treaties remains the same 'ever closer union'. The TEU does represent a departure by establishing an entity called 'a European Union', and a framework is created in the Treaty that is intended to give expression to this 'new stage in the process of creating an ever closer union'.[5]

Competing visions of the future direction that an ever closer union should take continue to rage. In the debate conducted in the United Kingdom, this spans a spectrum from whether the Union has reached its limits (and should be subject to roll-back), or whether a variant of federalism *in extenso* should be initiated.[6] However, speculation on the future of the EU is not the focus of this text. The substance of this study has a much more specific focus and is an attempt to engage in a systematic examination of one facet of the activities of the EU that are currently in existence. The assertion is that a new, distinctive and significant actor has entered the international system. The text will approach this through the examination of three inter-related assertions that both delineate the substance of the study and provide the methodology for their exploration.

Firstly, the operations of the European Union that are explicitly directed outwards from the Union can be characterised as the 'international identity' of the Union. The international identity is conceived both in terms of those instruments that are available to the Union to give expression to policy and furthermore how elements of the Union that define its *sui generis* nature also contribute distinctive facets to its international identity.

Secondly, the use of the notion of the international identity of the Union requires the development of a framework to facilitate analysis. A framework can be offered, drawing upon the literature of International Relations (IR), that provides a method for a unified consideration of all facets of the external policy of the Union. Throughout this book International Relations (IR) refers to the academic study of the phenomenon of international relations that it seeks to explain and interpret.

Thirdly, a consideration of the process by which this international identity is both constructed and represented requires an assessment of the nature of that process and the identification of sources of influence that impact upon the process.

DEFINING INTERNATIONAL IDENTITY

The three assertions that direct this text require further elucidation. The initial assertion is that the European Union has an identifiable and coherent international identity. The intention is to explore the nature of this international identity and the manner in which it is both constructed and represented. The use of the term 'international identity' requires clarification. There has been a convention, within the literature on the European Community (EC), of maintaining a distinction between the Community's external competencies as governed by the founding treaties, in contrast to European Political Co-operation – now superseded by the Common Foreign and Security Policy (CFSP) conducted among the then Twelve on an inter-governmental basis.

The external competencies of the European Community, are regulated by the Treaty of Paris and the two Treaties of Rome that are the legal foundations, respectively, of the European Coal and Steel Community (ECSC), the European Atomic Energy Community (EAEC) and the

European Economic Community (EEC).[7] The treaties demarcate areas of external competence for the Communities, for example a Common Commercial Policy (CCP), to which Member States subscribe with their accession to the Community. In these areas of competence powers are formally granted by the Member States to be exercised on their behalf by the institutions and instruments of the Community as laid down in the treaties.

The other dimension of the external relations of the Community are those that are usually designated as inter-governmental. The separation is on the grounds that this aspect of external relations stands outside the treaty-based relationship of the institutions. European Political Co-operation (EPC) has been designated in these inter-governmental terms by successive commentators upon the process. The assertion to be pursued is that with the foundation of the Union and with the identification of the instruments available to the Union this is a designation that provides only a limited insight.

The successor to EPC, that is initiated with the Treaty on European Union, is the CFSP, introduced by Title V, Article J of the Treaty on European Union, and operates alongside the external competencies of the EC and signifies a commitment by the Member States of the European Union to harmonise their foreign policies. Despite clearly identifiable differences between these two processes, which will be explored in Chapters 2 and 3, both are specifically directed outwards from the Union. The contention of this text is that separate consideration of these two processes, both empirically and conceptually, is at the cost of neglecting study of the factors that are common to both sets of policies and has led to neglect of conceptual frameworks that may accommodate both sets of processes.

There is an additional benefit in conceiving external relations and CFSP together. With the ratification of the Maastricht Treaty and the establishment of a three-pillar structure of the European Union there is now a single institutional framework that warrants study in totality. In the structure adopted to give expression to the European Union there is a departure from the manner in which the Community has organised itself previously.

The convening by the Member States of two inter-governmental conferences (IGCs), one on economic and monetary union, the other on political union, that were formally opened in Rome on 14 December 1990, started the negotiations for what was to become the Treaty on European Union. The structure for this Union surfaced in the *Draft Treaties Articles with a View to Achieving Political Union* issued by the Luxembourg Presidency on 20 June 1991.[8] The proposal eventually adopted was for two 'pillars' dealing with EPC and Justice and Home Affairs to be distinguished from that of the Community. Matters dealt with in the areas of EPC and Justice and Home Affairs were not to be a part of the Community legal system and the institutions of the Community were to enjoy different roles within the latter two pillars from those ascribed under the Treaty of Paris and Two Treaties of Rome. The three pillars, consisting of the Communities pillar, the Common Foreign and Security Policy pillar and the pillar for Co-operation in the Fields of Justice and Home Affairs (JHA), were adopted as the foundations for the Union, characterised in debates as a 'Greek temple' structure.[9] The three pillars are not accorded the same standing in the Treaty on European Union. The Communities pillar retains its primacy, as the Treaty states: 'The Union shall be founded on the European Communities, *supplemented by* [author's emphasis] the policies and forms of cooperation established by this Treaty...'.[10] Perhaps a more accurate pictograph of the European Union is a house in which the foundations have been laid (the European Communities) and for which a roof has been raised by means of supports (CFSP and JHA) with uncertainty as to their durability in their current form.

The intention in the Treaty on European Union is for the Union to be served by a single institutional framework and this is made explicit in the Common Provisions of the Treaty: 'The Union shall be served by a single institutional framework which shall ensure the consistency and the continuity of the activities carried out in order to attain its objectives while respecting and building upon the *acquis communautaire*.'[11]

The European Union has encompassed both the treaty-based external relations within its first pillar and EPC serving as the second pillar – albeit now extended and reincarnated as the Common Foreign and Security Policy. The subsumption of both facets of the policy that are explicitly directed towards the outside of the Union, accompanied by the commitment to a single institutional structure, gives us an identifiable entity worthy of attention. Furthermore, the objective that the European Union sets itself, 'to assert its identity on the international scene', requires a consideration of the instruments available to give effect to this aspiration.[12] This text intends to examine those instruments available to the Union for this purpose. It is important to note at this stage the distinction between a common instrument or policy from a single instrument or policy.

In the first proposition of this study, that the European Union has an identifiable and coherent international identity, an attempt is made to identify and characterise the international identity of the European Union at its inception. The notion of international identity is not intended as a synonym for 'foreign policy' or 'external relations' that, as has been mentioned above, have had currency in the literature on the European Community.[13]

The argument put forward in Chapters 2 and 3 is in empirical and conceptual terms the EU is to be considered *sui generis* and its engagement with the world beyond itself sufficient to constitute a distinctive label and framework for analysis.

ANALYSING THE INTERNATIONAL IDENTITY

The theoretical literature upon the international identity of the European Union reveals two main tendencies. Firstly, that the EU has been considered within the literature of IR against existing preconceived concepts of what constitute the significant actors for an understanding of International Relations. Secondly, there has been the construction of some new conceptual categorisations to fit the case of the EU and an attempt to measure the actor capability of the EU.[14] Both of these dimensions within the literature have given consideration to whether the EU is significant in the international arena.

The establishment of the European Union in the after-glow of the Cold War, and speculation as to the form and content of the post-Cold War international system, mark a confluence in which the question of the significant actors in contemporary international relations is urgent and will be explored in Chapter 4. Alongside this, the uncertainty as to the final form in which the Union will be manifest, and the context within which it is now operating, lends itself to different interpretations of the significance of the international role of the Union.

One possible response to this state of flux is a preference for empirical over theory applied study.[15] The safe harbour of case study offers a tranquil resting place away from the shifting currents of theory (that have recently been whipped up into a raging storm by post-modern and post-structuralist discourses). The literature is on the international role of the Union which explicitly considers that theory reveals a promiscuity in the use of methodology, epistemology and ontology.[16] In short, there is no commonly agreed theoretical perspective within which to consider the international role of the Union.

The *mainstream* of the contemporary literature within IR can be accommodated within three perspectives on international relations; 'Realism', 'Pluralism' and 'Structuralism'.[17] It is fully acknowledged that such a division is contested and may do violence to the complexities of the literature.[18] However, these are the terms within which the debate on the international role of the EU has been conducted to date.[19]

The three perspectives on international relations all stress different actors, processes and outcomes. In brief, the primary actor in international relations from the Realist perspective is 'the state', acting as a unified entity in pursuing a unified national interest in an anarchical international system characterised by competition and conflict. In the Pluralist perspective, the state operates alongside a variety of other actors. The state is not viewed as a unified entity but rather penetrated by a variety of other actors and unable to exercise exclusive control of its territory or external relationships. The Structuralist perspective takes the dominant international actors to be economic classes and their representatives. The process of international relations is characterised by exploitation and dependency with the nature of the world system expressed as a struggle between a 'centre' of developed capitalism and an underdeveloped 'periphery' – a relationship both within as well as across states.

The question that has prevailed is, whether there is sufficient explanatory potential within each (or any) of these three perspectives to help account for the international role of the EU, and, whether it is considered to be significant in international terms. Realist writers, with their emphasis on the nation states as the significant international actors, naturally downplay the role of the EU in international relations.[20] The thrust of such a position is that Western Europe cannot consider itself to be a 'power' in the international system unless it creates a defence identity free from reliance upon the military resources of the United States. However, even if a 'supranational' defence identity were created in Western Europe, this would be viewed as a source of weakness in defence policy rather than of strength; the nation states of Western Europe are seen as irreplaceable foci of loyalty and units for making war and thereby the real sources of power.[21]

The Realists' denial that the EU constitutes a consequential actor in the international system, since it lacks the means to project aggregated power (defined in strictly military terms), reveals a neglect of economic factors – especially where there is an apparent disaggregation between economic and military power.

The significant problem about using a Realist perspective to assess the international significance of the EU is that it defines actor capabilities and actorness in a particular fashion. To be considered as an actor of theoretical and empirical significance from the Realist perspective the EU has to adopt a particular set of characteristics or be denied international significance. The Realist conception of the state has undergone a considerable critique through a wider debate on definitions of the state.[22] This study argues that it is inadequate to the international significance of the

EU because it does not conform to one particular definition of 'actorness', that is defined as an exclusive ability by the Union to conduct foreign policy by the replacement of the foreign policies of the Member States.[23] By marginalising the form of the contemporary international presence that exists for the Union and by neglecting to conceptualise its contemporary role, in favour of judging its conformity to an ideal-type, an aspect of contemporary international relations is neglected.

International order in the Pluralist perspective does not derive directly from the balance of power between states but rather from accepted values and norms and forms of international governance that may, or may not, be reposed in institutions. The relevance of the Pluralist perspective for the study of the EU is two-fold. Firstly, its acceptance of the existence of international actors other than the state makes it possible to accommodate the European Union within the perspective. Secondly, the suggestion that there are other sources of order than the balance of power raises the possibility of a role for the Union in international governance. The questions of the form of the Union as actor and the international role of the Union are therefore opened up.

Three concepts as used within the Pluralist perspective are of particular importance in their application to the EU: interdependence, transnationalism and integration. Integration forms one of the sources of influence upon the international identity of the Union and will be explored in Chapter 6. 'Interdependence most simply defined means mutual dependence. Interdependence in world politics refers to situations characterised by reciprocal effects among countries or among actors in different countries.'[24] Furthermore, it challenges the Realist distinction between the domestic and the international on the grounds that 'the domestic power of the state can be sustained only through international economic co-operation and political accommodation'.[25]

'Transnationalism' is the assertion that there are actors *in addition to* states that play a central role in international affairs. International organisations may be seen as significant since they may encourage perceptions or interests among national governmental officials that may conflict with national interests. These concepts have been fruitfully applied to the EU; firstly, with regard to the dilution of the distinction between domestic and international politics:

> The EC's major policy responsibilities in the commercial, agricultural, and labour-related sectors traditionally used to be a part of a state's domestic concerns. Although the peculiarities of the Community's institutional mechanisms and the sheer depth and intensity of policy activity in

> these areas throw up new patterns which render traditional distinctions between foreign and domestic policies particularly inappropriate.[26]

The erosion of the distinction between the domestic and the international in particular policy areas in the European Union can be considered to be a manifestation of 'trans-governmental policy networks' and this phenomena is explored in Chapters 2 and 3.[27] However, we also have to distinguish between intra- and extra-EU phenomena. Transgovernmental policy networks concern an intra-EU policy-making process. The outcome of the policy-making process is a question of implementation into an extra-EU context. The distinction drawn between these two contexts rests upon the use of a systems methodology that is outlined in the last part of this chapter.

Pluralist/Liberalist perspectives appear to offer a variety of avenues for analysis, among them the intra-EU arrangements. However, the very plurality contained within the perspective, although acting as a useful counterweight to the rigidity of categorisation promulgated by Realists and to Realism's conflictual view of international relations, can merely describe phenomena rather than provide explanations of the way that units act.[28] In the context of defining the EU there can be a temptation to hide behind the *sui generis* nature of the entity at the cost of not exploring potential similarities and the effectiveness of the Union with other actors in the international system.

The Pluralist perspective also downplays two important areas with respect to the EU. Firstly, in so far as a clear hierarchy of issues exists and is *perceived* to exist within Union structures and decision-making, the distinction between high/low politics is still an important concern for Member States as the three-pillar structure of the EU initiated by the Maastricht Treaty illustrates. Secondly, Pluralism creates the expectation of the uniform coverage of phenomena. However the EU demonstrates a disjuncture between the logic of inter-dependence and transnationalism and Member State behaviour.

Realism came under attack, most notably by Pluralists, for its inability to incorporate transnational and transgovernmental actors in their explanation of the international system. Pluralists were contending that there could also be forces transforming the essence of the international system apart from the balance-of-power formulation of the Realists. Realists were deemed unable to comprehend or accommodate the growing complexity and increasing interdependence of the global economy. The Realist response was two-fold: firstly, to refine a systemic account of international relations – as exemplified by the work of Kenneth Waltz; and secondly, to attempt to modify Realism to accommodate international economic issues.[29]

'Neo-realism' can be seen as a part of a 'general lament/nostalgia' for a perceived decline in the status of the United States from a position as an economic 'hegemon' in the international system.[30] Advocates of 'Hegemonic Stability Theory' equated US dominance with international stability.[31] A relationship was suggested between hegemonic stability and the development of international 'regimes'. In an international system characterised by a hegemonic structure, international regimes will develop, and their rules, norms, principles and decision-making procedures will be relatively precise and obeyed.

The debate on hegemonic decline and the recognition of the emergence of international regimes marks the frontiers of dispute between neo-realists and neo-liberals. The area of dispute is how central regimes have come to be significant in international politics. For this reason attempts to define a regime encompass two perspectives on international relations which are problematic. States are still viewed as serving their own interest in seeking to maximise their power or minimise potential loss vis-à-vis other states but the dispute is around relative or absolute gains. As has been noted by Keohane, we are talking about co-operation, *not* harmonisation.[32] Cox has noted that international regime theory seeks to explain how co-operation is achieved and sustained without necessarily tying its existence to international organisations.[33] Regime theory within the Pluralist perspective has now been subsumed, alongside the study of international organisations and conventions, into approaches dubbed variously, neo-liberal institutionalism, new institutionalism or rational institutionalism.[34] Adherents of the latter perspective attest that elements of the literature have 'demonstrated that co-operation is possible even on realist premises', and the claim is also made that it represents a synthesis of realist and pluralist perspectives at the systemic level-of-analysis. [35]

The EU has thus attracted attention as an example of an international regime and more recently as the most significant test of theoretical virility in the on-going inter-paradigm between neo-realists and neo-liberals.[36] Hoffmann in the early 1980s, drawing upon the work of Krasner, stated that regimes are most likely to be established in areas where joint action is anticipated to produce better results than uncoordinated individual actions.[37]

> The experience of the EC confirms this. Its establishment resulted from the conviction of the members that purely national action in a variety of economic domains was no longer satisfactory, and that a number of

> major non-economic goals could best be served by setting up a collective regime.[38]

The EU, designated as a regime in this formulation, has not served to anticipate a 'European super-state', but rather to preserve, regenerate and adapt its constituent nation states. More recently, with the new insight offered by neo-liberal institutionalism, Keohane and Hoffmann have turned their attention to the EU and retained the analytical primacy of the nation state. The EU is viewed as an experiment in the pooling of sovereignty rather than the repository of its transference.[39]

The focus of this study is to give analytical primacy to the EU and not to its Member States. However, this does not diminish the utility of regime theory but rather suggests a manner in which we can conceptualise the relations that the EU conducts with other international actors. The network of multilateral and bilateral agreements that the EU has created, which have not displaced the bilateral diplomacy of the Member States, can be conceived as manifestations of international regimes and this can be seen as the chief characteristic of the integrative diplomacy of the Union.

Realism and Pluralism/Liberalism both share a common concern with actors and not structures of power. In contrast, in the Structuralist perspective – and this illustrates an overlap with the structuralist thinking of Waltz – structures and not actors are accorded primacy.

The Structuralist or neo-Marxist[40] perspectives have been a less popular means of conceptualising international relations.[41] The 'Structuralist' approach maintains the state conceived in economic terms, as central to its analysis, but in the sense of its role as representing economic interests. However, the centrality of the state is conditional upon the state servicing the interests of a dominant class. The relationship between states in the system is conceived in terms of the structure of a capitalist world economy.

More recently, the introduction of critical theory, associated with the Frankfurt School, has reinforced the notion that structures of power rather than actors are central to analysis and this represents the possibility for re-orientating the study of international relations.[42] Its impact upon the study of the EU is, as yet, undetermined.

The world systems perspective of Structuralism has been applied in relation to an examination of the EU.[43] The assertion is that the EU has engaged in an attempt to displace the United States from the primary core status within the capitalist system. The proposition is that to facilitate this goal the EU has engaged in a variety of activities. For example, by attempting to create favourable conditions for inward investment, promoting the development of European multinationals, creating a new monetary regime with the EMS and engaging in the Single Market project. The relationship between the EU and 70 African, Caribbean and Pacific (ACP) states regulated by the Lomé Convention has been offered as empirical evidence in support of the Structuralist perspective.[44]

World systems theory may have much to tell us about the permanence of Europe's economic relationship with some parts of the world. The role of the EU as a part of a centre–periphery relationship underpinned the analysis of Johan Galtung's attempt to see the EU as a 'superpower in the making' in a global perspective and part of an attempt to create a Eurocentric world, a world with its centre in Europe to which we return in our coverage of new conceptual categorisations on the EU.[45]

The above-mentioned perspectives within the discipline of IR remain distinct and offer, in turn, three separate views of the EU within three differing notions of what constitutes international relations. As has been suggested, each of the three perspectives either fails to concede an international role to the Union or else lacks the explanatory range to account for the activities of the entity in its entirety.

A debate on how to categorise the EU, in terms of its international significance, was conducted from the early 1970s by attempting to construct a new conceptual category. The debate focused around the issue of whether the EC was a 'civilian power' or a putative 'superpower'. A focus upon the EC as the manifestation of an integration processes emerged much earlier, and such theories will occupy us in Chapter 6 of this study. Suffice it to say at this stage that integration theories increasingly lost their currency from the mid-1960s and have regained adherents in the aftermath of the Single European Act.

François Duchêne's notion of a 'civilian power Europe' has resonated through the debate on the international identity of the EC.[46] Duchêne's concept of civilian power Europe is most striking for the unsystematic manner in which it was advanced. The contention was that maintaining a nuclear and superpower stalemate in Europe would devalue military power and give scope to 'civilian forms of influence and action':

> Europe would be the first major area of the Old World where the age-old processes of war and indirect violence could be translated into something more in tune with the twentieth-century citizen's notion of civilised politics. In such a context, Western Europe could in a sense be one of the world's civilian centres of power.[47]

Duchêne's conception of a civilian power Europe rested upon the inconceivability of a nuclear armed European federation and the banishment of war from Western Europe.

> The European Community's interest as a civilian group of countries long on economic power and relatively short on armed force is as far as possible to *domesticate* relations between states, including those of its own members and those with states outside its frontiers. This means trying to bring to international problems the sense of common responsibility and structures of contractual politics which have been in the past associated almost exclusively with 'home' and not foreign, that is *alien*, affairs.[48]

The changed European context post-Cold War and the tentative exploration of questions of defence (outlined in Chapter 4) within and around the EU framework would appear to render the civilian power hypothesis obsolete. However, it offers contemporary insights. Firstly, the wider European context within which the Union operates is crucial for understanding its own significance (a factor explored in Chapter 4). Secondly, the Union's pursuit of a distinctive integrative diplomacy would appear to be imbued with these ideas and is explored throughout this text. In short, there is the impact of a set of normative values on the international identity that the Union projects.

A view of the EU, contemporary to that held by Duchêne's, was Johan Galtung's assertion that the European Community was a superpower in the making. The EC was characterised as a *Pax Bruxellana*, an attempt to create a Eurocentric world with its centre in Europe and a unicentric Europe with its centre in the Western half of the continent.[49] The power of the emerging superpower is categorised as two-fold: resource power and structural power. The resource power of the Union is relative to that of the other superpowers then in existence, and structural power is considered to be the international structures which the EU is promoting and that will serve as instruments of structural power. Without accepting the premises of Galtung's argument, that the EU is a neo-imperial entity, it is possible to utilise two elements to explore the international significance of the Union. The Cold War context in which these latter approaches were articulated is no longer in existence, and the relevance of the notion of superpower, as then conventionally understood, is no longer useful. However, a comparison of the resource power available to the significant powers in the contemporary international system, compared to the resource power at the disposal of the EU would be one measure through which to explore the relative international significance of the Union. This is undertaken in Chapter 4. Secondly, the contemporary environment within which the EU utilises its instruments, also the focus of Chapter 4, illustrates both the influence of the Union and the external sources that, in turn, impact upon the Union.

Gunnar Sjöstedt had an original approach to the question of the EC as an international actor.[50] Instead of attempting to align the EC with an existing international actor category, Sjöstedt constructs a criteria of actor capability as a means of assessing whether or not the EC can be assessed as possessing actor capability. The properties that are identified as necessary for actor capability are seven-fold; a community of interests; a decision-making system; a system for crisis management; a system for the management of independence; a system of implementation; external communication channels and external representation; community resources and mobilisation system. The Union has developed elements of this typology, as will be illustrated throughout the text. However, the objection to the use of this framework is that it posits the prerequisites for actor capability without addressing the significant sources of influence that assist in giving an account of why the actor conforms to particular behaviour. In short, it ignores the environment within which the actor operates and through which it seeks to implement its policies.

A NEW METHODOLOGY

The alternative proposed in this study is to treat the construction and representation of the international identity of the European Union as a problematic that is amenable to the application of systems thinking. The organisational framework here is garnered from a theme within the literature of IR as was noted in the discussion of the making of foreign policy. The process of the construction and representation of the international identity of the EU is treated as a system *analogous* to the treatment of foreign policy elsewhere within the literature.[51]

The notion of system being utilised is different from those outlined in the coverage of the Realist, Pluralist or Structuralist perspectives. It does not imply that the EU is viewed as an actor in the international system, part of a world society approach or a world system. Rather, it seeks to define the EU as a totality for the purposes of analysis and, from that basis, it seeks to explore its operation within the environment within which it sits, and from which it can be distinguished. The elements contained within the system are not exclusively ascribed to the Union and it is possible to conceive of the Member States themselves as systems both overlapping and intersecting with elements of the EU system. Alternatively, the Member States could be viewed as subsystems of the EU system.

The application of systems thinking and systems analysis has, of course, been widespread across both the sciences and the social sciences.[52] Systems thinking makes conscious use of the particular holistic concept captured in the word 'system', to order thinking.

In order to adopt a system as the organising framework for the study, the sources of influence upon the international identity and their respective relationships have to be stated in a more explicit form. More specifically, in the field of International Relations, systems approaches have proved attractive in the search for a general theory of international relations.[53] In the field of foreign policy analysis, the work of Rosenau, articulated as an attempt to offer a pre-theory as the starting point for the construction of a general theory of foreign policy-making, has been adopted as the inspiration behind frameworks used for single nation-state, case-study approaches.[54] The set of sources of influence offered by Rosenau generated the thinking that underpins the selection of sources for the study of the Union.

The treatment of the EU in this manner requires qualification. The use of a systems approach is intended to act as a heuristic device and not as an attempt to assert that the EU can be classified taxonomically with nation states. Neither should it be seen as part of the aspiration to construct a general theory of foreign policy. The contention of this study is that systems thinking, as developed for application to foreign policy, can provide an insight into the construction and representation of the international identity of the European Union.

The intention is not to posit a theory to explain or predict the formulation of the international identity of the European Union. Rather, the intention is to refine and to make explicit the assumptions that inform the empirical work within the study. This text conceptualises the EU in a particular systematic manner: the assertion here is that there is a requirement to go beyond an administrative perspective, a focus upon the formal structure of policy-making.[55] There is a requirement to attempt to identify a variety of sources or influences that impact upon the policy-making and implementation process. In practice, these sources of influence are not formal parts of the policy-making and implementation process but can be viewed as having an impact upon the formulation of the international identity.

As has been already stated, the system that is being defined is that of the international identity of the European Union. This is not an attempt to examine the Union in its totality but rather to examine the elements that contribute to the construction and representation of the identity. We need to define what constitutes the elements of this system and the environment within which it operates. What are the inputs, the outputs and the process of constructing and representing the international identity of the European Union? The outputs of the system constitute what are being designated as the instruments of the international identity of the European Union. The inputs are an attempt to designate what factors are considered to be significant in accounting for the international identity.

The factors that are designated as the sources of influence upon the construction and representation of the international identity constitute the bulk of the text. These factors are designated within the study as the operational environment that impacts upon decision-making: external sources, legal sources, Member State sources, integrative sources and parliamentary sources.

The initial concern of this chapter was to clarify in what forms the EU has been accommodated within the literature of International Relations. Consideration has been given to the manner in which the European Union has been assessed from the standpoint of whether it is of international significance. As the diagram notes (Figure 1.1), the decision-making structure is central to our understanding of the Union and forms the focus of the next two chapters, alongside the identification of the typology of instruments at the disposal of the Union to give effect to policy.

With regard to the organising framework of this study, which is the adoption of a system as an organising device, the requirement is to identify the sources of influence in the construction and representation of the international identity of the EU. These sources of influence will be dealt with as the second strand of this text. The sources of influence constitute the operational environment within which decisions on the construction and representation of the international identity of the Union are undertaken.[56] They are intended to encompass all the inputs which affect decisions and decision-taking. These inputs, or sources as they are designated in this study, compose the operational environment of the Union and break down into two types: external and internal. The external sources are detailed in Chapter 4. The internal sources are outlined in Chapters 5, 6 and 7, and are composed of legal sources; Member State sources; integrative sources; and parliamentary sources. Additionally, each of these sources of influence, together with the decision-making structure of the Union, also contribute distinctive facets to the *sui generis* presence that the Union contributes as a new and significant actor in international relations.[57]

The sources of influence that are identified all impact upon the decision-making and implementation structure through which the EU seeks to both construct and represent its international identity. The decision-making and implementation structures of the Union are identified and impact of the sources of influence are illustrated. Analysis of the decision-making

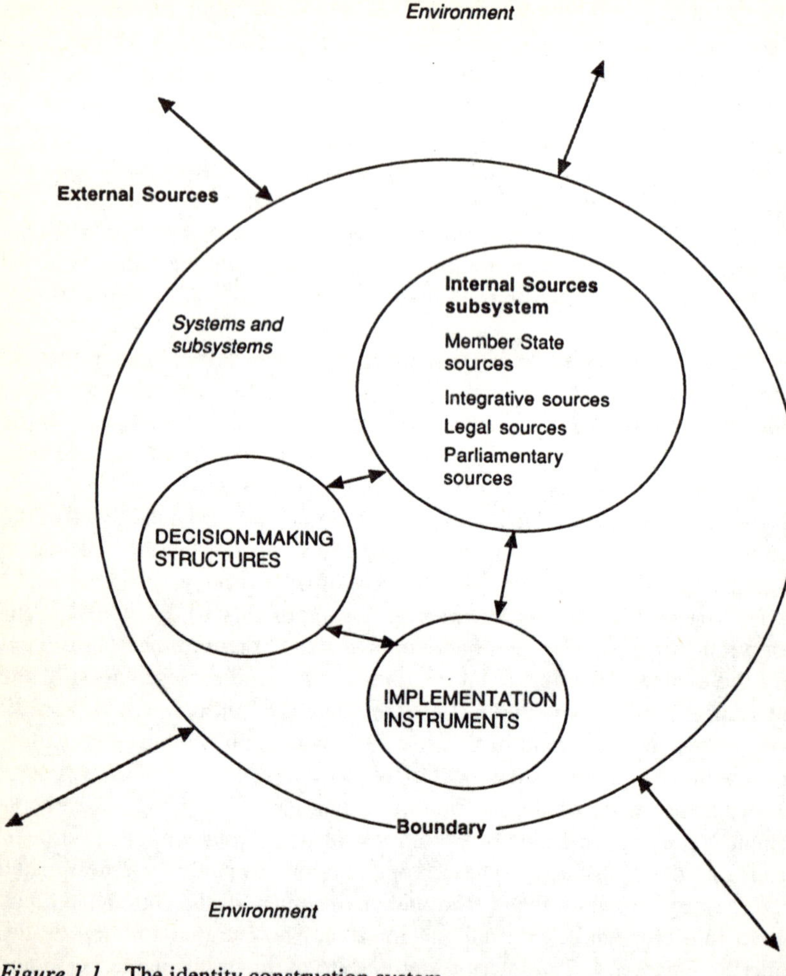

Figure 1.1 The identity construction system

structures focuses on a progressive drawing together of the decision-making structures for both the external relations of the Community and the CFSP.

With respect to the first of the sources of influence, the external sources, that impact upon the international identity of the European Union, it is necessary to clarify where the boundary is being drawn. Clearly, we are not distinguishing in terms of a domestic and an international environment.

The distinction being drawn between sources of influence is between *intra-* and *extra-*Union sources of influence. With external sources we are interested in extra-Union sources of influence, those elements that are outside the Union but are of substantial importance for accounting for the international identity of the EU.

The elements that constitute the external sources of influence upon the EU, that are apparent when we conceive of the EU in terms of the framework of a system, are conceived as follows and are illuminated by a survey of the literature. Firstly, there is the milieu which is comprised of the geographical, economic and technological status that coincide with the Fifteen and which in turn gives the Union significance and informs the areas of concern for the Union. Secondly, there are the changes in the structure of the international system which have been of particular significance to the Community, both within Europe and beyond. Thirdly, it is necessary to make clear the network of relationships that the Community has created for itself and defines its international environment.

The second of the sources of influence that have been examined are those that have been designated as legal sources. This section of the text considers both the formal system of rules under which the international identity operates and the differing legal instruments through which relations can be conducted. This has required the analysis of the requisite articles within the Treaties and the formal system of rules that have governed European Political Co-operation and now the Common Foreign and Security Policy. An examination of the requisite documents stresses the incremental extension of institutional and of instrumental competence. This work identifies what powers, in formal terms, are assigned to the respective Community institutions.

The third source of influence are the Member States. The Member States are considered as aggregated entities. As a source of the international identity the Member States are viewed as important in several areas. Firstly, there are the specific areas of foreign policy interest that their membership have placed upon the Community agenda and the consequence of each enlargement upon the international identity. Secondly, there are the areas of concern that have been retained by the Member States as unsuitable for Community consideration. Thirdly, there are the attitudes towards inter-governmentalism or integration and the impact upon the international identity.

The fourth source of influence of the international identity is integration as an informal and a formal process. The extent to which the literature on integration theory has given attention to questions of the external implications of the internal integrative process is considered. The assertion is that, without accepting the general logic of theories of integration, viewed over a historical time scale there has been an incremental development of the international identity.

With the fifth source of influence, it is asked whether the European Parliament has a distinctive role, beyond its formal competencies, contributing a dimension to the instruments available as part of the international identity of the Union.

It is important to bear in mind that these sources of influence are identified by their functions in the construction and representation of the international identity and not by their formal political or constitutional authority. This study contends that the specification of a set of sources that both impact upon, and articulate, the international identity is a systematic treatment of the Union which is both innovative and useful.

As has been made clear, the system that is being defined is that of the international identity of the European Union. It is necessary to define what constitutes the elements of this system. What are the inputs, the outputs and process of constructing and representing the international identity of the European Union? The outputs of the system constitute what is being designated as the instruments used in the implementation of the international identity of the European Union. The inputs are an attempt to designate what factors are considered to be significant in accounting for the implementation of the international identity.

Throughout the study, the instruments through which the international identity of the Community, now Union, is implemented will be identified along five inter-related parameters: informational, procedural, declaratory, transference and overt (Figure 1.2).[58] These instruments of the international identity that are being designated constitute the outputs of the decision-making system and, in turn, feed back into the decision-making process as inputs into the system.

The area of informational identity concerns the promulgation of overviews of the rationale of the Union's relationship with the world outside. The informational form of the identity designates the areas in which the Community has formally expressed a rationale for policy either in *strategic* or in *specific* terms. Examples of the strategic rationale include articles of the founding treaties (Article 110); or the declaration of the Rhodes Summit on the Europe of 1992; or the Luxembourg Report on the establishment of European Political Co-operation and now Title V of the Treaty on European Union establishing the CFSP.

Specific rationales are designed to designate the intention to establish or to re-orientate policy in a particular area. Examples of specific rationales include the Venice Declaration on the situation in the Middle East in

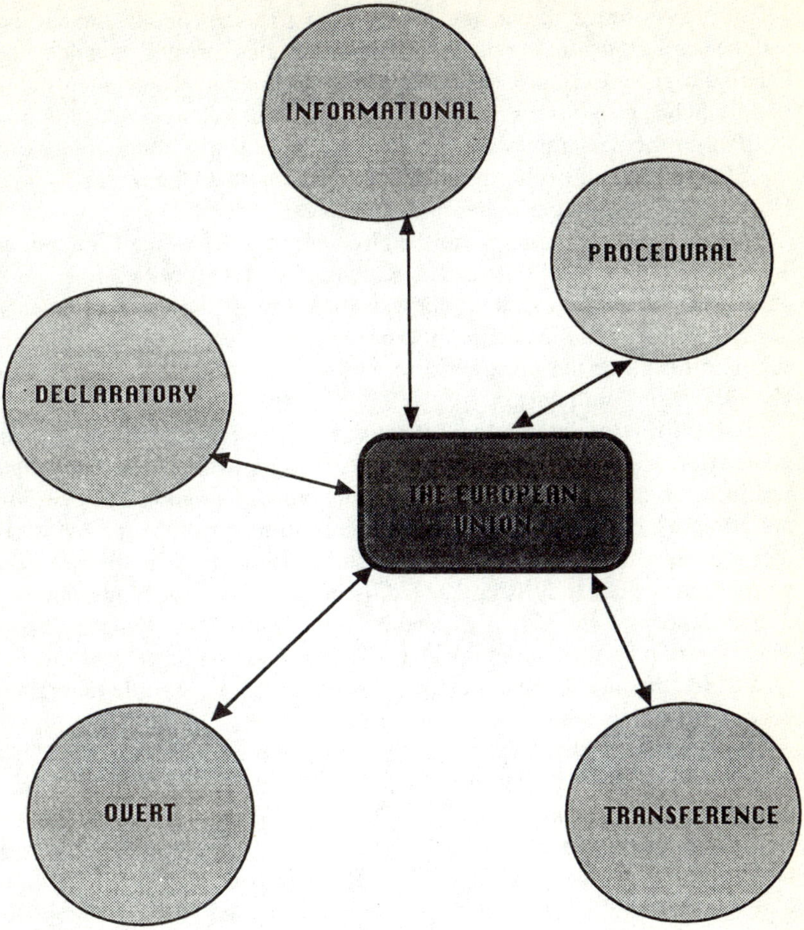

Figure 1.2 The implementation instruments of the international identity of the European Union
Source: Author

November 1973 and more recently the Council of Ministers agreement in January 1990 on association agreements with Central and Eastern European countries. Some of these latter rationales are given procedural expression, as in the instance of the Lomé Convention or the relationship with ASEAN.

The procedural dimension of the Community refers to the standing institutionalised relations that are established by the Community; for example, either in regionalised form, as noted above, or constituted on a bilateral basis, as with the United States.

The transference dimension denotes the financial and technical assistance relationships that the Community has created outside the Community; for example, the EC food aid programme. This dimension is important because it is an instrument that has been used to give expression to EPC. In the declaratory sphere, the well-documented communiqués of the EPC process illustrate the substantial use that the Community – now Union – and its Member States make of this dimension.

The overt dimension refers to the physical presence of the Community and its representatives outside the Community. This can be either on a permanent basis; for example, the establishment of the external delegations of the Commission, or more transitory, visits of the troika or the bicephalic troika or the dispatch of monitors, for example, to the former Yugoslavia or South Africa.

In short, how is international identity categorised? It is that which is given expression through the instruments that are available to the Union and facets of the EU that distinguish it from other international actors. The policies pursued by the Union through the instruments of the international identity represent recourse to common instruments. The framework, within which this study is conducted, is intended to identify the international identity of the Union as distinct from that of the Member States. The assertion is that, although the Member States inform, and are informed by, the international identity of the Union, it is possible to retain a conceptual and an analytical distinctiveness.

The concluding chapter assesses the utility of the concepts and analytical framework developed to help provide an insight into a facet of the activities of the European Union. The Conclusion also provides an assessment of the use of the framework for measuring the success of the Union through comparing the self-proclaimed aspirations of the Union with the reality of implementation. To summarise, the goal the Union has set itself, to paraphrase the words of the Treaty, is the assertion of its identity on the international scene. The goal of this text is use a distinctive and innovative methodology in order to explore the precise nature of the EU as an entity in contemporary international relations as of 1995.

NOTES AND REFERENCES

1. Council of the European Communities, Commission of the European Communities, *Treaty on European Union* [hereafter TEU] (Luxembourg, Office for Official Publications of the European Communities), Title I Common Provisions, Article B.
2. The implementation date for the Treaty of European Union was set in accordance with Title VII Article R.2. 'This Treaty shall enter into force on

1 January 1993, provided that all the instruments of ratification have been deposited, or, failing that, on the first day of the month following the deposit of the instrument of ratification by the last signatory State to take this step'.

3. For a survey of reform proposals from the mid-1970s see: M. Holland, *European Community Integration* (London, Pinter, 1993).
4. The Treaty of Rome establishing the European Economic Community stated in its preamble: '... determined to lay the foundations of an ever closer union among the peoples of Europe', Commission of the European Communities, *Treaties establishing the European Communities (ECSC, EEC, EAEC) – Single European Act – Other basic instruments*. Abridged Edition [hereafter TEC] (Luxembourg, Office for Official Publications of the European Communities, 1987), p.119.

   The Treaty on European Union updated this to state: 'This Treaty marks a new stage in the process of creating an ever closer union among the peoples of Europe, in which decisions are taken as closely as possible to the citizen'. TEU, Article A.
5. TEU, Article A.
6. For recent views reflecting these positions see respectively: S. Hill, *Visions of Europe: Summing up the Political Choices* (London, Duckworth, 1993), J. Pinder, *European Community: The Building of a Union* (Oxford, Oxford University Press, 1995).
7. It is important to note here that the Treaty establishing the European Economic Community is amended to the European Community under the provisions of Article G of the Treaty on European Union. TEU, Article G.
8. European Council, *Conclusions of the Presidency*, 26–28 June 1991 (European Community, Luxembourg).
9. For a discussion on the IGC on Political Union see: R. Corbett, 'The Intergovernmental Conference on Political Union', *Journal of Common Market Studies* XXX, 3 (September 1992): 271–98.
10. TEU, Article A.
11. *Ibid.*, Article C.
12. *Ibid.*, Title I, Article B.
13. D. Allen, R. Rummel and W. Wessels, *European Political Co-operation: Towards a Foreign Policy for Western Europe* (London, Butterworth Scientific, 1982); J. Redmond (ed.), *The External Relations of the European Community: The International Response to 1992* (London, Macmillan, 1992).
14. This as a distinctive approach to evaluating the EC is suggested in: 'Conclusion: The Community as an International Actor', O. Nørgaard, T. Pedersen and N. Petersen, *The European Community in World Politics* (London, Pinter, 1993).
15. R.O. Keohane and S. Hoffmann, 'Conclusions: Community politics and institutional change', W. Wallace (ed.), *The Dynamics of European Integration* (London, Pinter for RIIA, 1990), p.276.
16. See, for example, Chapters 1–5 in M. Holland (ed.), *The Future of European Political Co-operation: Essays on Theory and Practice* (London, Macmillan, 1991).
17. This three-fold division is outlined in a variety of texts although sometimes under slightly different labels. For example, P.R. Viotti and M.V. Kauppi, *International Relations Theory: Realism, Pluralism, Globalism* (New York, Macmillan, 1987).

18. There is an acknowledgement of the 'post-positivist' revolution which has challenged the utility of such a distinction – manifested in critical theory, post-modern, feminist and historical sociological guises. This has yet to make a sustained impact upon the study of the international role of the European Union.

    For the identification of these post-positivist approaches see: S. Smith, 'Foreign Policy Theory and the New Europe', in W. Carlsnaes and S. Smith, *European Foreign Policy: The EC and Changing Perspectives in Europe* (London, Sage, 1994).
19. See, for example, P. Ifestos, *European Political Co-operation: Towards a Framework of Supranational Diplomacy?* (Aldershot, Gower, 1987); A.E. Pijpers, *The Vicissitudes of European Political Co-operation: Towards a Realist Interpretation of the EC's Collective Diplomacy* (doctoral thesis, Leiden, 1990).

    A recent account has only explored this question through the realist and pluralist perspectives; B. Soetendorp, 'The Evolution of the EC/EU as a Single Foreign Policy Actor', chapter 6 in W. Carlsnaes and S. Smith, *European Foreign Policy, op. cit.*
20. H. Bull, 'Civilian Power Europe: A Contradiction in Terms', *Journal of Common Market Studies* 21: 151.
21. *Ibid.*
22. For a succinct summary see F. Halliday, *Rethinking International Relations* (London, Macmillan, 1994), chapter 4, State and Society in International Relations.
23. This is the approach adopted by Paul Taylor; P. Taylor, 'The EC in International Society', *Journal of European Integration* VI, 1 (Autumn 1982): 7–41.
24. R.O. Keohane and J.S. Nye, *Power and Interdependence*, 2nd edn (Glenview, IL, Scott, Foresman & Co., 1989).
25. W.F. Hanreider, 'Dissolving International Politics: Reflections on the Nation-state', *The American Political Science Review* 72, 4: 1276–1287.
26. C. Webb, 'Theoretical Perspectives and Problems', in H. Wallace, W. Wallace and C. Webb, (eds) Policy-making in the European Community second edition (Chichester, John Wiley & Sons, 1983).
27. Keohane and Nye, *op. cit.*, p.34.
28. M. Clarke, *British External Policy-making in the 1990s* (London, Macmillan for the RIIA, 1992), pp.4–5.
29. K. Waltz, *Theory of International Politics* (New York, Random House, 1979). For an indication of the backdrop to the rise of neo-realism and the response generated see: R.O. Keohane (ed.), *Neo-realism and its Critics* (New York, Columbia University Press, 1986).
30. D. Snidal, 'The Myths of Hegemonic Stability Theory: A Critique', *International Organisation* 39, 4: 580.
31. S. Krasner (ed.), *International Regimes* (Ithaca, NY, Cornell University Press, 1983). R. Keohane, *After Hegemony: Co-operation and Discord in the World Political Economy* (Princeton, Princeton University Press, 1984).
32. Keohane, *ibid.*, p.51.
33. R.W. Cox, 'Multilateralism and world order', *Review of International Studies* 18, 2: 161.

34. See, for example, R.O. Keohane, *International Institutions and State Power: Essays in International Relations Theory* (Boulder, CO, Westview Press, 1989).
35. O. Keck, 'The New Institutionalism and the Interparadigm debate' in F.R. Pfetsch (ed.), International Relations and Pan-Europe (Münster; Hamburg, Lit, 1993).
36. D.A. Baldwin, *Neo-realism and Neo-liberalism* (New York, Columbia University Press, 1993), p.5.
37. S. Hoffmann, 'Reflections on the Nation-State in Western Europe Today', *Journal of Common Market Studies* 21: 21–37.
38. Hoffmann, *ibid.*: 34.
39. R.O. Keohane and S. Hoffmann, 'Conclusions: Community Politics and Institutional Change', in Wallace, *op. cit.*
40. For the location of these perspectives within a Marxist heritage within International Relations see: V. Kubálková and A. Cruikshank, *Marxism and International Relations* (Oxford, Oxford University Press, 1989), especially post-script to the paperback edition.
41. Only about 10 per cent of the English language literature surveyed was considered to represent the Structuralist perspective in a recent survey: H. Alker and T. Biersteker, 'The Dialectics of World Order: Notes for a Future Archaeologist of International Savoir Faire', *International Studies Quarterly* 28, 2: 121–42.
42. M. Hoffmann, 'Critical Theory and the Inter-Paradigm Debate', *Millennium* 16: 231–49.
43. S. George, 'European Political Co-operation: A World Systems Perspective' in: M. Holland (ed.), *The Future of European Political Co-operation* (London, Macmillan, 1991).
44. A. Oyewuni, 'The Lomé Convention: From Partnership to Paternalism', *The Round Table* 318: 129–37.
45. J. Galtung, *The European Community: A Superpower in the Making* (London, George Allen & Unwin, 1973).
46. See, for example, P. Tsakaloyannis, 'The EC: from civilian power to military integration', in J. Lodge (ed.), *The European Community and the Challenge of the Future* (London, Pinter, 1989); F. Laursen, 'The EC in the World Context: Civilian power or superpower?' *Futures* (September 1991): 747–59.
47. F. Duchéne, 'Europe's role in World Peace', in R. Mayne (ed.), *Europe Tomorrow: Sixteen Europeans Look Ahead* (London, Fontana, 1972).
48. F. Duchéne, 'The European Community and the Uncertainties of Interdependence', in M. Kohnstamm and W. Hager, *A Nation Writ Large? Foreign-policy Problems before the European Community* (London, Macmillan, 1973), pp.19–20.
49. J. Galtung, *The European Community: A Superpower in the Making* (London, George Allen & Unwin, 1973), p.12.
50. G. Sjöstedt, *The External Role of the European Community* (Farnborough, Saxon House, 1977).
51. See, for example, C.W. Kegley and E.R. Wittkopf, *American Foreign Policy: Pattern and Process*, 4th edn (New York, St Martin's Press, 1991).
52. F. Emery (ed.), *Systems Thinking: 2* (Harmondsworth, Penguin, 1981). The variety of systems approaches requires clarification of the manner in which

it is being utilised here. A distinction is to be drawn between three systems approaches: General Systems Theory (GST), Systems Analysis and Systems Thinking. The notion of a GST, often caricatured, is more limited in scope than its name implies. In a celebrated article, 'General Systems Theory – the Skeleton of a Science', Kenneth Boulding declared,

> [GST] does not seek, of course, to establish a single, self-contained 'general theory' of practically everything' which will replace all the special theories of particular disciplines. Such a theory would be almost without content, for we always pay for generality by sacrificing content, and all we can say about practically everything is almost nothing. Somewhere however between the specific that has no meaning and the general that has no content there must be, for each purpose and at each level of abstraction, an optimum degree of generality. It is the contention of the General Systems Theorists that this optimum degree of generality is not always reached by the particular sciences. (K.E. Boulding, 'General Systems Theory – The Skeleton of a Science', *Management Science* 2, 3 (1956)).

The search for a GST has been institutionalised in the Society for the Advancement of Systems Theory with the runes regularly raked over in the *General Systems Yearbook.* Systems Analysis, an outgrowth of operational research during World War II, is associated in its origins with the RAND corporation (independent non-profit making advisory corporation). Systems Analysis, in its own terms, is a systematic appraisal of the costs and other implications of meeting a defined requirement in a number of ways. Systems Analysis was introduced to the Defence Department in the US by Robert McNamara and in 1965 there was an Assistant Secretary of Defence for Systems Analysis. Of course we neither have to have to embrace GST or be wedded to a behaviouralist methodology to make use of the concept of system.

53. The use of systems theory for the study of international relations can be identified from both macro and micro perspectives. From the macro perspective, see: M.A. Kaplan, *System and Process in International Politics* (New York, Wiley, 1957). For a micro perspective, see: J.N. Rosenau, *The Scientific Study of Foreign Policy* (New York, The Free Press, 1971).
54. Kegley and Wittkopf, *op. cit.*
55. For the notion of an administrative perspective, see: M. Clarke, *British External Policy-making in the 1990s* (Basingstoke, Macmillan for RIIA, 1992).
56. The notion of an operational environment is detailed in Chapter 4.
57. The idea of the then EC being identifiable as a distinctive presence in the international area was advanced by Allen and Smith. However, this was explicitly to offer an approach to the study of the EC without ascribing actorness. D. Allen and M. Smith, 'Western Europe's presence in the contemporary international arena', *Review of International Studies* 16 (1990): 19–37.
58. These forms of the international identity have been drawn, with modification, from M. Clarke, 'The Foreign Policy System: A Framework for Analysis', in M. Clarke and B. White (eds), *Understanding Foreign Policy: The Foreign Policy Systems Approach* (Aldershot, Edward Elgar, 1989).

Part I
Identifying the International Identity

2 The Development of the Framework of the International Identity: (1) External Relations

> L'Europe ne se fera pas d'un coup ni dans une construction d'ensemble: elle se fera par des réalisations concrètes créant d'abord une soldarité de fait.
>
> Robert Schuman, 9 May 1950[1]

> For the first time in the history of GATT, of which this was the eighth negotiating round since 1947, Europe acted as an international force capable of talking as an equal to the United States and Japan and gaining substantial concession from them, including in fields – agriculture, industrial goods and cultural and audiovisual policy – where we were in head-on conflict.
>
> Alain Lamassoure, 27 April 1994[2]

From the foundation of the European Coal and Steel Community (ECSC) in 1951 to the codification of European Union in 1993 there has been the progressive development of instruments that have given the Union the ability to operate internationally. In this chapter, an account is provided of the development of this set of instruments. However, the development of these international instruments available to the Union has not taken place within a vacuum. A changing international context within which the Union has both developed, and continually operated, has increased the importance of the Union and the instruments at its disposal. Therefore, an assessment of the international significance of the Union can only be offered after consideration is given to the changing international context within which the international identity of the Union has developed. The pattern adopted for the next three chapters reflects the importance of the context within which change has taken place. In this, and the following chapter, there is an exposition, and an analysis, of the development of the instruments available to the Union. In Chapter 4 we turn to the changing international context within which change has taken place in an attempt to offer a comprehensive account of the increasing international significance of the Union.

In this chapter we examine the development of the external relations of the Union. An account is provided of the development of the international instruments of the Union which are informed and generated as a consequence of the treaties that provide the foundations of the Union. In Chapter 3 we examine the counterpoint to the development of external relations, the inter-governmental arrangements that have contributed to the development of the international identity. The instruments of the international identity are considered to be a composite of both the treaty-based and inter-governmental arrangements. Before embarking upon an exposition of the development of the treaty-based competencies, it is worth recalling our working definition of international identity in this context: the existence of instruments or action which may ostensibly be under the control of Member States but are distinguishable in form from instruments or actions of Member States.

THE BIRTH AND DEVELOPMENT OF EXTERNAL RELATIONS

To chart the development of the external relations of the Union we have to give consideration to the treaties that have founded the three communities, the European Coal and Steel Community (ECSC), the European Economic Community (EEC) and the European Atomic Energy Community (EAEC). The concern of this chapter is to illustrate how provisions within these treaties, and their successive amendment, have formed the basis for the development of the instruments of international identity.

Two inter-related factors are significant in considering the contribution of the treaties to the formulation of international identity. These two factors illustrate that retaining a rigid differentiation between inter-governmentalism and integration is problematic when considering the international role of the Union. The first factor is that the Union is, in its essentials, a compact among nation states which are *not* subsumed by the Union. The second significant factor is that which is considered to take the Union beyond an inter-governmental international organisation – supranationalism. This is not to suggest that these two factors represent the only source of influence upon the development of the identity, the other chapters of this text highlight other substantive sources. However, these two factors represent the genesis of the international identity and the international identity remains a blend of these two elements.

THE GENESIS OF THE INTERNATIONAL IDENTITY

As was suggested above, two factors provide the genesis of the international identity of the Union, and illustrate that any account which focuses exclusively upon either inter-governmental or supranational dimensions of the international role of the Union is providing only a one-dimensional account.

The first of our two factors is that the basis for the Union are the treaties signed on behalf of the Member States. The Union is founded upon an inter-governmental bargain both struck and codified by the Member States. Two points are worth noting. Firstly, the Union is not founded upon a constitutional arrangement that places the citizens or peoples of the Union as its foundation. The creation of citizenship of the Union, as founded by Part Two of the Treaty on European Union, does not *fundamentally* alter the relationship between the citizen and the basis upon which the Union is founded.[3] Under Article 8 of the amended Treaty of Rome citizenship of the Union is dependent upon nationality of a Member State.[4] The second point is that amendments to the founding treaties require unanimous agreement among the Member States. Therefore, any deepening of the Community, and enhancement of supranationalism that is manifest in treaty amendments, requires both an inter-governmental bargain and ratification by the Member States before it can proceed.

In considering this first factor as one of the foundations of the international role of the Union the assertion of this study is that the development of an international identity does not require the displacement of the Member States or the emergence of a new, co-equal international actor. The process of the development of the international identity of the Union does not resemble a zero-sum game; the Member States have continued to inform, enhance and constrain the international activity of the Union.

The assertion that the international role of the Union is not usurping that of the Member States requires a clarification of what is understood by supranationalism, as this is the basis upon which the Union is contrasted with other inter-governmental arrangements. Supranationalism is therefore the second factor of the genesis of the international identity of the Union.

Supranationalism is a contested concept generally employed to denote the distinctive political and legal arrangements that characterise the Community. The term 'supranational' appeared in Article 9 of the Treaty of Paris that founded the ECSC but was subsequently repealed by Article 19 of the Merger Treaty of 1965.[5] The context in which it is used in the Treaty is a discussion of the members of the Higher Authority (the ECSC predecessor to the Commission): 'They will refrain from any Action incompatible with the supranational character of their duties. Each member state undertakes to respect this supranational character...'. [6]

The definitional problem stems from the essential circularity in the use of the term. The term 'supranationalism' is applied to the Community to reflect the *sui generis* nature of its arrangements, hence there is often an inferred tautology in its usage. Jean Monnet professed his dislike for the word but linked supranational to the Higher Authority, but in his interpretation it implied the task of the Higher Authority which was that its decisions should be binding.[7] The Union has not functioned in such a fashion and a consequence is that notions of 'supranationalism' have proliferated. Through the institutional arrangements Member States have retained key roles in both decision-making and implementation. However, this has been alongside the development of hierarchical arrangements, especially in relation to legal aspects of the Community. The Union cannot be characterised as supranational in the Monnet mould, understood as an uncomplicated hierarchical arrangement with the Member States subsumed to a central authority. Therefore there is also certain uneasiness in denoting both centrifugal and centripetal forces at work – used to distinguish between the institutions of the Community and the Member States. The reality, is that both facets are inter-meshed. It is the novel nature of this inter-meshed relationship that is worthy of consideration if the term 'supranationalism' is to retain any currency.

Built into the many definitions and uses of 'supranationalism' is the supranational dynamic: 'To define and give meaning and content to this term is to capture the essence of the particular model of integration experienced in Europe';[8] Thereby, 'supranationalism' becomes a synonym for an integrative process. Accounts of the development of the Community can then be broken down as tension between centrifugal inter-governmentalism and centripetal, and progressive, supranationalism.[9] Teleological accounts of the development of the Union have recently regained their vogue after a sustained period of discredit. Although the former represents a more considered account of the development of the Union, its teleological underpinnings distract from the permanency in which combinations of elements of inter-governmental and supranationalism have inter-meshed and attained legitimacy and permanency.

Ernst Haas, in launching the neo-functionalist account of integration, as applied to the EC, distinguished between structural-supranationalism and operation-supranationalism.[10] Structural-supranationalism concerned 'the existence of governmental authorities, closer to an archetype of federation than any past international organisation, but not yet identical to it'. Operational-supranationality is dependent upon the behaviour of individuals and groups of individuals. Haas's linking of supranationalism to an institutional-political structure as well as a form of behaviour weds supranationalism as process to the emergence of particular institutional structures that both modify, and are modified by, behaviour generated as a consequence of the emergence of those institutions.

Taylor has offered a typology of supranationalism against which it is possible to gauge the Union.[11] The essence of supranationalism is considered to be the inter-play between the constituent states and international institutions. The element upon which supranationalism is founded is the recognition of a general interest. The requirements for the supranational organisation to have supranational capability are the independence of the civil servants of the organisation, financial independence, voting by fluid majorities, an effective leadership and morale in the secretariat of the organisation. The national actor is constrained in two-fold fashion. Firstly, the integrity of its decision-making is compromised, and secondly, the national actor loses exclusive legal competence over its territory. Using this yardstick Taylor refutes the idea that the EU in totality is supranational and merely demonstrates supranational tendencies.[12]

Taylor, in offering a typology of supranationalism, offers a narrow set of criteria that act to refute the notion that the EC is supranational. Between Taylor's narrow definition of a 'completed' supranationalism and Haas's teleological account of supranationalism another definition is possible.

Distinctions can be drawn between supranational institutions, supranational decision-making processes and supranational implementation. These can also be kept separate from the question as to whether supranationalism is the outcome of an integrative process. The importance of this account of supranationalism is that the emergence of a supranational entity gradually displacing the national actors is not an essential prerequisite for the development of an international identity for the Union. This is not to suggest that the national states do not undergo a modification in their form and function but rather that there is not a requirement for their dissolution as international actors.

The neo-functionalist position, further explored in Chapter 6, was that a supranational feedback loop would develop with the results of supranational implementation generating inputs for more supranational decision-making enhancing the supranational institutions. More recent revisions of neo-functionalism have suggested that an inter-governmental bargain is required to facilitate such a process.[13] The hypothesis advanced here is that each of these three facets can operate independently. Reliance upon supranational institutions does not necessarily represent a loss or gain for supranationalism, the use of supranational institutions does not imply supranational decision-making and supranational implementation does not necessarily flow from supranational intentions. As Taylor remarked, 'The concept of supranationalism concerns the interplay between the state and international institutions.' This is ever the case in the development of the international identity of the Union.[14]

THE BIRTH OF THE UNION: THE SCHUMAN DECLARATION

The Declaration of Robert Schuman, French Minister of Foreign Affairs, on 9 May 1950 represented an unorthodox birth for an entity that has risen to become of such international significance. The Declaration represented a breach of diplomatic protocol: a substantive new direction for French foreign policy that was prepared without the knowledge or involvement of the French Foreign Ministry and without prior consultation with other Western countries (most notably the UK).[15] The Declaration also set the tone for much of the future development of the international role of the Union: a declaration of intent that lacked a blueprint for its execution.

The significance of the Declaration for the foundation of the international identity is four-fold. Firstly, it represented a departure from existent post-war international organisations that were configured as part of the Atlantic Community, such as the European Recovery Programme (ERP), the Organisation of European Economic Co-operation (OEEC), the North Atlantic Treaty Organisation (NATO) and the European Payments Union (EPU), because it explicitly excluded a direct role for the United States. The Schuman Declaration promoted a *European community* as distinctive from the Atlantic Community. Unlike the Convention establishing the OEEC signed in April 1948 and the North Atlantic Treaty of April 1949, the Schuman Declaration makes no explicit reference to the role of the United States.[16]

Secondly, the blend of both inter-governmentalism and supranationalism apparent in the Declaration went beyond the inter-governmentalism of the Council of Europe. The proposal for the pooling of French and German coal and steel production under a 'new high authority whose decisions will be binding', was to be preceded by intergovernmental negotiations assisted by an arbiter and were to 'be the subject of a treaty between the states to be submitted to Parliaments for ratification'.[17] The elements of supranationalism were conveyed through the proposition of a Higher Authority to oversee coal and steel production, the decisions of which would bind the members. A decision as to who would occupy the

Presidency of the Higher Authority was to be reserved for the Member States.

Thirdly, as these arrangements were conducted to eliminate the potential for armed conflict among participants, they marked the birth of the idea of a civilian power Europe. A wider peace in Europe to facilitate the 'uniting of the European nations' had as its prerequisite 'that the age-old opposition between France and Germany be eliminated'.[18] The proposition of a civilian power Europe did not require that the Member States subsume or neutralise their foreign policies in the interests of a common ideal. Indeed, the French quest for security had reformulated itself into a new form with the intent of binding Germany to Western Europe or, as one commentator succinctly suggested, France proposed that Germany should participate in its own containment.[19]

However, the proposals were also couched in such a manner as to make them acceptable to the United States, which was to remain the guarantor of the feasibility of a civilian power Europe and for this reason has remained the primary bilateral influence on the construction and representation of the Union.[20] The feasibility of a departure from the notion of civilian power Europe was to be predicated upon both the elimination of superpower rivalry in Europe and the ability and desire of the Member States to seek defence arrangements for this *European community*. These, of course, represent the conditions of the post-Cold War era and suggest how the external context has contributed to the modification of the international role of the Union.

Fourthly, the declaration demonstrated a consciousness of the significance of the idea for the international system. Civilian power Europe was, at its foundation, creating an international presence aware of its international responsibilities. The declared ethos was the promotion of peaceful relations of nation states conscious of their collective responsibilities. The Schuman Declaration explicitly noted this responsibility with respect to three dimensions. The coal and steel produced by the pooling of production was to 'be offered to the world as a whole without distinction or exception, with the aim of contributing to raising living standards and to promoting peaceful achievements'.[21] The increased resources generated by the pooling of production was to facilitate the development of Africa. The United Nations was charged with providing a representative to report 'on the functioning of the new organisation, particularly with respect to protecting its peaceful aims'.[22]

At the Inter-governmental Conference launched on 20 June 1950 France and the Federal Republic of Germany were joined by the Benelux states and Italy. The outcome of the negotiations, the Treaty of Paris establishing the European Coal and Steel Community was signed on 18 April 1951 with a commitment to a 50-year operation. The Treaty of Paris gave the international identity of the Union its first codification. The Treaty contained no provision for the withdrawal of signatories prior to its expiry.

The ECSC also established the parameters across which to measure the development of international identity: *national coverage, functional activity and instruments for action.* It is the progressive expansion of these inter-related elements that serve to illustrate the increase in the international presence of the Union. The progressive enlargements of the Union have increased its international significance, as have the increase in scope of its activity and its sources of influence, as explored in Chapter 6.

The inter-governmental negotiations substantially modified the role and function of the Higher Authority. This was in two respects: the creation of the institutions of the Court and Council of Ministers placed constraints upon the activity of the Higher Authority. The Treaty eventually signed bears the imprint of the differing national interests of the Member States, most notably the Dutch push for the establishment of a Council of Ministers.[23]

The ECSC was envisaged in the Treaty under Title Two as functioning through four institutions: the Higher Authority (assisted by a Consultative Committee), the Common Assembly, the Court of Justice and the Council of Ministers.[24] Eight of the nine members of the Higher Authority were designated with the consent of all governments. The ninth was to be chosen by the eight already elected. The Higher Authority was charged with making all decisions by a simple majority vote. The Council of Ministers, its Presidency rotating six-monthly between the Member States, was to take decisions by simple majority, two-thirds majority, five-sixths majority or unanimity, dependent on the situation. In some situations the votes were weighted in accordance with the value of the coal and steel output of each of the Member States.[25] The Council of Ministers, although not representing a remarkable innovation like the Higher Authority, is significant for our purposes in that it is a hybrid of inter-governmentalism and supranationalism. Although composed of governmental representatives and therefore often considered to be an inter-governmental body, the Council also constitutes a supranational body in performing its function as a legislature. The Council of Ministers is an institutional manifestation of the blend of supranationalism and inter-governmentalism that is the essence of the international identity of the European Union and, as will be explored, is the institution in which both the external relations and the Common Foreign and Security Policy (CFSP) are drawn together.

Explicit consideration was given within the Treaty to the role and function of the ECSC with respect to the international system. Article 3 of the Treaty provided a codification of the ethos that was intended to guide the ECSC's relations with the international arena:

> The institutions of the Community shall, within the limits of their respective powers, in the common interest...ensure an orderly supply to the common market, taking into account the needs of third countries...promote the growth of international trade and ensure that equitable limits are observed in export pricing.

In addition, in Article 6 the Community was granted legal personality (not granted to the European Union).

> In International Relations, the Community shall enjoy the legal capacity it requires to perform its functions and attain its objectives.

The Higher Authority acting alone was given the power under Chapter X, 'Commercial Policy' (Articles 71–75) to propose means of harmonising relations with third countries, advise on changes in tariff rates vis-à-vis third countries, supervise the administration of export-import licence system and to propose measures to Member State governments for joint action against third countries in cases of dumping. The Member States commercial policies in areas excepting coal and steel were to remain the preserve of the Member States. Therefore, an area of functional activity in international affairs exclusive to the Community was created, which was to operate alongside the existing commercial policies of the Member States.

Under Article 79 the Treaty was to apply only to the European territories of the Contracting Parties but any preferential treatment that the coal and steel of a Member State enjoyed in its non-European territories was to be extended to all. The Higher Authority was explicitly charged with maintaining the relations of the Community with the OEEC and the UN:

> The Higher Authority shall maintain all appropriate relations with the United Nations and the Organization for European Economic Cooperation and shall keep these organizations regularly informed of the activities of the Community'

The invocation of these provisions at an early stage of the ECSC set a precedent for the later forms of its development as an international entity. The ECSC was granted observer status in the meetings of the OEEC Council, Executive Committee and within its technical commissions.[26] Within the OEEC the Six granted the ECSC the status of sole spokesperson on matters concerning coal and steel. In areas where responsibility was shared between the Higher Authority and the Member States, prior co-ordination and declarations were required to ensure the commonality of positions.[27]

Under Article 94 relations were to be maintained with the Council of Europe. However, the conduct of these relations was not explicitly reserved for the Higher Authority. The Council of Europe, like the OEEC, covered a gamut of activities, with coal and steel only peripheral to its activities. The link between the Council of Europe and the ECSC went beyond common purpose to institutional overlap. Delegates to the ECSC Common Assembly were drawn from the representatives of the Consultative Assembly of the Council of Europe. The Common Assembly was to meet in the premises of the Council of Europe in Strasbourg.

Relations with other international organisations were a pressing concern in the foundation of the ECSC and the early stages of development. Indeed, the ECSC was formulated within the existing framework of rules established by the General Agreement on Tariffs and Trade (GATT). The Six were all signatories to the GATT and bound by its principle of equality of treatment and the extension of Most Favoured Nation (MFN) to all members. As the ECSC was a preferential trading arrangement a derogation had to be sought from the member states of GATT. The ECSC had to seek exemption from MFN treatment which required the support of a two-thirds majority of GATT members. In September 1952 the Higher Authority gained authorisation from the Council of Ministers to appoint a joint representative of the Six to the GATT session of October 1952.[28] The result was a bicephahlic representation of both a Member State representative and a Higher Authority representative. This is a form of representation which the Union has maintained and developed since that date. The GATT agreed on 10 November 1952 to regard the ECSC 'as if the European territories of these states constituted the territory of a single contracting party as concerns coal and steel.[29] However, it was the Member States and not the ECSC itself that was the contracting party to the GATT, a situation that is still maintained with the Union. As with the OEEC, the Six instructed the Higher Authority to act as their representative and to submit the annual report on its operations upon which the GATT insisted. From 1956 onwards the Higher Authority was to act as the negotiator of the Community in GATT tariff bargaining.[30]

The most significance advance in the development of the international instruments of the Union, and that which has become the most effective of the procedural instruments of the Union, was the policy of Association. Despite recent accounts to the contrary, associationism was not born with the Treaty of Rome.[31] Although the United Kingdom had declined to take part in the ECSC at this stage it was to engage in a relationship with the ECSC which was to set the pattern for the Union's international relations by progressively institutionalising its relations with third parties.

The United Kingdom accredited the first permanent delegation to the ECSC in Luxembourg on 1 September 1952.[32] In November 1952 a Joint Committee of members of the Higher Authority and a UK delegation met to work on the establishment of an association agreement for the United Kingdom.[33] The agreement signed in December 1954 established a Council of Association composed of representatives of the United Kingdom and the Higher Authority. Both sides were accorded equal authority, the Higher Authority was being treated in a manner analogous to a sovereign nation state. Alongside the Association Council there was also the provision for meetings of the Council of Ministers, Higher Authority and UK representatives. Again, the creation of the overt instrument of Association and its attendant bodies like the instrument of bicepahlic representation detailed above have become significant instruments for the Union and have their origins in the ECSC.

The Higher Authority, in establishing a mission to the United Kingdom was accorded the same immunities and privileges as an international organisation.[34] The Higher Authority representative in London became known as the 'first European ambassador' in Luxembourg.[35] The Association Agreement was subject to a ratification process both in the United Kingdom and in the six Member States.

The United Kingdom appointed its representatives to the Council of Association from the Board of Trade, the Ministry of Fuel and Power and the Coal and Iron and Steel Boards. Relations with the United Kingdom deepened with the Council of Association meeting six times between November 1955 and October 1957.[36] A number of committees were created to study various activities and the Common Assembly involved itself in this work by calling for a tighter association agreement and the creation of an inter-parliamentary commission.[37]

Relations with the United States were also crucial to the development of the international identity of the ECSC. The United States had been involved in the preparation of the anti-cartel provisions contained within the Treaty of Paris.[38] The United States had also acted as a strident defender of ECSC as it sought GATT approval. The US also accredited a representative to the ECSC in Luxembourg in August 1952, ahead of the United Kingdom.[39] The relationship with the United State was not conducted along the formal lines of an association agreement.

Switzerland, Austria, Norway, Denmark, Sweden and Japan all followed the United States and the United Kingdom in setting up permanent foreign missions in Luxembourg.[40] The Higher Authority was active in seeking two objectives in its conduct of international affairs: the Higher Authority sought tariff concessions from third countries and attempted to extend the common market by concluding Treaties of Association. In both capacities the High Authority acted under the instructions from the Council of Ministers acting unanimously in giving authority for negotiations to proceed. The Council was also permitted to appoint observers at the negotiating sessions with third countries. Following the agreement with the United Kingdom, a Consultation Agreement was signed with Switzerland in May 1956. The ECSC, in establishing differing degrees of relationship with third parties, was establishing a pattern that has been both expanded and enhanced as an instrument of the Union over the succeeding period.

The Swiss agreement merely provided for regular consultation between the Higher Authority and the Swiss government. As with the agreement with the United Kingdom, a joint committee was established, composed of an equal number of Higher Authority and Swiss Federal Council members. This agreement did not require the ratification by the Member States. The Higher Authority had conducted and formulated an international agreement under its own auspices, again the starting point for succeeding agreements.

The Higher Authority co-ordinated its international role through the External Relations Working Party. The Higher Authority's significance was curtailed in the role it played at the Messina Conference and the work of the Spaak Committee.[41] The Higher Authority's role was to be merely consultative. A pattern was thereby established by which any move towards a deepening of integration and significant enhancements of the international role of the Union were to be inter-governmental and advanced through the process of the inter-governmental conference. The Higher Authority was not to be the sole author of the international destiny of the Union.

After the withdrawal of the British from the Spaak Committee, which was to result in the proposal for the European Economic Community, Spaak requested that all other international organisations withdraw and the Higher Authority then took no further role in the proceedings.

REFORMULATING THE IDENTITY: FROM MESSINA TO ROME

The Spaak Report represented a departure from the sectoral model of integration that had been conducted within the ECSC (excepting nuclear energy) and instead proposed the creation of a general common market with the institutions necessary for its functioning. The Higher Authority was not to be the model for the institutions of the new Communities.

In 1956, whilst the deliberations of the Spaak Committee continued, the Higher Authority took part in tariff negotiations within the GATT, as mandated by the Council of Ministers, in the areas that fell within its remit. Tariff reductions on steel were negotiated with the United States and Austria in 1956 and in November 1957 a tariff reduction agreement was signed with the United Kingdom under the auspices of the Association Agreement.

The early functioning of the ECSC, envisaged as the starting point for a sectoral approach to European integration, was overshadowed by the advocation, formulation and eventual rejection of proposals for a European Defence Community (EDC) launched by René Pleven in October 1950. The ratification and enactment of the EDC would have constituted a maximalist approach to the creation of an international identity for the emergent European community. The institutions of the ECSC were closely involved in the EDC project. At the first ECSC Council of Ministers meeting, chaired by Konrad Adenauer in Luxembourg on 8 September 1952, the Common Assembly drafted a political constitution for the six Member States as a corollary to the EDC.[42]

The EDC belongs in both inter-governmental and supranational accounts of the development of an international identity. The EDC was also proposed by Monnet as a parallel supranational authority.[43] Article 38 of EDC Treaty, which called for the establishment of a supranational political authority and the statute for a European Political Community, was drafted by the ECSC Assembly. The draft envisaged the unification of the EDC and the ECSC together with foreign, economic and monetary policy co-ordination.[44] Although inter-governmental meetings in 1953 and early 1954 diluted the more supranational dimensions of the draft Treaty, some of its provisions were to re-emerge in the EEC Treaty. One of the European Political Community proposals had been to abolish quotas and tariffs on trade and to establish a joint external tariff and unify trade policy as parts of organising a single market.[45]

The failure to ratify the EDC Treaty acted as the spur to reinvigorate integration through different means. However, this was not to be generated by applying the deep sectional model of the ECSC. Rather, the approach adopted was to construct a framework establishing objectives, and their method of attainment, as the facilitator of an on-going process.

The process began with an inter-governmental initiative. The personnel of the Council of Ministers from the ECSC, meeting as foreign ministers, launched this process at their conference in Messina in June 1955. They were determined that an effort should be made to complete a Western European atomic energy community and a general common market. Under their auspices, a committee of experts was convened under the chairmanship of Belgium's Paul Henri Spaak to frame the proposals for an atomic energy community and a general common market. Monnet's earlier hope, dashed with respect to the ECSC, that an extra-territorial district would be set aside for the location of the institutions was not realised in the proposals.

The work of the inter-governmental expert committee was speedily completed in spring 1956 and its deliberations, in the form of two reports, passed to the Ministers in Venice in May 1956.[46] The reports, committed to treaty form, were signed in Rome in March 1957 and came into effect on 1 January 1958.

The Spaak reports advanced two objectives: the continuation of sectional integration with atomic energy and a framework within which wider economic integration would be generated. Each Member State left its imprint upon the proposals; clauses that favoured France's overseas possessions were granted for France, supported by the other colonial powers, Belgium and the Netherlands; and German concerns that the Community would be protectionist and would distort world trade were addressed through commitments to free trade.

The central pillar of the new construction was to be the creation of a common market, understood as an economic area in which goods, services, persons and capital could enjoy free movement. The mechanism was a programmed elimination of tariff and quantitative restrictions on trade together with an end to discrimination based upon national origin. The Treaty was based on market and liberal economics (not dirigisme). Exceptions to this general stance were agriculture, not viewed as a suitable candidate for elimination of barriers, but rather more suited to a common policy. In the Treaty a common agricultural policy and a common transport policy were no more than a joint commitment. A common commercial policy was viewed as the outcome of a customs union and the adoption of the common external tariff. Industrial policy and regional policy did not gain attention. The creation of a European Investment Bank and a European Social Fund were included as measures designed to help the least developed areas of the Community.[47]

The dominance of the dollar at this time made a regional monetary system unthinkable: even the liberalisation of capital movements was to be somewhat limited (Article 67). The Member State governments retained control of their fiscal and monetary policies. In the first year of the EEC all the Member States were to restore the external convertibility of their currencies.

The EEC Treaty was much less specific in its provisions but wider in scope than the Treaty of Paris. The two new Communities retained the quadri-institutional structure but the powers of the Higher Authority, renamed 'Commission' in the new treaties, were considerably curtailed. The provisions of the treaties denote that this not to be the blueprint for a super-state subsuming the role and functions of its constituent Member States. Vast swathes of core policy for the nation state were directly excluded from the provisions of the EEC treaty and its modification was dependent upon the unanimous support of all its members. The leading role in the maintenance and functioning of this community was to be its Member States *accompanied*, not dictated, by the Community institutions. It is the absence of an overall constitutional settlement ascribing clearly defined powers between Member States and Community institutions that has been both a strength and a weakness in the overall development of the Union. Gauging the development of the Union against criteria considered requisite for the successful functioning of the nation state in the international arena belies the subtlety of the instruments and network of influence through which the Union has sought to have international influence.

The development of the instruments of an international identity proceeded from the foundation of the EEC, building upon the practices established by the ECSC enhanced and developed through the relevant provisions of the EEC Treaty.

The preamble of the EEC indicated the ethos that was to guide the fledgling international role of the EEC: 'Desiring to contribute, by means of a common commercial policy, to the progressive abolition of restrictions on international trade'.[48] The establishment of a common market with its consequential common customs tariff and a common commercial policy towards third countries (Article 2) was to provide the backbone of the international role of the EEC. Association, with overseas countries and territories (Article 3.k), was also to be a foundational principle of the EEC and not merely an instrument of policy.

The common market was to be progressively established over a period of 12 years.[49] This transitional period was to provide the impetus behind the period considered here to be the *developmental* stage of the international identity of the Union. The stage is delineated by developments in both the external relations and the inter-governmental elements of the international identity and is not intended to be a comment on, or indication of, any wider integrative process.

Articles 18 to 29 of the EEC Treaty covered the establishment of the common customs tariff to be introduced in its entirety, at the latest, by the end of the transitional period (Article 23). The substantive measures dealing with the common commercial policy were contained within Articles 110–116 of the Treaty.

Article 110 committed the Community through the foundation of a customs union: '...to the harmonious development of world trade, the progressive abolition of restrictions on international trade and the lowering of customs barriers'. The intent was that by the end of the transitional period the Member States would have implemented 'a common policy in the field of external trade'. Article 111 dealt with the enactment of commercial policy during the transitional period. The Commission was charged with making recommendations to the Council in connection with tariff negotiations with third countries. The Council, after authorising the Commission to open negotiations, was to appoint a special committee to oversee the action of the Commission. There was a provision for progressively tightening the means through which decision-making would take place from unanimity during the first two periods to a qualified majority in the final period.[50]

Article 112 called for the progressive harmonisation of exports from Member States to third countries. This would be achieved by directives subject to the same transitional scheme of decision-making. Post-transitional period commercial policy was to be governed by Articles 113–116. The common commercial policy would then 'be based on uniform principles, particularly in regard to changes in tariff rates, the conclusion of tariff and trade agreements, the achievement of uniformity in measures of liberalization, export policy and measures to protect trade such as those to be taken in case of dumping or subsidies'.[51] These policies would be pursued by the Commission acting under the direction of the Council, as during the transitional period. The committee subsequently established by the Council to monitor the activities of the Commission was to become known as the Article 113 Committee and is detailed below. The Council was committed to acting in this area by a qualified majority.

From the end of the transitional period under Article 116 the freedom of individual action of the member states within international organisations was to become constrained:

> Member States shall, in respect of all matters of particular interest to the common market, proceed within the framework of international organizations of an economic character only by common action. To this end, the Commission shall submit to the Council, which shall act by a

qualified majority, proposals concerning the scope and implementation of such common action.'

The Community was granted legal personality under article 210 of the Treaty, ensuring that the Community had the power to enter into international agreements. Therefore unlike the ECSC Treaty, the EEC expressly conferred the power on the Community to negotiate international treaties; Article 113 had conferred the power to make commercial agreements with third countries; and Article 238 provided the Community with the power to make much more substantive agreements under which article Association Agreements have been conducted:

> The Community may conclude with a third State, a union of States or an international organization agreements establishing an association involving reciprocal rights and obligations, common action and special procedures.

Provisions in the Treaty (Articles 229–231) specified particular organisations with which the Community was explicitly charged with maintaining relations. The Commission was explicitly charged with 'the maintenance of all appropriate relations with the organs of the United Nations, of its specialised agencies and of the General Agreements on Tariffs and Trade. The Commission shall also maintain such relations as are appropriate with all international organisations.'[52] It was the Community at large which was charged with co-operation with the Council of Europe and the OEEC. The Treaty also contained a residual provision in Article 228 to catch elements of agreements that were not specified in the previous articles outlined.

The Treaty contained an article that has been used extensively with respect to international agreements to facilitate agreement in areas not explicitly provided for in the Treaties:

> If action by the Community should prove necessary to attain, in the course of the operation of the common market, one of the objectives of the Community and this Treaty has not provided the necessary powers, the Council shall, acting unanimously on a proposal from the Commission and after consulting the European Parliament, take the appropriate measures.[53]

The development of the doctrines of 'implied powers' and 'parallelism' have taken the powers of the Community beyond these express competencies and will be explored in the legal sources of influence (Chapter 5). In short, the case law of the European Court of Justice has established that wherever the treaties contain powers to act internally the Community has the external competence to deal with that matter. Therefore, as areas of internal integration increase the functional extent of the international identity expands. Hence integrative sources are one of the dimensions of influence to be explored in Chapter 7.

Part Four of the Treaty acknowledged the continuing colonial interests of the Member States. In the provisions dealing with the Association of Overseas Countries and Territories the non-European countries and territories of Belgium, France, Italy and the Netherlands extended the provisions of the Common Market beyond Western Europe and thereby provided the foundations for the successive Lomé Conventions. At its inception the Common Market extended beyond the physical boundaries of Europe and established a geographical reach that has progressively expanded. The principle of collective Community responsibility for development was also established, which again was to be extended, although it did not preclude, the perpetuation of bilateral development relationships.

The EEC Treaty established a timetable for the accomplishment of a common market. With the progressive enactment of the Treaty provisions over the transitional period and the establishment of the Common External Tariff, the Community embarked upon a development of its international role. As integration has gradually weakened, new common instruments have been created and there has been an undoubted shift in the division of external policy competencies between EC and national institutions. The Community has utilised the economic instruments at its disposal in pursuing political objectives.

The 1960s can be judged a success for the international identity of the Union. The Union clarified and consolidated its international practices and laid the foundations of a network of international agreements. The Union sought to engage with the international arena under the auspices of the post-war international organisations established to provide for international governance. Of course, the Cold War also overlaid these arrangements, and the impact of the Union within the changing international context provides the focus of our next chapter. Four issues of significance for identity can be identified in the 1960s; the GATT, association agreements, EFTA and membership applications and the Luxembourg compromise.

The first Commission of the EEC distributed its nine portfolios and accorded international affairs two – one commissioner for external relations and another for overseas countries and territories.[54] The on-going tariffs-cutting process of the transitional period commenced on 1 January 1959 and simultaneously the community embarked upon the erection of a common external tariff.

The Commission assumed responsibility for representing the Community in both the Dillon and Kennedy GATT rounds.[55] The Community embarked upon the development of its network of preferential trading arrangements, with association agreements signed with Greece (1962), Turkey (1964), and the Yaoundé Convention that entered into force in June 1964 established an association with 18 African states.[56] The Community accorded priority to its neighbours and former colonies.

The foundation of EFTA, also in January, offered an inter-governmental alternative to the arrangements of the Communities. EFTA lacked the CCP and the CET of the Union and its attractions as an alternative to Community membership were demonstrated with the membership applications from the United Kingdom and Denmark in 1961, with the Irish Republic acting alongside. Norway submitted a membership application the following year. The 1963 and 1967 vetoes of the UK application to the Community demonstrated that the development of the national extent of the international identity was unequivocally in the hands of the Member States.

The decade was framed by two inter-governmental proposals that illustrate the change in the long-term acceptability of the Union as the form through which the nation states should pursue their relations. The Fouchet proposals of 1960 for a confederation of European states were an attempt to supplant the Community method.[57] Although not realised at the time, the subsequent Franco-German Treaty of Friendship and Reconciliation signed in January 1963 established an inter-governmental arrangement at the heart of Western Europe, albeit one that the Bundestag subordinated to the European Communities by an amendment to the preamble of the agreement.[58]

By 1969 the Community had begun to consider the cohabitation of inter-governmentalism and supranationalism as an alternative to displacement and a more effective strategy in exerting the influence of the Union on the international scene. The year 1969 represents one of the turning points in the development of the international identity, as there was a move from a phase of development to a phase of unspectacular consolidation.

However, prior to 1969, obstructive inter-governmentalism was to reach its peak. The 1965 crisis was to prove the most enduring obstacle to the internal integration of the Community and its aftermath was to resonate until the 1980s and the enactment of the Single European Act. Although ostensibly a dispute on how to finance the Common Agricultural Policy (CAP) from the expiration of its initial financial regulation in July 1965 until the end of transitional period in 1970, the 1965 crisis was the last gasp of chauvinistic inter-governmentalism of a Member State within the

Community. This was demonstrated when the issue moved beyond the proposed budgetary mechanism that would have enhanced the powers of the Commission and the Parliament to a refusal to accept the qualified majority voting provision in the Treaty due to be implemented on 1 January 1966. The text of the so-called Luxembourg Compromise suggests that the event ended in a cessation of hostilities rather than a peace treaty.[59] In essence the issue has been resolved by a mixture of methods, opt-outs, derogations and the consigning of certain topics to inter-governmental discussion that have, over time, become bound ever closer to the Union. Another event of institutional importance was the enactment of the Merger Treaty signed in April 1965 and brought into effect on 1 July 1967 which ended three sets of institutions for the Communities.

The Customs Union was fully enacted on 1 July 1968, 18 months earlier than had been stipulated in the Treaty. In 1968, following the formation of the Customs Union, the Council of Ministers adopted a common list of products imported without quantitative restrictions from contracting parties to the GATT outside the Community. A general rule was adopted that Member States abstain from introducing quantitative restrictions on products featured on the common list. Between 1969 and 1974 the list was progressively extended. It has now been transferred from a coarse tariff list to much more detailed 'Nimexe' categories.[60] Although the various GATT rounds have progressively reduced the level of tarification and non-Tariff barriers to trade have been increasingly important tools deployed by the Community, the establishment of the CET provided a substantive tool for use by the Community as the increasing importance of political economy became apparent.

The Hague Summit of 1969 set the agenda for the consolidation of international identity that was to take place in the period up to 1988. The Hague Summit was an inter-governmental meeting of the Heads of State and Government of the Member States. The Hague Summit launched a programme for reinvigorating internal integration by the strengthening of Community institutions and the commitment to establish economic and monetary union. The Hague Summit also agreed upon the enlargement of the Community and launched the process of European Political Co-operation covered in the following chapter. As the following chapter notes, EPC was not to be without its problems but, by 1987, the viability of the process was recognised by its codification into the Single European Act (SEA). Inter-governmentalism was not only to sit alongside the Community but also to be intertwined in its operations with the creation of the European Council.

CONSOLIDATING AN INTERNATIONAL IDENTITY, 1969–1988

As Chapter 4 illustrates, from the 1960s renewed economic development for the Member States of the Community coincided with changes in the structure of the international environment that has accorded the Union greater international significance.

The period of consolidation of an international identity from 1969 to 1988 witnessed the progressive enlargement of the Union from six to nine, ten then twelve Member States, thereby introducing additional sources of influence on the the construction and representation of the international identity of the Union, as detailed in Chapter 6. During this period of consolidation the Union constructed a network of relations that encompassed the globe. By 1988 the Union had concluded Association Agreements or Co-operation Agreements with all the states of the Mediterranean basin not covered by earlier Association Agreements (excluding Libya and Warsaw Pact Member States); concluded the third Lomé Convention with 75 states in Africa, the Caribbean and the Pacific; had established Co-operation Agreements under Articles 113 and 235 with the states of the Andean Pact and the states of Central America, the ASEAN states and the Gulf Co-operation Council; and created framework bilateral agreements with other Asian and Latin American countries. Indeed the list of states *excluded* from such agreements was easier to cite: the United States, Japan, Australia, New Zealand, the Soviet Union and COMECON states, South Yemen, Nepal, Burma, Laos, Cambodia, Bhutan, Afghanistan and South Korea, Iran and Iraq.

Article 110 had committed the Community to the pursuit of liberal external trade policies, and in this regard the Community acted as a party to the various GATT negotiating rounds. As a consequence the Common External Tariff (CET) had been progressively reduced, reaching an average of 5 per cent after the Tokyo round was implemented.[61] However, as tariff barriers to trade have decreased in importance, 'new protectionism' increasingly became the issue in the 1980s. The Tokyo round of the GATT was mainly concerned with Non-Tariff Barriers to Trade (NTB) and the result was a series of Codes but these were to have a limited impact, and the NTB issue returned to the GATT agenda for the Uruguay round. Although the EC's commitment to trade liberalisation was manifested through the low level of the CET, an assessment of the openness of the EC in the early 1980s needs to be qualified because of the extensive use of other instruments of external protection detailed below.

Article 113 did not rely purely upon tariffs as the instrument through which to give effect to the Common Commercial Policy (CCP). As the EC became progressively the largest trading bloc in the world, its international significance has increased. Alongside this newly acquired status there was also the increasing competition from developing states. The EC responded with the whole gamut of measures available under Article 113: quotas, voluntary export restraints, anti-dumping measures and countervailing duties.

The EC had applied quota restrictions on industries of the developing world considered to enjoy an unfair cost advantage. For example, the Long Term Arrangement (LTA), dating from 1962 and replaced in 1974 by the first Multi-Fibre Arrangement (MFA), provided a framework for bilateral agreements between importing and exporting countries for quantitative restrictions on low-cost products originating from the developing world.[62]

The steel trade had also become a regulated industry, especially after 1974 with the growing challenge of Third World producers. Bilateral Voluntary Export Restraints were used in this sector to impose prices and ceilings on imports into the Community. In 1982 the EC found the tables turned on itself when it was forced to sign such an agreement with the United States which had threatened to impose heavy countervailing duties.[63]

During the 1980s the EC made increasingly frequent use of anti-dumping instruments to protect national producers.[64] Rules were also developed on minimum local content in an effort to alleviate a perceived influx of screw-driver assembly plants.[65] Despite the provisions for a Common Commercial Policy, it proved difficult to put an end to national differences in areas such as exports of textiles and clothing and motor vehicles. The communitisation of these fields was only accomplished with the foundation of the single market.

The latter stages of the period of the long decade were marked by a flurry of internal integrative activity that was the consequence of the 1985 White Paper on the forging of the internal market.[66] The White Paper is remarkable in that it gives no attention to the external dimension of the single market. The adoption of the White Paper also coincided with the Uruguay round of the GATT launched at Punta del Esta in September 1986.

The codification of the White Paper through the anonymously named Single European Act belied the content of what was the first substantive amendment to the treaties since the Treaties of Rome were signed. Perhaps the French title of the original text is a more accurate reflection of its contents – *Acte Unique*.

The *Acte* derived its impetus from the Solemn Declaration of Stuttgart of 19 June 1983 in which the Member States committed themselves to becoming a European Union. Thus the *Acte* was merely a staging post in a longer process. As is outlined in the following chapter, the *Acte* codified the European Political Co-operation process. The *Acte* also codified the role and function of the European Council. Consisting of amendments to the Treaty of Paris and the Treaties of Rome, the *Acte* suffered from the same inaccessibility of its successor, the Treaty on European Union. Although a significant codification of the period of consolidation in the sphere of EPC, the Single European Act did not represent the turning point in the process of consolidation of the international identity. It was not the decisive point in acquiring the status of a single actor.

The turning point of this process was the termination of the Cold War in Europe, which made the political and economic integration of both halves of Europe a codified goal across the vast majority of the nation states of Europe. Scenarios envisaging a European Union stretching from Portugal to the borders of the Slavic states of the former Soviet Union, from the Arctic circle to Limassol, could now be subject to a time scale of 20 years.

The 1988 Joint Declaration of COMECON and the EC opened a totally new situation on the eastern frontier of the Union. The first generation of Trade and Co-operation Agreements aimed at the progressive elimination of quantitative restrictions and the application of MFN treatment gave way to Association Agreements and then the acceptance at the Copenhagen European Council in June 1993 of eventual membership.[67] The EC developed a series of new instruments to deal with the technical assistance through the PHARE programme, gradually extended from Hungary and Poland to all the countries of the region, including the Baltic states. The EC also acted as the co-ordinator of the bilateral aid provided by the OECD states, the G-24, and provided a major role in establishing the European Bank for Reconstruction and Development (EBRD).

The demise of the Cold War in Europe eliminated the barriers against Europe moving beyond a civilian power as envisaged by Duchêne and outlined in Chapter 1. The recasting of relations between East and West Europe potentially pushes the boundaries of the international system to the frontiers of Europe. The establishment of a Union extending across more than 25 nation states would create a political community encompassing over one-eighth of the total number of nation states. The question then becomes not what is the international identity of the Union but rather what of the continuing identity of the international?

The changing situation with respect to Eastern Europe was matched by the changing attitudes of the non-Member States in Western Europe. In a declaration in 1984, the EC and EFTA committed themselves to the creation of a European Economic Space which should comprise all the 18 countries of the EC and EFTA. The agreement for the European Economic Area (EEA) was signed in May 1992. The agreement extended the single market to EFTA countries (excluding Switzerland, which declined to ratify the EEA after public opposition expressed in a referendum). The exclusion of the EFTA countries from the decision-making process for the rules to guide the single market resulted in membership applications from Austria, Sweden, Finland and Norway. Norway, Iceland, Switzerland and Liechtenstein remain the only EFTAs outside the Union.

1989– : PROTO-TRANSFORMATION FROM INTERNATIONAL IDENTITY TO THE STATUS OF A SINGLE ACTOR?

The period from 1989 onwards witnessed the accelerated transformation of Eastern and Central Europe, the rise and fall of the New World Order and the re-emergence of civil war within Europe. All of these events have raised questions about the competence and ability of the Union to operate effectively in the post-Cold War era, and have nudged the Union into developing a new set of international identity instruments more attuned to the demands of the late twentieth century.

The period leading up to the establishment of the two inter-governmental conferences that were to generate the Treaty on European Union was dominated by the Gulf crisis. The Union was able to respond to the conflict with the economic instruments at its disposal by imposing the first economic embargo two days after the invasion of Kuwait, as outlined in the next chapter.

The Gulf War focused attention within the Inter-governmental Conference (IGC) on the creation of a common foreign and security policy, as outlined in Chapter 3 on inter-governmentalism. In the midst of the on-going IGC process, war erupted in Yugoslavia. The dispatch of the troika of foreign ministers Michaelis, Poos and van den Broek (Italy, Luxembourg and the Netherlands) on a mediation mission on the first day of the Luxembourg European Council held on 25–26 June 1991 was to be the start of the Union's long involvement in seeking a solution to the conflict. Over the next six months this external context was to see the Dutch presidency giving greater attention to foreign policy at the cost of attention to the IGC.

The provisions of the Treaty on European Union greatly enhanced the international identity of the Union, not only through the CFSP, but also through the relocation of fiscal and monetary policy under the auspices of the Union.

THE DECISION-MAKING STRUCTURE

The conduct of the external relations of the EU are based upon the provisions of the Treaty of Paris and the two Treaties of Rome. A number of the relevant Treaty articles have been detailed in this chapter, and the relevant legislative processes and the other relevant Treaty articles are detailed in Chapter 5. The role of the Union institutions in the process of constructing and representing the international identity of the Union in the CFSP process differs from that which exists for external relations, and are detailed in the following chapter. The role of the European Court of Justice and the European Parliament in both processes is detailed in Chapters 6 and 8 respectively. The focus here is upon the European Commission, the Council of Ministers and the European Council. The role that each of these actors plays in the CFSP process is detailed in the following chapter. The focus here is upon the role of these institutions in constructing and representing the external relations of the EU.

The issue of primary importance for the role ascribed to the Commission and the Council of Ministers is the legal foundation and processes detailed in the treaties. The Commission performs three primary roles with respect to external relations: initiative, negotiation and representation. In considering the Commission, a distinction has to be made between the 20 members of the Commission, their *cabinets* and the civil service which is answerable to the Commission. The distribution of portfolios across the Commissioners is the formal responsibility of the Commission President, but due account has to be taken to ensure that there is an appropriate allocation across the Member States of the more significant portfolios. Of the current body of Commissioners four Commissioners have direct responsibilities for external relations defined geographically and functionally.[68] Hans van den Broek, the former Minister for Foreign Affairs of the Netherlands, is responsible for the CFSP and relations with Eastern Europe, the former Soviet Union, Turkey, Cyprus and Malta; Sir Leon Brittan, the former British cabinet minister, is responsible for international trade, relations with the United States, Japan and other industrialised countries and China. Manuel Marin is responsible for relations with the Mediterranean, the Middle East, Latin America and Asia; and Joao de Deus Pinheiro is responsible for relations with the ACP countries. However, because, as is detailed in Chapter 6, the ECJ has ruled that the Community has responsibility for external relations where an internal policy exists, and because an increasing number of policy areas detailed in the treaties have articles explicitly dealing with external activity, the competencies covered by all the Commissioners include an international dimension. Members of the Commission also hold a variety of portfolios of which one or more may be of external significance; for example, Emma Bonino, one of the two Italian members of the Commission, is simultaneously responsible for consumer affairs, humanitarian aid and fisheries. Additionally, the *modus operandi* of the Commission is one of collective responsibility and this ensures that all commissioners will have an involvement in external relations.

The private office of Commissioners, their *cabinets*, are crucial for inter-Commissioner communications and impact upon the degree of involvement of the commissioners in the portfolios held by other commissioners. The *chefs de cabinet* play a central role in intra-Commissioner communication and act as policy filters. In the Delors Commission the *cabinet* was crucial to the control that Delors exercised across the entire Commission structure.[69]

The organisation of the civil servants of the Commission who support the Commissioners in their work is divided into Directorates General. These do not coincide with the portfolios distributed across the Commissioners. Therefore, despite four Commissioners being involved in external relations there are three Directorates General that encompass external relations: DGI External Economic Relations; DGIA external political relations; and DGVIII Development. Additionally, DGIII Industry and DGVI Agriculture have major interests in external relations. The Commission has a separate European Community Humanitarian Office (ECHO) and a Forward Studies Unit, a think tank whose remit encompasses all areas of Community competence and is directly responsible to the President. The President himself, currently Jacques Santer, plays an additional important role as both an overt instrument of the Union as a figurehead and as President of the Commission who oversees the Commission's role in the Common Foreign and Security Policy. However, Santer does not hold the Presidency of the Union, which rotates between the Member States within the Council on a six-monthly basis.

Directorates General are headed by a Director General, a Commission civil servant responsible to the relevant Commissioner, and supported by assistants, administrators and advisers. The breakdown of the Directorate General then differs according to its responsibilities. DGVIII, Development, is responsible for the economic and development assistance that is provided for the African, Caribbean and Pacific signatories of the Lomé Convention. In DGVIII two Deputy Directors General are responsible for different directorates, the sub-divisions into which the Directorate General is divided. One Deputy is responsible for the directorates dealing with development policy, the management of instruments that encompass food aid, relations with NGOs, private investment and the Stabex and Sysmin systems of commodity price support under the Lomé Convention, and finance. A second Deputy Director General is responsible for three geographical Directorates dealing with, respectively, West and Central Africa; East and Southern Africa; and the Caribbean, Pacific and Indian Ocean. There are also a number of separate administrative units that deal with functional responsibilities, including a unit for health and AIDS programmes.

The primary responsibility of DGI is the Common Commercial Policy and for the conduct of dialogue with third countries and organisations with which the Union conducts relations. It is also responsible for the aid and co-operation arrangements that exist with non-ACP states. It also acts in a co-ordinating function with the other Directorates General in the Commission in the conduct of external relations. DGI is larger than DGVIII and has four Deputy Directors responsible for Directorates as follows: North–South relations, Mediterranean policy and relations with Latin America and Asia; North America, South Africa, Australia, New Zealand and the Far Eastern countries; analysis and policy-planning, the World Trade Organisation (WTO) and, prior to the foundation of the WTO, a Uruguay Round Steering Group, agriculture and fisheries, OECD, sectoral commercial questions, export credits, export promotion and external relations in the research, science, environment and nuclear energy fields; relations with Russia and members of the CIS, Central and Eastern Europe and including the Baltic States. DGI is directly concerned with the policy-making and execution of the external relations of the Union and therefore has primarily dealt with matters of trade. However, in 1993 Commission President Jacques Delors created a new Directorate General, DGIA, responsible for External Political Relations. The new DG reports to Hans van den Broek and also encompasses the control of the external delegations of the Commission (detailed in the following chapter). The perspective within the Commission as to what purpose this new DG should serve is clear: 'The object being to create, all the time, something like a single external service, like the Foreign Office, out of what had been rather dispersed elements up to now'.[70]

The involvement of the Commission in the political dialogue that the Union conducts with third countries and the wide-ranging nature of the dialogue is provided for in the geographical breakdown of the Directorates of DGIA encompassing political relations with European countries and the CIS; North America, Asia, Australia and New Zealand; and Latin America, Africa and the Middle East. DGIA also has two functional directorates dealing with the management of its external missions and multilateral political relations that encompass security aspects, human rights, the United Nations, OSCE and the Council of Europe.

The creation of DGIA, dealing explicitly with external political relations and reporting directly to a former Foreign Minister, illustrates both a relaxation of the Member States' attitude to the Commission's role in the processes of EPC and CFSP (charted in the following chapter) and an increased willingness to utilise the political significance of the Union that derives from its economic strength.[71]

As was noted above, Article 113 of the EC Treaty gives the responsibility for the conduct of trade policy to the Commission. However, the power of decision resides with the Council of Ministers. As Article 113 also notes, the Council authorises the Commission to engage in any negotiations and these are conducted in the framework of directives issue by the Council. The composition of the Council of Ministers is dependent upon the topic under discussion at any one time. The General Affairs Council is the forum in which the relevant Commissioners propose action to the ministers. As detailed in Chapter 5, the Council acts as the legislature within the Union in the conduct of external relations, and in matters of trade policy the Council can act by a qualified majority vote.

The work for the Council is prepared by the Committee of the Permanent Representatives (COREPER) which is either composed of the ambassadors of the Member States, the Permanent Representatives (COREPER II) or their deputies (COREPER I). The Member States Permanent Representations accredited to the Union are composed of staff drawn from a variety of national ministries. For instance, the UK Permanent Representation is headed by a diplomat from the Foreign and Commonwealth Office and his deputy is drawn from the Department of Trade and Industry and given the diplomatic rank of Minister. Staff accredited to the Permanent Representation are drawn from a variety of ministries and their responsibilities encompass the gamut of activities of the Union.[72] The staff accredited to the Permanent Representation participate in the working committees of COREPER that have progressively expanded over time and encompass Commission representatives.[73] The Permanent Representations play a dual role in that they both keep the Member States informed of developments and also act to represent and defend the positions of the Member States.

COREPER is central to the interaction between the Commission and the Member States in the development of external relations. The staff of the Permanent Representations spend the vast majority of their time engaged in the examination of Commission proposals in the subcommittees and working groups of COREPER. They are joined by experts from their capitals in dealing with technical questions. The working groups prepare reports on the Commission proposal which is passed to COREPER indicating areas in which there is agreement designated 'Points I'. The report is considered by either COREPER I or II. COREPER II usually deals with external relations and has its agenda prepared by the Antici Group of Counsellors or First Secretaries who establish the agenda for COREPER meetings. COREPER will normally approve Points I without discussion and will then proceed to resolving matters left from the working groups. Those proposals on which COREPER reaches agreement appear on the agenda of the Council of Ministers as 'A points' which are approved en bloc by the Ministers. Unresolved points appear on the agenda under the heading of 'B points', together with suggestions for debate and decision by the Ministers. The Permanent Representatives and their deputies are also in attendance at Council meetings to advise and assist the Ministers on the agenda. As noted in the next chapter, the Council is the forum in which questions of external relations and the CFSP are brought together on the same agenda.

The existence of committees through which the Member States advise the Commission on its proposals and the implementation of Directives is called 'Comotology'. An important committee in this process is the Article 113 Committee, from the relevant clause in the EC Treaty creating a special committee that oversees the Commission in its task of negotiating trade policy. The Member States have taken full advantage of this provision of the Treaty. The membership of the Committee is made up of a Commission representative and officials drawn directly from each Member State. They are directly responsible to the relevant Minister and not drawn from the Permanent Representation. The Article 113 Committee plays a major role in establishing the mandates that the Council gives the Commission for negotiations and these mandates are sometimes approved by the Ministers without discussion. The Committee also meets at the level of Deputies and has met at Ministerial level, most notably during the GATT ministerial conference in Geneva in November of 1982, to provide direct instructions fro the Commission in its negotiations with the US Trade Representative.[74]

The creation of the European Council in 1974 also provided a level above the Council at which difficult decisions could be resolved. The

European Council often makes strategic rationales for the future direction, and examples that relate to the international identity are detailed throughout this book. The focus on the decision-making structure for external relations illustrates that the Member States are intimately involved in the policy-making and implementation process. Therefore, although the Commission, in the treaties, is envisaged as the primary proposer and interlocutor of trade policy, a role summed up in the refrain the 'Commission proposes the Council disposes', the relationship in decision-making is more inter-twined. It now remains to illustrate the policies that have been pursued by the Union in the realm of external relations which are the outcome of this decision-making process.

Trade defence instruments

The importance of the EU in the international trading system is demonstrated in Chapter 4. Since the EU is the world's major trading bloc, its decisions impact upon the world economy. The 1992 programme to create the single market abolished or transformed the Member State non-tariff barriers to trade and replaced them with Union instruments. Chapter 4 notes the hierarchy of trade preferences that exist for the groupings detailed above and illustrates the sources and destinations of Union imports and exports.

The existence of the Common External Tariff detailed below provides tariff protection to the EU but tariff barriers are negligible, with the Union having a substantial number of preferential trading relationships in place. However, the Union retains a number of non-tariff barriers (NTBs). The EU increased the use of its NTBs in the early 1980s, a period dubbed one of 'new protectionism'. The Union's economic strength makes it possible for it to persuade trade partners to abide by 'voluntary' export restraints (VERs) and orderly marketing arrangements (OMAs). Tariff Quotas applied under the Generalised System of Preferences, detailed above, also constitute a form of NTB protection, as does the Multi-Fibre Agreement.

The EU also deploys anti-dumping duties against those states it believes are engaged in unfair trade practices. In particular, the EU adopted the New Community Trade Instrument in 1984 which consisted of a mix of instruments and measures enabling the Commission to initiate anti-dumping actions that the Council has to approve within 30 days. During the period 1980–1991 the Community relied heavily upon anti-dumping regulations, particularly against Eastern Europe and China.[75] The charge was increasingly levelled that the Union was using anti-dumping rules that were provided for under the GATT as protectionist instruments and was endangering the international trading system through its actions.[76]

Table 2.1 Anti-dumping actions, 1990–1994

	1990	*1991*	*1992*	*1993*	*1994 (Jan–June)*	*1994 (July–Dec)*
Initiations	20	39	21	34	9	
Measures taken	22	16	19	14	9	
thereof: definitive duties	19	16	19	8	9	
price undertaking	3	0	0	2	0	
Findings of no dumping	1	1	1	5	0	
Findings of no injury	6	4	1	1	0	
Measures in force	142	158	150	n/a	156	

Source: World Trade Organisation (1995)[78]

The conclusion of the WTO Agreement and its enactment will cut tariffs, create a framework that will restrain the use of trade defence instruments detailed above, and gradually liberalise trade in agriculture, textiles and clothing. The EU itself has modified its response to anti-dumping and countervailing duties by replacing the New Commercial Policy Instrument with a new 'Trade Barriers Regulation', which permits the Union to act by a simple majority rather than by a qualified majority in the Council of Ministers.[77]

The new Trade Barriers Regulation was part of a general reorganisation of the trade defence measures in response to the conclusion of the Uruguay round. The Union continues to be one of the most frequent users of anti-dumping procedures (Table 2.1).

THE EUROPEAN UNION AND EXTERNAL POLICY: A NETWORK OF AGREEMENTS

The enactment of the European Union on 1 November 1993, in the aftermath of the completion of the single market programme, provided the Union with both a deepening of internal integration and the creation of new instruments, and an objective, to assert its identity on the international scene. Since 1993 the Union has modified both its trade policy and the framework through which it conducts its policy.

In particular, four major sets of agreements have come into force or have been signed. Firstly, the accession agreements for Austria, Sweden and Finland; secondly, the European Economic Area; thirdly, 'Europe Agreements' with the six Central and Eastern European countries, which have been accepted as prospective applicants to the Union, and subsequently extended (although not yet ratified) with Estonia, Latvia and Lithuania.; fourthly, the partnership and co-operation agreements that have been signed with Russia and other members of the Commonwealth of Independent States (CIS).

In its 1994 legislative programme, the first enacted since the establishment of the European Union, the Commission detailed its intentions for the Union's role on the international scene:

> Strengthening new international responsibilities in the new architecture of Europe in order to contribute to the future equilibrium of the continent and to the harmonious development of international relations, by giving fresh and visible impetus to the process of cooperation at international level by the conclusion and implementation of the results of trade negotiations under the Uruguay Round, and by new initiatives with respect to the countries of Eastern Europe and the Third World; ensuring that the Community's external activities are based on and backed up by strong and stable common internal policies, so as to affirm the Community's role as an open and reliable partner in the world, and with a view to strengthening Europe's trading capacity and its competitive status on world markets.[79]

The Commission was noting both the changed external environment in which the Union was operating and the impact of internal integration upon the conduct of the Union's identity.

The Commission's legislative programme provides the measures it intends the Union to enact but also acts as an informational instrument in detailing specific rationales for the conduct of the Union's external relations during the period it encompasses. Alongside a re-affirmation of the declarations on the general principles that are intended to underpin the policies of the Union, the legislative programme also details elements of the procedural instruments of the Union for creation or enhancement.

In the 1994 programme the countries with which the Union has procedural instruments are broken down by both geography and the depth of their procedural relationship with the Union. The Commission declares five broad areas under the heading of 'affirming the Union's identity on the international scene'.[80] These headings will be used to explore the extent and the depth of the contemporary procedural instruments and trade policies of the Union.

Enlargement

The accession of Austria, Sweden and Finland required changes to the EU institutions to accommodate three new members but there was also a consequential impact upon the trade policies of the Union. As EU members, Austria, Finland and Sweden adopted the Common External Tariff and the other non-tariff measures of the Union. The three new Members withdrew from EFTA and Finland and Sweden from free-trade agreements that they had with the three Baltic states. Because of differences in the tariff and non-tariff arrangements of the new applicants the Commission, displacing the three states, sought to negotiate compensation arrangements demanded by third countries.[81]

The European Economic Area and with Member States of the European Free Trade Association

The agreement on the European Economic Area (EEA) that came into force on 1 January 1994 extended the single market to the five EFTA members, Iceland, Norway, Austria, Finland and Sweden. The EEA remained in place with the accession of the latter three entering the Union on 1 January 1995. Switzerland remains outside the EEA following a negative referendum vote in December 1992. This required the re-ordering of the customs union in existence between Switzerland and Liechtenstein and the latter acceded to the EEA on 1 May 1995. The EEA created the world's largest free trade zone encompassing 372 million people and at its introduction accounted for 40 per cent of world trade, thereby exceeding NAFTA (which came into effect on the same date) in both measures.[82] The EEA replaced free-trade agreements that the Community had established with EFTA in 1972 and 1973 and which, essentially, covered trade in industrial products. The EEA also created an institutional framework consisting of an EEA Council, Joint Committee and an EEA Consultative Committee to facilitate, respectively, 'political impetus' and guidance and enactment, as well as 'closer mutual understanding', and for contacts between 'representatives of the social partners'.[83] The EEA agreement also made provision by the EFTAs for interest-rate subsidies and grants, totalling 500 million ecu, to Portugal, Ireland, Greece and Spain.[84]

Countries of central and eastern Europe and the independent countries of the former Soviet Union

The EU has signed Europe Agreements with nine Central and Eastern European states. The Agreements require ratification in the national parliament of each Member State, the parliament of the associated state and EU assent under EC Treaty Article 238 (detailed in Chapter 5). The Agreements with Hungary, Poland, Bulgaria, the Czech and Slovak republics and Romania are all in force. Europe Agreements were signed with the three Baltic states in June 1995. The Agreements required both Union and Member State ratification because they were mixed agreements covering both Member State and Community competencies; they provided for trade, commercial and economic co-operation alongside cultural co-operation and a political dialogue.[85]

The Europe Agreements replaced earlier Trade and Co-operation Agreements that were concluded between October 1988 and March 1991 in the aftermath of the Joint EEC/COMECON Declaration of 25 June 1988.[86] The Agreements provide for free-trade areas in industrial goods between the EU and the signatories, with exceptions for trade in steel, textiles and clothing products which are covered by tariffs and quotas.[87] Trade in agriculture remains restricted. The trade provisions of the Agreements are alongside measures encompassing economic, monetary and industrial co-operation, culture, education and training. The Agreements also provide for grants and loans including loans from the European Investment Bank. The Union also co-ordinates the assistance offered by the OECD alongside its own PHARE programme of grants to facilitate economic restructuring and to encourage the creation of market economies.

The Agreements also established a number of institutions: Association Councils meeting at Ministerial level; Association Committees for enactment of the agreements; and Association Parliamentary Committees (detailed in Chapter 8).[88] The Union accepted the principle of the admission of the European Agreement countries at the European Council meeting in Copenhagen in June 1993, and at the European Council meeting in Essen in December 1994 agreed to adopt a pre-accession strategy to set out the exact requirements for all of these states to accede to the Union.[89]

In the legislative programme for 1994 the Commission also detailed the intention to create partnership and co-operation agreements with Russia, the Ukraine, Moldova, Kazakhstan, Kyrgyzstan, Belarus, Uzbekistan and Turkmenistan. These Agreements, which replace a trade and co-operation agreement signed with the Soviet Union in 1989, have been signed with all but the latter two states.[90] Like the Europe Agreements, the Partnership and Co-operation Agreements cover political, cultural and economic matters and therefore require both signature and ratification by the EU institutions, Member State parliaments and the relevant authorities of the third parties. The Agreements create Co-operation Councils meeting at Ministerial level, Co-operation Committees and Parliamentary Co-operation Committees. The trade provisions do not provide for free-trade areas but eliminate quotas except in the areas of textiles, coal, steel and nuclear products. The Union has also deployed the positive transference instrument of TACIS (Technical Assistance for the CIS) programme that has been in operation since 1991. Between 1991 and 1994 TACIS has provided 1,870 million ecu in three main areas: nuclear safety and energy; support for measures to create a market economy (including privatisation and military conversion); and human resources.[91] The Union has also provided 1.75 billion ecu in loans for the purchase of food and medical supplies, and 654 million ecu in food and emergency aid.[92]

Mediterranean policy

In October 1994 the Commission produced a report proposing the creation of a Euro-Mediterranean Economic Area to encompass the EU and the states of the Mediterranean basin.[93] The Commission proposed the creation of a vast free-trade area encompassing all the states by the year 2010. The Commission proposed a strategy of variable geometry progressively updating the existing agreements that exist with the states of the region but also creating sustained support through a programme comparable to PHARE and costing the Union 5,500 million ecu between 1995 and 1999.

As noted above, the EEC began to develop its relations with the region in 1963 with the signing of an Association Agreement with Turkey. The relationship was scheduled for upgrading to a customs union in 1995 if the European Parliament provided assent. Cyprus and Malta both currently have Association Agreements with the Union, and like Turkey have submitted applications for membership of the Union. The Union has committed itself to opening accession negotiations with Cyprus and Malta within six months of the completion of the 1996 Inter-governmental Conference of the Union. The decision to set a date for the negotiations was a *quid pro quo* required by Greece for the conclusion of the Turkey customs union agreement.[94] The institutions of the Association Agreements in force with Turkey, Cyprus and Malta mirror those of the Europe Agreements.

Between 1976 and 1977 the Community established Co-operation Agreements with the countries of the Maghreb, Morocco, Algeria, Tunisia, and the Mashreq countries of Egypt, Israel, Jordan, Lebanon and Syria signed agreements providing for trade concessions, quotas for access to the EC market and economic aid.[95] Between 1973 and 1991 the Union used the positive transference instrument of aid to provide 1,337 million ecu in aid and 1,965 million ecu in loans from the European Investment Bank (EIB).[96] Financial protocols covering the years 1992–1996 under the new Mediterranean Policy adopted in December 1990 allocate 1,075 million ecu in aid and 1,300 million ecu in EIB loans, together with 300 million ecu in support of structural adjustment.[97]

The Commission envisages creating a series of Euro-Mediterranean Agreements, Association Agreements, with Egypt, Israel, Morocco, Tunisia, Jordan and Lebanon as soon as possible to replace the existing co-operation agreements in place.[98]

Countries of Africa, the Caribbean and the Pacific

As was noted above, an association system was enacted under Part IV of the EC Treaty creating a trade and aid relationship between the six founding Members of Community and the colonial possessions or connections which they all, bar the Federal Republic of Germany, maintained in 1957. The relations between the EC Member States and its associate partners have progressively evolved. The Yaoundé Conventions I and II, negotiated by the newly de-colonised Associated African and Malagasy States, were in force from 1964 to 1969. This was succeeded by the first of the four Lomé Conventions initiated to encompass the Commonwealth countries of the United Kingdom on its accession, and in force from 1975.

The Lomé IV agreement, which has been in force since 1990, provides duty-free access and therefore no quantitative restrictions on products originating in the ACP states. Lomé IV, established for a 10 year duration, has recently undergone a mid-term review. This was ostensibly to assess the financial protocol for the remaining five years of the agreement, but other factors have also entered the discussions including the view that the Lomé process is unlikely to continue in its present form beyond the expiry of the agreement. There is currently disagreement among the Member States as to the amount that should be allocated to the European Development Fund (EDF). The EDF is financed by direct contributions from the Member States, not the Union budget, and is therefore, central to the aid component of Lomé, providing grants and operating alongside other forms of financial support. The EDF operates alongside the EIB, that provides low-interest loans.

The Lomé Convention is ostensibly a dialogue of equals with the institutions of the ACP-EU Council of Ministers, the Committee of Ambassadors and the Joint Assembly (detailed in Chapter 7) providing a forum for dialogue. The Lomé Convention is notable both for the longevity of the agreements and for the comprehensive approach encompassing all aspects of co-operation, from aid, trade concessions, to agricultural and industrial assistance and the stabilisation of export earnings. It also provided the Union with a wide geographical spread of interests, albeit sectorally limited. However, the number and spread of the states involved in the agreement has provided the EU with a universality of coverage. This is of especial importance now that the Union overseas delegations who used to deal with the convention in third countries have been incorporated into a single structure along with all the Union's other delegations (detailed in Chapter 4).

The total sums committed under the first five-year protocol of Lomé IV are detailed in Table 2.2. The bulk of this is for grants and soft loans, although Stabex, the stabilisation fund from which countries heavily dependent upon one of more primary products can draw to overcome severe fluctuations in export earnings, and Sysmin, which encompasses minerals, have accounted for substantial amounts in recent years. EC

Table 2.2 Lomé IV: development expenditure, 1993 (million ecus)

Sector	*1993**
Trade promotion	81.802
Cultural and social development	334.341
education and training	88.566
water engineering, urban infrastructure,	129.155
housing health	116.619
Economic infrastructure	165.624
transport and communications	165.624
Development of production	816.919
rural production	225.839
industrialisation	142.319
campaigns on specific themes**	448.760
Exception aid, Stabex	138.137
rehabilitation	–0.072
disasters	110.103
Stabex	2.465
refugees and returnees	25.640
Other***	62.890
Total	1,599.715

* Provisional

** Including desertification and drought, disasters, major endemic and epidemic diseases, hygiene and basic health, endemic cattle diseases, energy-saving research, sectoral imports programme and long-term schemes

*** Including information and documentation, seminars, programmes and general technical co-operation, general studies, multisectoral programmes, delegations, administrative and financial costs, improvements to public buildings, project-linked multisectoral technical co-operation (all projects)

Source: European Commission (1994)

financial aid to the Lomé Convention constitutes the bulk of the financial aid that the EU gives to developing countries (Figure 2.1).

Countries of Asia and Latin America

The EU's relations with Asia were established in 1973 when non-preferential trade agreements were entered into with India, China, Pakistan, Sri Lanka and Bangladesh. In 1980 the Community concluded a more broad-ranging agreement with ASEAN, extended to Brunei when it joined the organisation in 1984. Similar agreements were then concluded with India, China and Pakistan in 1980, 1984 and 1985 respectively. These commercial, economic and development agreements included development aid. These states are covered by the EC's generalised system of preferences introduced in 1971 but also benefit from development aid, food aid, emergency aid and aid for NGO projects. The Union has also created a similar system to Stabex for the region called Compex.

The EC's priorities were altered with the passage of a Council Regulation on aid and economic co-operation with the Asian and Latin American Developing countries of 25 February 1992. It provided for all of the states of these regions to be eligible for financial aid, technical assistance and economic co-operation. But such aid and co-operation could be amended or suspended for violations of human rights and democracy. These new priorities were reflected in 'third generation' agreements signed with Macau and Mongolia in 1992 and India in 1993.

Co-operation agreements have been concluded with Sri Lanka, India, and Vietnam, and an agreement is currently being negotiated with the Republic of Korea. The 1994 programme of the Commission set up no new special arrangements with Latin America, and no proposals to update the co-operation agreement in force between the EU and the GCC. But a proposal for an inter-regional framework agreement for negotiation was approved at the Essen summit, alongside an agreement to strengthen relations with Mexico and Chile.

The Union's relations with Latin America in the area of trade have been through 'third generation' co-operation agreements signed with the Andean Pact and with individual countries.

Multilateral and bilateral relations with the industrialised countries

The Commission envisaged the implementation of the Uruguay round and pursued a closer dialogue with the United States and Canada under the Transatlantic Declarations of 1990 and 1991. Relations with Japan were to

In 1992: 3.28 bn ecu from the Community budget, European Investment Bank and the European Development Fund

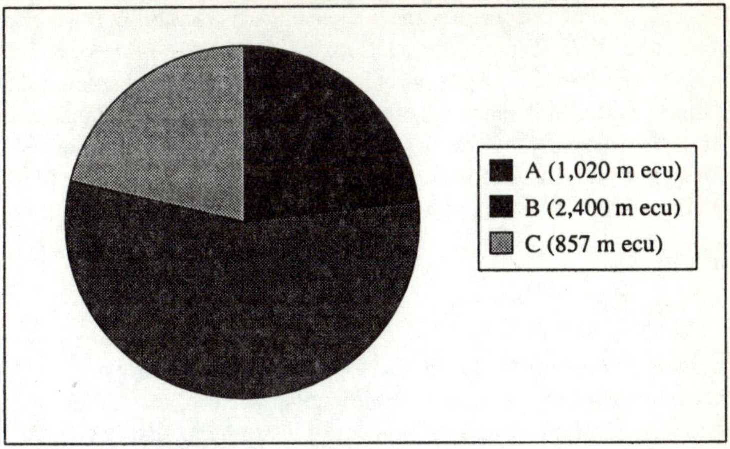

A Asia, Latin America, S. and E. Mediterranean
B Lomé Convention aid
C Food aid, emergency aid, developing country co-operation and projects

Planned yearly aid to ACP countries 1990–1995
Total: 12 bn ecu
Average: 2,400 m ecu

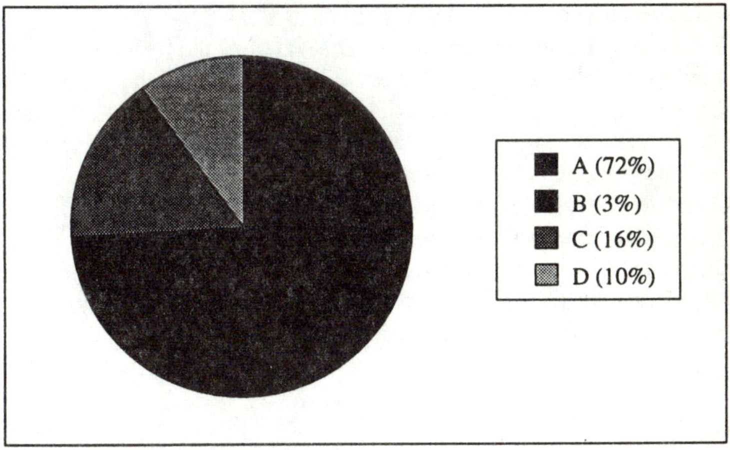

A Projects: grants and soft loans
B Emergency and refugee aid
C Stabex and Sysmin
D European Investment bank loans

Figure 2.1 EC financial aid to developing countries
Source: European Commission (1994)

be continued under the Joint Declaration of July 1991. The inter-relationship between these actors is explored in Chapter 4.

The excitement concerning the conclusion of the Uruguay round has occupied the EU's recent trade relations with industrialised countries but there have also been proposals to enhance the bilateral dialogue with both the United States and Japan. The recent disagreement with Canada about fisheries illustrates that trade generates its own crisis diplomacy and demonstrates that in questions of trade the historical ties of the Member States impact upon foreign policy, a question pursued in Chapter 7.

CONCLUSION

This chapter contends that from the foundation of the European Coal and Steel Community in 1951 to the codification of European Union in 1993 there has been progressive development of instruments that have given the Union the ability to operate internationally. Furthermore, the successive enlargements of the Union have enhanced the size and scope of the operations of the external relations undertaken by the Union. The international identity of the Union has increased in size and significance through the widening of the Union by expanded membership, the accompanying expansion of external relations activity and the range of instruments through which to conduct external relations.

Within this chapter an account was provided of the development of instruments available to the Union as a consequence of the Treaty provisions and commonly called external relations. The contention is that an account of the development of the instruments cannot be considered in a vacuum but requires us to explore the inter-governmental arrangements of EPC and the changing international context within which the Union has both developed and continually operated.

Therefore we first turn to these inter-governmental arrangements prior to considering the changing international context within which the international identity of the Union has developed.

NOTES AND REFERENCES

1. S. Patijin (ed.), *Jalons dans l'Europe unie* (Leyden, A.W. Sijthoff, 1970).
2. Alain Lamassoure, Minister Delegate, attached to the French Minister of Foreign Affairs, with responsibility for European Affairs, *Le Figaro*, 27 April 1994; *Speeches and Statements*, Ambassade de France á Londres, Service de Presse et d'Information, SS/94/80.

3. TEU, Title II, Part II.
4. *Ibid.*, Part Two, Article 8.
5. *Treaty Establishing a Single Council and a Single Commission of the European Communities*, Brussels, 8 April 1965.
6. *Treaty Establishing the European Coal and Steel Community*, Title One, Article 9.
7. J. Monnet, *Memoirs*, transl. Richard Mayne (London, Collins, 1978), p. 297.
8. J.H.H. Weiler, *Supranationalism Revisited – Retrospective and Prospective: The European Communities after Thirty Years*, EUI Working Paper No. 2 (European University Institute, San Domenico, Italy, March 1981), p.3.
9. M. Holland, *European Community Integration* (London, Pinter, 1993), chapter 2.
10. E.B. Haas, *The Uniting of Europe: Political, Social and Economical Forces 1950–1957* (London, Stevens & Sons, 1958), pp.58–9.
11. P. Taylor, 'Supranationalism: The Power and Authority of International Institutions', in A.J.R. Groom and P. Taylor, *Frameworks for International Co-operation* (London, Pinter, 1990).
12. *Ibid.*, p.120.
13. R.O. Keohane and S. Hoffmann, 'Institutional Change in Europe in the 1980s', in R.O. Keohane and S. Hoffmann, *The New European Community: Decision-making and Institutional Change* (Oxford, Westview Press, 1991).
14. Taylor, *op. cit.*, p.109.
15. R. Bullen, 'An Idea Enters Diplomacy: The Schuman Plan, May 1950', in R.J. Bullen, H. Pogge von Strandmann and A.B. Polonsky, *Ideas into Politics* (London, Croom Helm, 1984).
16. For the text of these treaties, see: R. Vaughan, *Post-War Integration in Europe* (London, Edward Arnold, 1976).
17. Déclaration de M. Robert Schuman, Ministre des Affaires Etrangéres de la France, le 9 mai 1950, in Patijin, *op. cit.*, pp.49 and 51.
18. *Ibid.*, p.47.
19. Bullen, *op. cit.*, p.195.
20. Detailed in Chapter 4.
21. Patijin, *op. cit.*, p.49.
22. Patijin, *ibid.*, p.51.
23. For an illustration of how differing national interests impacted upon the negotiations and their outcome, see: K. Scwabe (Hrsg.), *Die Anfánge des Schuman-Plans 1950/51: Beitráge des Kolloquiums in Aachen, 28.30. Mai 1986* (Baden-Baden, Nomos Verlagsgesellschaft, 1988).
24. Under the Treaty of European Union Article H the Court of Auditors was added as an institution of the ECSC.
25. Haas, *op. cit.*, p.45.
26. D. Spierenburg and R. Poidevin, *The History of the High Authority of the European Coal and Steel Community: Supranationality in Operation* (London, Weidenfeld & Nicolson, 1994), pp.193–5.
27. *Ibid.*, p.196.
28. *Ibid.*, p.187.
29. Quoted in Haas, *op. cit.*, p.98.
30. *Idem.*

31. For an account dating associationism the Treaty of Rome, see: E.R. Grilli, *The European Community and the Developing Countries* (Cambridge, Cambridge University Press, 1993).
32. Spierenburg and Poidevin, *op. cit.*, p.202.
33. *Idem.*
34. *Ibid.*, p.217.
35. *Ibid.*, p.350.
36. Haas, *op. cit.*, p.101.
37. *Ibid.*, pp.101–2.
38. G.W. Ball, *The Past Has Another Pattern* (New York, Norton, 1982), p.88.
39. Spierenburg and Poidevin, *op. cit.*, p.219.
40. *Ibid.*, pp.223–6.
41. For accounts of the role of the Higher Authority in the Spaak Committee, see: F. Duchêne, *Jean Monnet: The First Statesman of Interdependence* (London, W.W. Norton & Co., 1994), chapter 8; Spierenburg and Poidevin, *op. cit.*, chapter 13.
42. E. Fursdon, *The European Defence Community: A History* (London, Macmillan, 1980), pp.212–7.
43. The role of Monnet in initiating the proposed defence community is detailed in Duchêne, *op. cit.*, chapter 7.
44. Fursdon, *op. cit.*, pp.215–7.
45. Duchêne, *op. cit.*, chapter 7.
46. For details of these events see: D.W. Urwin, *The Community of Europe: A History of European Integration* (London, Longman, 1991), pp.74–5.
47. For a commentary on the early years of Community operation, see: H. von der Groeben, *The European Community: The Formative Years: The Struggle to Establish the Common Market and the Political Union (1958–66)* (Luxembourg, Office for the Official Publications of the European Communities, 1987).
48. TEU, Preamble. The numbering system of the Articles is in accordance with the Treaty of Rome as amended by the Single European Act in 1987.
49. *Ibid.*, Article 8.
50. *Ibid.*, Article 111.4.
51. *Ibid.*, Article 113.1.
52. *Ibid.*, Article 229.
53. *Ibid.*, Article 235.
54. Von der Groeben, *op. cit.*
55. R.C. Hine, *The Political Economy of European Trade: An Introduction to the Trade Policies of the EEC* (London, Harvester Wheatsheaf, 1985), pp.4–8.
56. For the background to the Yaoundé Convention, see Grilli, *op. cit.*, chapter 3.
57. 'The Fouchet Plan for a European political union: draft treaty of 2 November 1961', in R. Vaughan, *Post-War Integration in Europe* (London, Edward Arnold, 1976).
58. For the text of the Treaty and the Preamble, see: 'Text of the Franco-German Treaty signed in Paris, 22 January 1963; with preamble to the Act of Ratification adopted by the Bundestag on 8 May 1963', in Patijn, *op. cit.*, pp.145–61.

59. 'The Luxembourg Agreement, 29 January 1961', in Patijn, *op. cit.*, pp.174–9.
60. Hayes, *op. cit.*, pp.14–5.
61. For details of the negotiations and their outcome, see: Hine, *op. cit.*, pp.221–32.
62. For details of the transition from the 1961 Short Term Arrangement, through the LTA to the MFA, see: K.A. Koekkoek and L.B.M. Mennes, 'Some Potential Effects of Liberalising the Multi Fibre Arrangement', chapter 6 in L.B.M. Mennes and J. Kol (eds), *European Trade Policies and the Developing World* (London, Croom Helm, 1988).
63. M.C.E.J. Bronckers, *Selective Safeguard Measures in Multilateral Trade Relations: Issues of Protectionism in GATT European Community and United States Law* (Deventer, Netherlands, Kluwer, 1985).
64. I.V. Bael and J. Bellis, *International Trade Law and Practice of the European Community: EEC Anti-Dumping and other Trade Protection Laws* (Bicester, CCH Editions, 1985).
65. Hayes, *op. cit.*, pp.20–5.
66. Commission of the European Communities, *White Paper on Completing the Internal Market* (Luxembourg, Office for Official Publications of the European Communities, 1985).
67. For an account of the changed relationship between the EC/EU and Eastern Europe, see: J. Pinder, *The European Community and Eastern Europe* (London, Pinter for RIIA, 1991).
68. *Interinstitutional Directory: European Union,* March 1995 (Luxembourg, Office for Official Publications of the European Communities, 1995).
69. For a full study of the Cabinet of Delors conducted through participant observation, see: G. Ross, *Jacques Delors and European Integration* (Cambridge, Polity Press, 1995).
70. Interview with Head of Unit, Inspection of Delegations, DGI(A), Commission of the European Communities, 15 July 1993.
71. The Commission has placed both its Political Director and European Correspondent in DGIA who are the key participants in the CFSP process below the level of Minister, as will be detailed in Chapter 4. The Commission has been directly connected to the COREU communications network of CFSP since 1982.

    For the latter information, see: A. Pijpers, E. Regelsberger and W. Wessels, *European Political Co-operation in the 1980s: A Common Foreign Policy for Western Europe?* (London, Martinus Nijhoff, 1988), p. 106.
72. For the composition of all the Permanent Representations, see: General Secretariat of the Council, *Guide to the Council of the European Communities* (Luxembourg, Office for Official Publications of the European Communities, 1994).
73. For details of the historical development of COREPER and its attendant working parties and committees, see: F. Hayes-Renshaw, C. Lequesne and P.M. Lopez, 'The Permanent Representations of the Member States to the European Communities', *Journal of Common Market Studies* XXVIII, 2 (December 1989): 119–38; F. Hayes, 'The Role of COREPER in EEC Decision-making', *Administration* 32, 2: 177–200; E. Noél, 'The Committee

of Permanent Representatives', *Journal of Common Market Studies* (March 1967): 219–51.

74. R. Gray, 'How does the EC Set Trade Policy? Article 113 Committee plays key role in determining Community Position', *Europe* (September/October 1985): 24–5.
75. P. Nicolaides (ed.), *The Trade Policy of the European Community: Legal Basis, Instruments, Commercial Relations* (Maastricht, EIPA, 1993).
76. For a discussion, see: P. Messerlin, 'the Anti-dumping Regulations: A First Economic Appraisal, 1980–85', *Weltwirtschaft Archiv* 125, 3: 563–87; R. Weidermann, 'The Anti-Dumping Policy of the European Communities', *Intereconomics* (January/February 1990): 28–35.
77. Council Regulation 3286/94.
78. World Trade Organisation, *Trade Policy Review European Union: Report of the Secretariat* WT/TPR/S/3, 30 June 1995.
79. 'The Commission's legislative programme for 1994, Resolution of the European Parliament on the 1994 legislative programme, Council declaration on the 1994 legislative programme, Joint declaration of the European Parliament and the Commission on the 1994 legislative programme', *Bulletin of the European Union* Supplement 1/94 (Luxembourg, Office for Official Publications of the European Communities, 1994) [hereafter *Bulletin*]: 21.
80. *Ibid.*, pp.21–4.
81. World Trade Organisation, *Trade Policy Review of the European Union: Report by the Secretariat* Geneva, WTO, 30 June 1995. *Unpublished.*
82. 'Bloc bigger than Nafta "from many points of view"', *Guardian*, 1 January 1994, p.33; 'EEA links 17 nations in world's largest free trade zone', *Financial Times* weekend January 1–2, 1994, p.1.

    The figures quoted were EEA 372 million people and $7,501 bn GDP, NAFTA 360 million and $6,770 bn GDP.
83. 'European Economic Area – Background Briefing', *Background Report,* Commission of the European Communities, London, 13 January 1994.
84. *Idem.*
85. 'Bilateral Relations of the European Community with the Countries of Central Europe: Association Agreements, known as "European Agreements"', MEMO/92/94, *Commission of the European Communities*, London, 26 February 1992.
86. 'EEC-Eastern Europe Relations', MEMO/92/27, *Commission of the European Communities*, London, 21/05/92.
87. *Idem.*
88. *Idem.*
89. 'Summit's route map to the future', *The European*, 9–15 December 1994, p. 1.
90. 'The European Union and the New Independent States of the ex-USSR', Background Report, *Commission of the European Communities*, ISEC/B20/94.
91. *Idem.*
92. *Idem.*
93. 'Strengthening the Mediterranean Policy of the EU: Establishing a Euro-Mediterranean Partnership', COM (94) 427 Final.

94. *The European*, 28 July–3 August 1995, p.4.
95. 'Europe and the Mediterranean', Background Report, ISEC/B21, *Commission of the European Communities*, December 1994.
96. *Idem.*
97. *Idem.*
98. 'Strengthening the Mediterranean Policy of the European Union: Proposals for implementing a Euro-Mediterranean Partnership', COM (95) 72 Final.

3 The Development of the Framework of the International Identity: (2) From EPC to CFSP

> The Member States shall support the Union's external and security policy actively and unreservedly in a spirit of loyalty and mutual solidarity. They shall refrain from any action which is contrary to the interests of the Union or likely to impair its effectiveness as a cohesive force in international relations. The Council shall ensure that these principles are complied with.[1]

Chapter 1 considered the means of assessing the construction and representation of the international identity of the European Union. The chapter concluded by advocating a focus upon the instruments and the sources of influence that have given expression to the international identity. In the previous empirical chapter we commenced identifying the emergence of a set of instruments at the disposal of the Union. Furthermore, there was an examination of the progressive development and codification of the decision-making and implementation framework that has facilitated the expression of the international identity of the European Union.

In the previous chapters it has been noted that there has been a convention of distinguishing between two facets of the international identity of the European Union: namely, the external relations of the Union as regulated by the Treaty of Paris and the two Treaties of Rome; and the dimension that is usually designated as inter-governmental by successive commentators upon the process. In this, as in the previous chapter, we begin analytically to unite these two processes by illustrating the set of instruments that are available to the Union within a single typology. In addition we seek to a clarify the two frameworks that underpin and delineate any recourse to those instruments and chart their progressive coming together. Our focus now turns to the process commonly understood as inter-governmental.

The inter-governmental dimension has recently undergone a transformation from European Political Co-operation (EPC) to the Common Foreign and Security Policy (CFSP). It is suggested in this chapter that the development of the framework to facilitate EPC and its transition, under the Treaty on European Union, to the CFSP has been an uneven and incremental process. The establishment of the CFSP does not represent a new process but, rather, can only be understood by the consideration of its predecessor, EPC. The eventual end-point of the process remains, as yet, uncertain. As with the process of development outlined in the previous chapter, both internal and external imperatives that are to explored here, and within the other chapters, distinguish sources of influence on the international identity. This chapter explores how the inter-governmental element of the framework of the international identity has undergone a progressive codification over time.

It is not suggested that the Union has developed all the accoutrements of diplomacy. The Union has not displaced the arrangements of the Member States by creating a single, permanently unified foreign ministry, or a single network of embassies or permanent diplomats. The development of the inter-governmental framework has created a structure that is composed of elements drawn from the Member States, but simultaneously these operate as facilitators and manifestations of the international identity of the European Union.

The intention is to stress how the inter-governmental part of the framework has progressively developed to facilitate the projection of European Union influence. Some commentators have credited this facet of the identity as constituting one of the elements of a foreign policy.[2]

The ability of the Union to assert its international identity has not required the construction of a single foreign policy infrastructure. The international significance of the Union is, in part, a consequence of its heterogeneous composition. Whether this makes for the most efficient projection of the international identity of the Union is a matter of no small significance.

However, as was asserted in Chapter 1, the Union does not readily fit into existing conceptualisations of what constitute international actors and the accompanying conceptions of their effectiveness. What is needed here is to clarify the framework and set of instruments available to the Union and then to make an assessment of its effectiveness. In this chapter an outline is provided of the development of the framework of EPC and its transformation into the CFSP. Furthermore, the actions that have been implemented under the CFSP are examined.

THE ORIGINS OF EUROPEAN POLITICAL CO-OPERATION

Attempts to create a European foreign policy involving the Member States of the EC predate the Treaty of Rome founding the European Economic Community (EEC). The earliest attempt has been dated to 1952, the year following the creation of the first EC institution, the European Coal and Steel Community (ECSC).[3] The ill-fated attempt to create the European Defence Community (EDC) by the six members of the ECSC had been accompanied by the de Gasperi initiative to create a federalist European Political Community with a common foreign policy.[4]

President de Gaulle, as an opponent of increased power to supranational European institutions, promoted as an alternative notion to a federal Europe, the *L'Europe des parties*. In this vein, a French initiative for quarterly inter-governmental meetings of the foreign ministers of the Six for 'consultation' was initiated in 1960.[5]

Inter-governmentalism gained a further boost with the first conference of the 'Heads of State and Government and Foreign Ministers' of the Six, held in Bonn in February 1961. The conference mandated a committee, headed by Christian Fouchet, to examine methods of achieving a European Union. The Fouchet Committee proposed European Union under terms favoured by the French government – 'a union of states' – as opposed to the 'union of European peoples' favoured by the other five states.[6] Under the union of states proposal, European Union would be directed by a council composed of the heads of state and government. The union of European peoples approach envisaged a merger of the ECSC, EEC and Euratom executives and an increased role for the European Parliament (which was to become directly elected). In the face of these irreconcilable differences between the Member States, the Fouchet proposals were shelved.

The question of European Union returned to the agenda at the Hague Conference of heads of state and government in December 1969. The secession of Pompidou to the French Presidency (and his announcement in July 1969 that France no longer opposed the entry of the United Kingdom to the EEC) provided a new context for the deliberations of the Six. The international back-drop to the Summit saw the United States deeply embroiled in Vietnam; the Middle East in crisis following the 1967 war; the Soviet invasion of Czechoslovakia; and domestic unrest experienced in the Member States in 1968. The Hague summit marked the end of the transitional period of the Community and consequently it was agreed progressively to replace the financial contributions of the Member States with own resources for the Communities, thereby securing financing for the Common Agricultural Policy.[7] The summit also launched a project for economic and monetary union as well as negotiations for the enlargement of the Union.[8] The flavour of the communiqué issued at the end of the conference was that the Communities had attained a certain maturity and there was a need to reflect these new circumstances by going further. This was provided for in the communiqué issued by the Heads of State and Government that:

> a united Europe capable of assuming its responsibilities in the world of tomorrow and of making a contribution commensurate with its tradition and its mission...conscious of the role it has to play in promoting the relaxation of international tension...agreed to instruct the Ministers of Foreign Affairs to study the best way of achieving progress in the matter of political unification within the context of enlargement.[9]

THE LUXEMBOURG REPORT

Acting under the mandate of the Hague summit, the Foreign Ministers of the six Member States established a committee staffed by the heads of the political departments of their respective foreign ministries to give expression to the summit conference resolution. The subsequent report prepared by the committee chaired by the Belgian Etienne Davignon was adopted by the Foreign Ministers meeting in Luxembourg on 27 October 1970.[10]

The Luxembourg Report was explicit about the teleological thrust of the undertaking that it was advocating; that the six Member States 'being concerned to achieve progress towards political unification, the Governments should decide to cooperate in the field of foreign policy'.[11] However, the telos of the undertaking was tempered by the two objectives of this co-operation:

> (a) To ensure greater mutual understanding with respect to the major issues of international politics, by *exchanging information and consulting regularly*; [author's emphasis]
>
> (b) To increase their solidarity by working for a harmonization of views, concertation of attitudes and joint action *when it appears feasible and desirable* [author's emphasis].

Clearly, what was not envisaged at this stage was a joint foreign policy consisting of a universal coverage and binding upon all six participating states.

The Luxembourg Report initiated the institutions and procedures that were intended to facilitate 'exchanging information and consulting regularly'.[12] A President-in-Office was intended to initiate 'Ministerial Meetings' of the foreign ministers of the six states at least once every six months.[13] The position of President-in-Office was to be rotated among the Foreign Ministers to ensure that the meetings were headed by the country that was occupying the Presidency of the Council of the European Communities.

The groundwork for the meetings of the Foreign Ministers was to be conducted by a 'Political Committee' consisting of the heads of the political departments of the Member States – those who had prepared the Luxembourg Report – who would meet at least four times a year. The chairing of these Political Committee meetings was to be determined by the same formula as that of the Ministerial Meetings. The Political Committee was empowered to form 'working parties' for 'special tasks'.

The Luxembourg Report outlined procedures that were to be parallel, but outside, the existing institutions of the European Community. The relationship between the Luxembourg institutions and the Commission was expressed in one sentence: 'The Commission will be consulted if the activities of the European Communities are affected by the work of the Ministers.'[14] Informal meetings between members of the European Parliament's Political Affairs Committee and the Foreign Ministers were to be scheduled every six months to ensure a 'democratic process' in the construction of political union.[15] Additionally, the President-in-Office was to give an annual report on EPC to the full Parliament.

A short section entitled 'General' clarified three questions of practical importance.[16] Firstly, as all meetings were to be held in the country of the 'chairman', the host state would incur the burden of administration and each state was to appoint one of its officials as the 'correspondent' to counterparts in the other participating states. Hence, day-to-day control and administration of the process outlined in the Luxembourg Report was to be kept firmly in the hands of individual governments. An attempt to create a 'Political Secretariat' floundered on the question of where it should be located.[17] France, keen to ensure that EPC was kept separate from the EC, insisted on Paris over Brussels – the location favoured by the other five Member States.

The Luxembourg Report envisaged that 'the Foreign Ministers will submit their second general report two years at the latest after the introduction of consultation on foreign policy', by which time three other states would have acceded to the European Community – the United Kingdom, the Irish Republic and Denmark.

The first European Political Co-operation meeting took place on 19 November 1970 with two main items on the agenda that were to pre-occupy EPC over the next five years: the proposed Helsinki Conference and the Middle East.[18] Although for Willy Brandt, Chancellor for the Federal Republic of Germany, writing in retrospect, 'it still remains doubtful whether their formal statement of views on the situation in the Middle East was the right curtain-raiser'.[19]

THE COPENHAGEN REPORT

In a speech delivered on 23 April 1973, Henry Kissinger, then National Security Advisor, had declared 1973 the 'Year of Europe' and launched a proposal for a new Atlantic Charter. In the speech Kissinger denigrated the notion of a world role for the Community, stating, 'The United States has global interests and responsibilities. Our European allies have regional interests.'[20] Kissinger's analysis was at variance with the role that the Heads of State and Government, meeting for the first time as an enlarged group of nine, had claimed for the Community six months earlier:

> Europe must be able to make its voice heard in world affairs, and to make an original contribution commensurate with its human, intellectual and material resources. It must affirm its own views in international relations, as befits its mission to be open to the world and for progress, peace and co-operation.[21]

The Community went further than this aspiration by preparing a 'Document on the European Identity', published on 14 December 1973. The Document had a specific purpose for the Nine, '[to] enable them to achieve a better definition of their relations with other countries and of their responsibilities and the place which they occupy in world affairs'.[22] The European identity was defined in a three-fold fashion: the degree of unity already achieved within the Community; the extent to which the Nine were already acting together in world affairs; and the dynamic of European unification itself. The Foreign Ministers had declared that the role of the Community in international relations was informed by three sources – the existence of formal integration; past practice through EPC and external relations; and the process of integration.

Furthermore, within the Document a number of principles that were intended to dictate relations with the world can be discerned; firstly, defence of the principles of representative democracy, rule of law, social justice and human rights;[23] secondly, a willingness to extend membership to all

European nations who shared these ideals;[24] and thirdly, that the historical ties the Member States had created with other parts of the world should be maintained;[25] fourthly, the Community should favour an open world economy and the wealth the Community gained from its trading should be used to benefit all economic relationships;[26] and finally, that military defence should be assured by the Atlantic Alliance, US nuclear weapons and US forces stationed in Europe.[27]

There were also three internal principles that were explicitly stated as governing relations with third countries:

- the Nine acting as a single entity, will strive to promote harmonious and constructive relations with these countries. This should not however, jeopardise, hold back or affect the will of the Nine to progress towards European Union within the time limits laid down
- the future when the Nine negotiate collectively with other countries, the institutions and procedures chosen should enable the distinct character of the European entity to be respected
- In bilateral contacts with other countries, the Member States of the Community will increasingly act on the basis of agreed common positions.[28]

The Foreign Ministers were making clear their understanding of the Community as a distinctive, if unique actor, in its own right *but* one that would not displace the diplomacy of the component states and would rather seek to ensure harmonisation. The Document provided the first informational strategic rationale for the content of EPC. Furthermore, it went on to define interests by stating the regions (Africa, the Mediterranean, Latin America, Asia, USSR and Eastern Europe); multilateral organisations (Council of Europe, United Nations); and bilateral partners (China, Japan, Canada) with whom they wanted to strengthen links.[29] A special passage was reserved for describing relations with the United States, and stated that the Nine collectively intended to conduct relations 'on the basis of equality'.[30]

Earlier in the same year the 'Second Report on European political co-operation on Foreign policy' was approved by the Foreign Ministers of the Nine meeting in Copenhagen in July 1973.[31] This report was largely concerned with describing measures that had been adopted to further EPC since the Luxembourg Report.[32]

In the preamble to Part II of the Copenhagen Report it was noted that at the Conference of Heads of State or of Government held in October 1972 an objective had been established to 'transform, before the end of the present decade, the whole complex of the relations between the Member

States of the European Communities into a European Union'.[33] The measures for the EPC outlined in the Copenhagen Report were intended to further the move towards European Union.

The bulk of Part II of the Report was concerned with outlining procedural changes. The formal Foreign Ministers' meetings were henceforth to take place four times a year. Additionally, other consultations would take place: 'They may also, whenever they consider it necessary to consult each other on specific subjects between meetings, meet for the purpose when they happen to come together on other occasions.'[34] The formal separation between the meetings of Foreign Ministers in the mode of the Council of Ministers of the EC and the mode of Ministers considering questions of EPC was still in existence, but had been noticeably loosened.

The extra preparation that the increased frequency of Ministerial Meetings had created was acknowledged in the statement that meetings of the Political Committee 'will be held as frequently as the intensification of the work requires'.[35] The role of the Correspondents within each foreign ministry was enhanced with the assignment of the 'task of following the implementation of political and of studying problems of organization and problems of a general nature'.

The Political Committee's capacity to set up working parties was strengthened; it was envisaged that departmental heads from the respective foreign ministries would meet on a regular basis and study 'common medium- and long-term positions' on subjects proposed by the Political Committee.[36]

Importantly, the Copenhagen Report also outlined the role of the embassies of the Nine in the EPC process. Embassies in the capitals of Nine were to appoint one of their staff to maintain contact with the foreign ministry of the government to which they were accredited for EPC purposes. The foreign ministry of the country of residence was to supply 'information on a Community basis' and '*occasionally* [author's emphasis] entrusted with consultations on specific subjects'.[37] In addition, the President-in-Office may meet the ambassadors of the other states between the meetings of the Foreign Ministers to keep them informed of issues of political significance.

Embassies of the Nine in third countries were to be formally involved in EPC only when contacted direct by the Political Committee 'when it considers it necessary to obtain a contribution on a specific item on its agenda', with the provision for a common report to be produced by the nine embassies 'where appropriate'.[38]

The day-to-day burden that EPC created for the state holding the Presidency was acknowledged. However, the response was not to create an inter-governmental secretariat but rather to permit the sharing of the administrative burden and, importantly, 'to establish a communications system with a view to facilitating direct contact between their departments' – realised by the creation of the COREU telex network.[39]

The Copenhagen Report strenuously maintained the separation of the Commission of the EC from the EPC process:

> The political machinery, which deals on the intergovernmental level with problems of international politics, is distinct from and additional to the activities of the institutions of the Community which are based on juridical commitments undertaken by the Member States in the Treaty of Rome.[40]

No additional role was outlined for the Commission in the EPC process outside of Treaty of Rome issues; with respect to the European Parliament, informal meetings were increased to four times a year between the President-in-Office and the Political Committee of the Parliament.

In an appendix to the Copenhagen Report, the section, 'Results Obtained from European Political Cooperation', makes clear that the measures outlined in the bulk of the Report were, in fact, already existing practice.

The only additional information supplied is the role of the Nine with respect to the Conference on Security and in Europe. The CSCE was characterised, by a Foreign and Commonwealth Office official of the time, as crucial in the development of EPC as 'the first major test of their ability to work together'.[41] A Sub-Committee of the Political Committee, a *Sous-Comité CSCE*, was established and met in Helsinki, and the capital of the country holding the Presidency, in order to create a common position for the Nine on political humanitarian and cultural matters. This committee excluded the Commission, and was responsible to the Political Directors. In addition, the *Groupe ad hoc* was established, including representatives of the Member States together with the Commission, to examine areas concerning economic and technical interests. The division of work increased during the process by the creation of a *chef-de-file* system whereby each of the nine delegations was given responsibility for one subject area dealt with by the Conference.

In operating within the CSCE itself a number of innovations were introduced. The negotiations conducted within the second basket were conducted by civil servants of the Commission who were added to the delegation of the Member State which held the Presidency of the EC and spoke as members of the Commission when questions of Community competence arose.[42] In the concluding documents the President-in-Office signed on behalf of the EC to indicate that the Community was complying with the measures covered by the Treaty of Rome and thereby the EC was the only grouping represented officially involved in the process. The CSCE represented a learning process in attempting to cope in a context in which matters of EPC and economic issues were co-existent. Furthermore, the nature of the CSCE process was perfectly suited to EPC, as been noted by one commentator: 'These confidence-building measures between sovereign states, with no supporting enforcement apparatus, were the very stuff of EPC consensus.'[43]

The reactive nature of the Copenhagen Report suggested that the EPC process developed in a dynamic manner after the Luxembourg Report. One commentator has qualified this view by suggesting that the period 1970–1973 was one in which 'most participants were concerned more with institutional questions than with matters of substance'.[44] It is maintained that is was external imperatives, the war in the Middle East in October 1973 and the increasing difficulties in transatlantic relations that forced issues of substance on to the agenda and the experience gave a short-term impetus to the EPC process. However, there was a gradual decline in the process until the crises of 1979/80 in Iran and Afghanistan, which again acted to galvanise the EPC process by virtue of the incoherent European reaction to events.

The period from late 1972 to 1975 was indeed a period of substantial importance in the maturation of EPC and most importantly, for the purposes of this study, set the framework of instruments through which EPC was given effect. The preparations and involvement of the Community in the Conference on Security and Co-operation in Europe, that commenced in November 1972 and culminated in the Final Meeting in Helsinki from 30 July to 1 August 1975, also coincided with an increased Community involvement in the Middle East and the development of a number of other substantive instruments.

Although it has been described as a 'meaningless palaver', the Euro-Arab Dialogue between the Community and the 22 members of the Arab League created innovative relationships between EPC and Community structures.[45] Region-to-region dialogue was a largely unknown phenomenon in 1973, unlike the alacrity with which it is undertaken in the mid-1990s. Previously, within the confines of EPC the Foreign Ministers had declared their support for a settlement of the Arab-Israeli conflict on the basis of Security Council Resolution 242.[46] This position was re-affirmed when belatedly the Nine collectively responded to the attack by Egypt and Syria on Israel in October 1973 eight days after its occurrence.[47] In the declaration the Nine requested a cease-fire and negotiations on the basis of

Security Council Resolution 242. However, divisions between the Member States became apparent with the decision by the Organisation of Arab Petroleum Exporting Countries (OAPEC) to create three categories of consumers: friends, neutrals and enemies. As 'friends' the United Kingdom and France suffered no cut in oil supplies; as an enemy the Netherlands was subject to a total embargo alongside the United States. The remaining six classified as neutrals suffered a monthly 5 per cent reduction in supply. Although, the Nine may have viewed themselves as acting collectively, this experience demonstrated that outside actors were both able and willing and could discern differently against individual members. The upshot of the direct external pressure was a declaration by the Nine on 6 November 1973 that went further than previously declared positions, by recognising that any lasting peace settlement required full consideration of the legitimate right of the Palestinian people. The new Declaration is interesting in illustrating that declaratory diplomacy can be substantive, generating hostility from Israel, the United States and a lifting of the 5 per cent cutback on the neutrals. However, the embargo on the Netherlands was maintained.

The arrival of a delegation of Foreign Ministers from Arab states at the European Council meeting on 14–15 December 1973 was also innovative, in that it placed the Nine under direct and immediate pressure to respond directly to outside actors. The Community was treated as a substantive entity and this resulted in a commitment from the Nine to put into effect a dialogue.

Although agreeing in principle to a dialogue in March 1974, opposition from the United States prevented a response being made immediately and the rules for the dialogue were not declared until 1975 in a joint memorandum.[48] What was new was the creation of a central body, the General Committee, created to undertake this dialogue. On the Community side a Co-ordinating Group was established, reporting both through COREPER and the Political Committee. The structure adopted for the General Committee on the Community side was joint representation of the Presidency and the Commission. The Arab side also adopted a bicephalic presidency of both the Secretariat of the Arab League and the state holding the Presidency. The Euro-Arab Dialogue is based upon a non-existent legal framework with most of the Arab participants linked through other trade agreements (Gulf Co-operation Council, as parts of the Mediterranean policy or through the Lomé Convention). The rules and structures of procedure are contained within the Joint Communiqué of the first meeting of the General Commission, consequently the proliferation of working groups and subcommittees has taken place on a pragmatic basis.[49]

THE LONDON REPORT

The demands of the international events of 1979–1980 generated amendments in the EPC procedures that were given expression in the 'Report on European Political Co-operation' approved by the ten Foreign Ministers in London on 13 October 1981 (Greece acceded to the EC on 1 January 1981).[50] The substance of the London Report is the more efficient operation of the EPC process. The Report deals first with advice for governing Ministerial meetings, which was divided into two sections.

The first section dealt with the formal meetings of the Ministers; the agenda of these meetings was to be reserved only for items of major importance, and all texts submitted to the Ministers were to be accompanied by precise recommendations or a clear choice of options. The second section concerned informal or 'Gymnich' meetings.

The first informal weekend meeting was instituted at Gymnich in Germany in April 1974. Each Presidency-in-Office thereafter adopted the practice of holding one such meeting in a comfortable setting during its six-month Presidency. These meetings were to have no formal agenda and only the Foreign Ministers and a presidency note-taker were to be present. Only information approved for release by all ten of the participants would be transmitted to the press.

The Political Committee's agenda management for the Ministers' meetings was to be supported by the Correspondents' Group, who would act as a filter to the Political Committee by identifying work produced by the working groups that required substantive discussion. The Working Groups, in turn, were to both provide summaries of their reports and identify matters requiring further attention by the Political Committee.

The London Report explicitly addressed two criticisms that had been levied at the EPC process: namely, the reactive nature of its consultations and continuing divergence of issues of substance. There was a commitment to the Political Committee taking 'a long term approach to certain problems, and to institute studies to that end' and additionally for the Ten to 'prepare studies on areas where their positions diverge'.[51]

The fact that the Ten were increasingly being acknowledged as a single actor in international affairs was acknowledged and a 'troika' form of representation established, suggesting a desire to ensure continuity: 'If necessary, and if the Ten so agree, the Presidency, accompanied by representatives of the preceding and succeeding presidencies, may meet with representatives of third countries.'[52] The move towards representational harmonisation was also envisaged at the level of missions in third countries. Heads of Mission were to meet regularly and to seek to exchange information and co-ordinate views. Joint reports prepared by the Heads of Mission and submitted to the Political Committee were actively encouraged. The London Report also noted that 'in certain capitals of the Ten the practice has developed of regular meetings between the nine heads of Mission and the political director of the host government.'[53]

The drive to achieve continuity between Presidencies, reflected in the move towards a troika of Foreign Ministers, was also to be carried forward in other areas, with the Presidency 'assisted by a small team of officials seconded from preceding and succeeding presidencies'.[54] These seconded officials were to be accredited to their embassy in the capital of the country holding the Presidency. The President-in-Office was also empowered to share responsibilities by permitting the preceding Presidency to complete tasks outstanding from its term of office and delegating work to the successor President.

The London Report also acknowledged the changed role of the European Parliament that had been directly elected since 1979. However, there was no commitment to follow its will on foreign affairs, only 'the possibility of more frequent reference to resolutions adopted by Parliament'.[55]

The location and frequency of the meetings of the Foreign Ministers was no longer to be constrained by the desire to underline the distinct separation of the EPC and the EC. It was envisaged that political meetings could take place on the same occasion as the Foreign Affairs Ministers met together as the Foreign Affairs Council of the EC. Additionally, acknowledging the need for better crisis reaction, an emergency meeting requested by three Member States would convene within 48 hours. A similar procedure was also available to Heads of Mission in third countries.

THE SOLEMN DECLARATION

The creation of European Political Co-operation had originally been for the purpose of assisting further moves towards European Union. However, EPC had remained outside the remit of the Treaty of Rome and was conducted as an inter-governmental process outside the institutions of the EC. EPC had also remained a consultation process with no commitment by the participants either to agree or to act together.

In the early 1980s, the EC was under considerable strain internally with increasing criticism of the cost of the Common Agricultural Policy and the issue of the UK contribution to the EC budget. In spite, or rather because of these economic problems, the German and Italian Foreign

Ministers, Genscher and Colombo, sought to revitalise the concept of European Union by offering a 'Draft European Act'.[56] On the occasion of the presentation of the Act to the European Parliament, Genscher stated:

> we cannot focus our efforts solely on economic issues. We must, instead, set our sights on the grand design of the political unification of Europe, for it is from that design that we shall draw the strength to act as one and take decisions, on economic matters, and others, which will not simply paper over the cracks but provide forward looking solutions.[57]

The Draft Act proposed that Member States should move beyond consultation on foreign affairs and adopt a 'common foreign policy'. To facilitate the formulation of a common foreign policy it was envisaged that 'The decision-making structures of the European Communities and European political shall be brought together under the responsibility of the European Council'.[58] The Draft Act ran into a variety of obstacles from the Member States.[59] The Foreign Ministers were given the task of considering the Draft Act and the result was the preparation of a 'Solemn Declaration on European Union' signed on 19 June 1983.[60]

The Solemn Declaration made no mention of the merger of the EC and EPC institutions proposed in the Draft Act. In place of a commitment to a common foreign policy and a merger of the EPC into EC institutions, the Solemn Declaration stressed that within EPC there must be 'intensified consultations' and the 'progressive development and definition of common principles and objectives'.[61]

It was during this period that the Community first adopted a negative transference instrument implemented in the form of sanctions as the counterpoint to the positive transference instrument of aid. In between 1966 and 1968 the Member States had implemented the Security Council sanctions against Southern Rhodesia as individual acts. In 1980, in response to the taking of American hostages, the Member States discussed sanctions against Iran but implemented sanctions individually. On 4 January 1982, in response to the imposition of martial law in Poland, and in the aftermath of an informal meeting of Foreign Ministers of the Community, the Member States issued a declaration 'on the development of the situation in Poland' that contained a clause that 'Other measures will be considered in the light of developments of the situation in Poland, in particular measures concerning credit and economic assistance to Poland'.[62] The Ministers, as the Council of the Communities, then announced that they had instructed COREPER and the Commission to examine the feasibility of trade policy measures. In response to a Commission proposal the Council adopted a Regulation, a legal act, enforcing restrictions on imports.[63]

The next occasion on which the Member States utilised the negative transference instrument of sanctions was a much less satisfactory experience and illustrates the impact of domestic political processes upon policy formulation. With the occupation of the Falkland Islands on 2 April 1982, the British government requested sanctions at a Council meeting on 6 April. Although the principle was agreed, a Danish parliamentary requirement for consultation on measures of trade policy, delayed the passage of Regulation until 14 April and which came into force for one month from 16 April.[64] On the expiry of the sanctions, parliamentary opposition in Italy and Denmark, and domestic opposition in Ireland, saw sanctions renewed for only seven days at the Council of Ministers' meeting on 17 May. The Council, meeting again on 23 May, agreed extension without time limits, but Ireland and Italy refused to continue their enactment.[65]

Prior to the birth of European Union on 1 November 1993, sanctions were enacted through the Community in the EPC process on three other occasions. Firstly, against South Africa in 1986 through a Council Regulation prohibiting the import of gold coins, and decisions on the prohibition of iron and steel products (within the framework of the ECSC) and a Council decision on a ban on new investments. In the latter instance the decision lacked a legal basis and was ignored by the British government from February 1990.[66] Secondly, against Iraq, following its invasion of Kuwait on 2 August 1990, when the Community also used positive transference by humanitarian aid to Turkey, Jordan and Egypt. Thirdly, against Serbia and Montenegro during fighting in Croatia in 1991.

The use, and experience, of sanctions illustrates that in the implementation of policy the Community was reliant upon Community institutions for common decision-making and codification of the decision but these measures are reliant upon the Member States for their implementation. A variety of Community Articles (EC Treaty Articles 113, 224 and 235) can be utilised to impose sanctions and these will be detailed in Chapter 5.

THE SINGLE EUROPEAN ACT

EPC was eventually to achieve legal recognition in the Single European Act (SEA) that came into force in 1987. Until this date EPC had been operating without a legal basis guided by the reports, declarations and procedures outlined above. However, Title III, 'Treaty Provisions on European Cooperation in the sphere of foreign policy', was *not* an amendment to either the Treaty of Paris or the Treaties of Rome and therefore EPC remained formally outside the remit of the EC institutions. Title III of the

SEA was, for the most part, a codification of existing practice acting to 'confirm and supplement the procedures agreed in the reports of Luxembourg (1970), Copenhagen (1973), London (1981), the Solemn Declaration on European Union (1983) and the practices gradually established among the Member States.'[67]

The SEA made one important contribution to the EPC process by establishing a full-time secretariat based in the Council of Ministers building in Brussels charged with the preparation, implementation and administration of EPC matters.[68] The Secretariat was headed by a senior diplomat appointed for two and a half years. In support there were to be five other diplomats – two drawn from the two previous Presidencies, one from the present and two others drawn from the two succeeding Presidencies. Thus each diplomat was intended to serve for two and a half years, with one new diplomat joining every six months. The members of the European Political Secretariat were to enjoy full diplomatic privileges and immunities.[69]

The period from the commencement of the two inter-governmental conferences until the eventual enactment of the TEU represents the twilight years of EPC. They coincided with the Gulf War and the outbreak of the conflict in the former Yugoslavia. The perceived inadequacy of the Community response towards these events mocked EPC in its old age. Although the Union had been presented with crisis management situations in the 1970s, with the invasion of Cyprus and the democratic revolutions in Portugal and Spain, the magnitude of the two major conflicts of the early 1990s overwhelmed the instruments available through EPC and primacy was accorded to other fora, such as the United Nations and NATO. Against the backdrop of these events the Community was transforming itself into the Union and a more robust set of instruments was soon to be enacted.

THE TREATY ON EUROPEAN UNION AND THE COMMON FOREIGN AND SECURITY POLICY

The Treaty on European Union agreed at Maastricht on 11 December 1991 reflected aspirations for a common foreign policy and went beyond the modest aims of the EPC process. To quote Article B:

> The Union shall set itself the following objectives:... – to assert its identity on the international scene, in particular through the implementation of a common foreign and security policy including the eventual

> framing of a common defence policy, which might in time lead to a common defence.[70]

The Common Foreign and Security Policy has transformed EPC into an integral part of the three-pillar structure of the Union. The CFSP retains a style of decision-making distinct from that which operates under the Community pillar of the Treaty, but the two decision-making systems have been brought very much closer under the CFSP and, as Article C of the Treaty states, 'The Union shall be served by a single institutional framework.'[71] However, the Article goes on to give particular attention to the international identity, asserting:

> The Union shall in particular ensure the consistency of its external activities as a whole in the context of its external relations, security, economic and development policies. The Council and the Commission shall be responsible for ensuring such consistency. They shall ensure the implementation of these policies, each in accordance with its respective powers.[72]

Title V of the TEU covers the 'Provisions on a Common Foreign and Security Policy'. The objectives of the policy established by Article J.1.2, and attempts to achieve their realisation, will be explored below after an exploration of the CFSP decision-making and implementation process.[73]

The CFSP process of decision-making has been altered from that which operated under EPC. As was noted in Chapter 1, Article C of the Maastricht Treaty requires that the Union shall be served by a single institutional framework. The General Affairs Council of the European Communities has now adopted the title of the Council of the Union (hereafter, 'the Council'). The distinction between EPC Ministerial meetings and General Affairs Council meetings, as was outlined above, had been progressively eroded, and now EPC ministerial meetings have been terminated altogether. The Council is now the sole forum for CFSP. This means that the formal EPC ministerial meeting, that was held each six months in the capital of the country holding the Presidency, has been abolished. The Gymnich informal meetings remain in place.

The Council, in its meetings, now operates with a single agenda and in a single setting with CFSP and other Union business taken together. As a member of the Council has noted, the content of meetings increasingly concerns the international identity:

> [the] Council now concentrates the bulk of its discussions on the Union's external relations. To confine myself to the Councils held since 1 January, under the French Presidency, out of 61 agenda items,

39 – two thirds – concerned external relations, 18 of them actions embarked on under the CFSP proper.[74]

In the TEU notice was also given that the existing relationships between institutions involved in the process were to be reconsidered:

> the division of work between the Political Committee and the Committee of the Permanent Representatives will be examined at a later stage, as will the practical arrangements for merging the Political Secretariat with the General Secretariat of the Council and for cooperation between the latter and the Commission.[75]

Changes have occurred in these arrangements. The preparation of CFSP items remains, as under EPC, the responsibility of the Political Committee. The Political Directors meet on a monthly basis with the European Correspondent responsible for day-to-day contacts. The EPC Secretariat has been merged with the General Secretariat of the Council. The Secretariat is now staffed by 15 diplomats seconded from each Member State and an equal number of officials from the Council Secretariat.[76] The COREU network which conducts communications in English and French, was to continue 'for the time being' but all common foreign and security texts that are considered or adopted in Council or European Council meetings were to be in all community languages.[77] Within the Foreign Ministries EPC units, responsible for co-ordinating the positions of the individual Member States and supporting the Correspondents and the Political Directors, underwent a renaming rather than a restructuring anticipating 'work as usual'.

The Commission for its part responded to the recognition of its full association with CFSP and its ability, shared with the Member States, to submit any proposals to the Council, by dividing the main department, the Directorate General, with responsibilities for external relations into two parts: DGI for External Economic relations, and DGIA for External Political Relations.[78] This new assertiveness was reinforced with the appointment of the Hans van den Broek, a former Minister for Foreign Affairs of the Netherlands, as the Commissioner with responsibility for external political relations.[79]

The Presidency of the Union is explicitly granted the responsibility for the implementation of the CFSP under the TEU and the troika and bicephalic troika are also retained as other overt instruments at their disposal.[80] A number of other overt instruments have been deployed under the CFSP and these are detailed in Chapter 4.

In pursuance of the objectives of the CFSP two approaches are provided for. The first approach is 'establishing systematic cooperation between

Member States in the conduct of the policy, in accordance with Article J.2'.[81] Article J.2 requires that the

> Member States shall inform and consult one another within the Council on any matter of foreign and security policy of general interest in order to ensure that their combined influence is exerted as effectively as possible by means of concerted and convergent action.[82]

This requirement does not represent a substantial departure from EPC; however, the Member States have made it possible to go beyond this process by creating 'common positions'.[83] It is then imperative upon Member States to ensure that their national policies conform to the common positions and furthermore to ensure that these are upheld in international organisations and conferences, even when all the Member States are not participants.[84]

The TEU also goes further and provides for 'by gradually implementing, in accordance with Article J.3, joint action in the areas in which the Member States have important interests in common'. The introduction of joint actions has also generated a new decision-making process through which these positions are formulated. Joint actions are intended to provide for self-contained 'packages' of foreign policy:

> Whenever the Council decides on the principle of joint action, it shall lay down the specific scope, the Union's general and specific objectives in carrying out such action, if necessary its duration, and the means procedures and conditions for its implementation.[85]

The decision as to what should be the subject of a joint action resides with the Council, acting under general guidelines from the European Council. Both common positions and joint actions require unanimous agreement in the Council. However, voting has been introduced, albeit in limited circumstances, and this has broken the previous EPC practice of unanimity. 'The Council shall, when adopting the joint action and at any stage during its development, define those matters on which decisions are to be taken by a *qualified majority*. [Author's emphasis][86]

The introduction of security questions under Article J.4 of the Title represents a substantive widening of the EU's agenda, to which we give consideration in Chapter 5. At this point it is noteworthy that under the provisions for the Western European Union to 'elaborate and implement decisions and actions of the Union which have defence implications', the Council remains the sole Union institution explicitly charged with cultivating the relationship.[87]

The Treaty on European Union appears to augment a new era in European foreign policy: it appears to signify that EPC is to give way to a more binding inter-governmental process. The planned use of Community institutions also appears to signify a relaxation of the attempt to maintain control over EPC by governments at all levels of the process. However, the role of the Parliament remains marginal, and this is detailed in Chapter 7.

As a central part of the aspiration of the Union, in the words of the TEU, 'to assert its identity on the international scene', the Member States under the auspices of the CFSP have defined a set of broad objectives and sought to implement the policy. The clutch of broad objectives for the CFSP, as defined in Article J.1(2) of the Treaty are:

- to safeguard the common values, fundamental interests and independence of the Union;
- to strengthen the security of the Union and its Member States in all ways;
- to preserve peace and strengthen international security, in accordance with the principles of the United Nations Charter as well as the principles of the Helsinki Final Act and the objectives of the Paris Charter;
- to promote international cooperation;
- to develop and consolidate democracy and the rule of law, and respect for human rights and fundamental freedoms.

In the aftermath of the signing of the TEU on 7 February 1992, and with the expectation that the Treaty would come into force on 1 January 1993, the Foreign Ministers of the then Twelve presented a report 'on the likely development of the CFSP with a view to identifying areas open to joint action vis-à-vis particular countries or groups of countries' to the European Council meeting in Lisbon in June 1992.[88] The European Council meeting in Maastricht in December 1991 had given the Foreign Ministers the task of preparing this informational instrument and to provide the beginnings of a strategic rationale within which to conduct the CFSP.

The Foreign Ministers made clear that the CFSP should both be seen as the successor to EPC but went further, in that

> With specific aims and means, the CFSP represents a 'saut qualitatif' in the sense that it integrates the 'Acquis' of EPC and gives it greater potential, principally by means of joint action, an additional instrument which implies a strict discipline among Member States and enables the Union to make full use of the means at its disposal.[89]

In particular CFSP was to ensure that the external action of the Union was to be less reactive to events and 'more active in the pursuit of the interests of the Union and in the creation of a more favourable international environment'.[90] The intention, clearly influenced by the experience of the Community in the early stages of the Yugoslav conflict, was that the Union would engage in preventive diplomacy.[91]

The Lisbon Report proposed both 'geographical areas' and 'horizontal domains' as the basis on which to implement the CFSP. Each area identified for activity was to be on the basis of specific objectives and a set of these was outlined in the Report.

- strengthening democratic principles and institutions, and respect for human and minority rights;
- promoting regional stability and contributing to the creation of political and/or economic frameworks that encourage regional cooperation or moves towards regional or sub-regional integration;
- contributing to the prevention and settlement of conflicts;
- contributing to a more effective international coordination in dealing with emergency situations;
- strengthening existing cooperation in issues of international interest such as the fight against arms proliferation, terrorism and the traffic in illicit drugs;
- promoting and supporting good government.[92]

The Foreign Ministers cast the strategic informational rationale of the CFSP in terms of an integrative diplomacy, promoting both regional integration but more broadly supporting the creation and perpetuation of international regimes for co-operation. The Ministers went further than specific objectives by listing a three-fold set of factors that should be considered in determining the common interests of the Union: geographical proximity; an important interest in the political and economic stability of a region or country; the existence of threats to the security interests of the Union.[93]

Recognising that the Union had common interests, the Foreign Ministers set out their definition for the first phase of the CFSP. The Ministers were moving beyond questions of seeking to harmonise foreign policies of twelve individual states and were identifying a set of interests for a single actor. These interests were defined in two-fold terms: firstly, in terms of areas of 'geographical interest', and secondly, of 'horizontal domains'. These areas can be taken as both the primary interests of the Union as a single actor and provide an indication of the order in which that actor, the Union, might define its interests.

Geographical interests were ordered largely in accordance with geographical proximity and divided into two broad regions with a breakdown within those regions. The first priority was accorded to Central and

Eastern Europe, encompassing, in order; 'Russia and the Former Soviet Republics'; 'Other countries in Central and Eastern Europe including the Balkans'; and 'Former Yugoslavia'. The second broad region was 'Maghreb and the Middle East', then broken down into its two component parts described respectively as the 'Union's southern border' and 'one of the constant preoccupations of the Community and its Member States'.[94]

Africa, Asia, Latin America and the Caribbean are also mentioned in passing, and treated as a collective group with which 'the Union may want to develop gradually in a consistent and coordinated manner its external activities'.[95] The industrialised nations of the United States, Canada and Japan are mentioned and it was made clear that these relations are to be conducted on the basis of existing joint bilateral declarations previously made with these states.

Within horizontal domains, which encompass security, priority was accorded to the then CSCE process: disarmament and arms control in Europe; nuclear non-proliferation; economic aspects of security defined as control of arms exports and the transfer of military technology.[96]

To give practical effect to its interests and in accordance with the provisions of Article J.3(1) on decision-making within the CFSP, the European Council has laid down general guidelines for the areas that the Council of Ministers should consider to be the subject of joint action. At a European Council meeting in Brussels on 29 October 1993, the European Council primed the CFSP pump by asking the Council of Ministers to outline the basis for joint action in five areas: the reinforcement of the democratic process and development of co-operation in Central and Eastern Europe via the promotion of a stability pact; the use of the political, economic and financial resources of the Union in support of the Middle East peace process; support for the transition towards multi-party democracy in South Africa, through the assistance of preparation and monitoring of elections and the creation of a framework for economic and social assistance; the search for a solution to conflict in the former Yugoslavia by means of contributions to the implementation of the peace plan and humanitarian action; support for democratic process in Russia by the despatch of observers to the Russian Parliamentary elections on 12 December.[97]

At another two European Council meetings in 1994, in Corfu and Essen, another two joint action areas were added: joint action on the preparation of the 1995 Nuclear Non-Proliferation Treaty Conference; and control of exports of dual-use goods.

These joint actions represent a manifestation of European Union 'actorness' in that the Union has created distinctive arrangements for their implementation. In EPC, as was noted above, the EC sought to draw on the economic significance of the Union. This is still a component in the CFSP and explicitly provided for in one area of the Treaty of Rome, as amended by the TEU. Under Article 228a of the CFSP the EU can utilise economic sanctions as a negative transference instrument

> Where it is provided, in a common position or in a joint action adopted according to the provisions of the Treaty on European Union relating to the common foreign and security policy, for an action by the Community to interrupt or to reduce, in part or completely, economic relations with one or more third countries, the Council shall take the necessary urgent measures. The Council shall act by a qualified majority on a proposal from the Commission.[98]

The relevant legislative process for the enactment under a qualified majority is detailed in Chapter 5. Sanctions have been enacted under Article 228a in support of common positions on Libya, Sudan, Haiti and the former Yugoslavia. The enactment or termination requires a Regulation to be passed that takes effect, without the need for measures at the level of the Member States, either once the Regulation is published in the 'L' (Legislation) series of the *Official Journal of the European Communities*, or on the date contained in the Regulation.[99]

However, the Union has gone beyond drawing upon existing Community strengths in the joint actions that it has undertaken thus far by seeking to create specific instruments to serve particular joint actions. Although these draw upon the resources of the Community and the Member States they are explicitly for furthering the CFSP and, in turn, enhance the international identity and represent an operationally tentative, but profoundly symbolic, advance on EPC. In particular, the WEU has been used for the implementation of joint actions, and this will be explored in Chapter 4. Under CFSP the Union has gone beyond CFSP in creating a structured relationship with the Europe Agreement countries. Once per Presidency a special Council meeting is convened and, as with the WEU, the Union has involved the prospective applicants in CFSP actions through both half-yearly political committee meetings and working group meetings.[100] Operationally the Associates were invited to create 'Shadow European Correspondents', and a mechanism has been put in place to permit the alignment with the Union in common declarations, the implementation of joint actions and co-ordination within international organisations. Therefore, under the CFSP the Union has created a status of Association analogous to that existing within the WEU and as an attempt to broaden and deepen the relationship with the Associates beyond the Community pillar. Other innovative features of the joint actions are detailed after outlining the other manifestations of CFSP which place the joint actions in perspective as only a minor part of a relatively undeveloped process.

If we examine the CFSP between its implementation on 1 November 1993 until 31 December 1994 it becomes clear that the Union has relied heavily upon the use of declaratory instruments. Declarations issued under CFSP have departed from the practice under EPC of using a plural expression, 'the Community and its Member States', to distinguish between the two entities.[101] Declarations under the CFSP refer to the 'European Union' in the singular.[102] Despite the ordering of interests detailed in the Lisbon Report, the majority of the 110 CFSP Declarations of the period have concerned the African region (geographical breakdown detailed in Figure 3.1).

The Declaration is used by the Union as a reactive instrument to respond to unfolding international events. But, it is perhaps the silences rather than the Declarations that are of interest. Declarations are a public expression of consensus among the Fifteen and largely either welcome or condemn events. The paucity of Declarations on the Mediterranean basin, despite the intensity of the violence in Algeria during the period, can be read as a lack of substantive agreement among the Member States as to an appropriate response. Likewise, the use of troops by the Russian Federation in Chechnya on 11 December 1994 did not generate a Declaratory position by the Union until 18 January 1995. Speaking on the events in Chechnya the Belgian Foreign Minister Frank Vandenbroucke

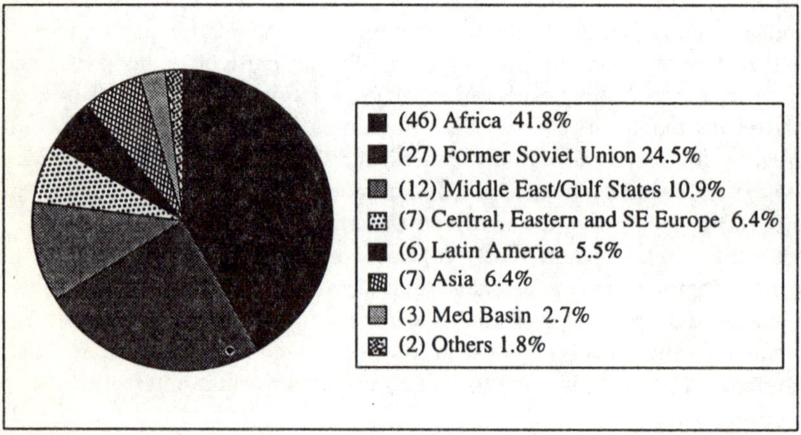

Figure 3.1 CFSP Declarations from November 1993 to December 1994 by region
Source: Author

characterised the difficulties in a Union response by stating, 'European foreign policy is handicapped by the requirement for unanimity by member states for each decision.'[103]

The other two areas through which the Union can pursue these objectives are 'Common Positions' and 'Joint Actions' areas, both of which, as was noted above, also require a unanimous decision by the Member States. During the period from 1 November 1993 to 31 December 1994 the Council adopted six Common Positions. Four of these provided for either embargoes (Sudan, Haiti, Federal Republic of Yugoslavia) or the use of Common Position to detail the objectives and priorities for the Union's relations with two countries (Rwanda and Ukraine).

The joint actions initiated during the period were outlined above. They are of particular interest because of the development of new instruments through which to give them effect. Joint Actions of the Council are legal acts and have effect when published in the *Official Journal* alongside other Community legislation. The first two Joint Actions covered the convoying of aid in Bosnia-Herzegovina and the sending of observers to the Russian elections and were adopted by the Council at its meeting as the Council of the European Union on 8 November 1993.[104]

The expenditure for the Bosnia-Herzegovina humanitarian aid Joint Action was divided between the Commission and the Member States.[105] A total expenditure of 48 million ecu was allocated to fund the Action.[106] The Joint Action with respect to the Russian elections was given effect through a Moscow-based European Union Observer Centre for the Russian elections on 12 December 1993. The centre was staffed by one representative of the Belgian Presidency, one from the European Parliament and two from the Commission as well as locally engaged personnel.[107] The Centre, which reported to the Council, was responsible for providing transport and communications assistance to the 24 observers sent by the European Parliament and monitors sent by the national parliaments and NGOs of the Member States. Furthermore, the Union employed the German-based NGO, the European Institute for the Media (EIM), to monitor election coverage.[108]

A similar unit was created for the Joint Action on the South African elections, fielding 312 observers. The Union established in South Africa a 'European Electoral Unit' headed by Jacob de Ruiter, a former Dutch Minister of Justice and Minister of Defence, and with a budget of 12 million ecu.[109] The unit (dissolved one month after the elections), monitored the electoral process and administered and oversaw the deployment of European Union monitors and, in particular, co-ordinated the Union's efforts with those of the United Nations.[110]

The Joint Action on the Conference for Stability in Europe illustrates the importance of the role of the Member States both as a source of influence on the CFSP and in generating initiatives conducted under its auspices. The proposal, originally floated by then French Prime Minister Balladur (and subsequently dubbed the Balladur Pact), was adopted by the Council as a Joint Action on 20 December 1993.[111] The inaugural conference to launch the initiative was convened in Paris on 26–27 May 1994. The purpose of the initiative was to 'implement preventative diplomacy, aimed at arousing neighbourly relations and to encourage the countries, notably through concluding appropriate agreements, to consolidate their frontiers and settle the problems of national minorities which they may face'.[112] The Union explicitly used the aspiration of Central and Eastern European Union states to join the Union as leverage to ensure their compliance.[113] The then Union Presidency of Greece, the troika including Germany and Belgium, and France, as the host country of the inaugural conference, were all deployed, both bilaterally and multilaterally and through their respective embassies in the region, to promote agreements.[114] The initiative eventually resulted in a collection of over 100 bilateral treaties and a Declaration on good neighbourly relations between East and Central European states, which were collectively handed to the Organisation for Security and Co-operation in Europe for the monitoring of compliance with the agreements.[115] The Stability Pact illustrates how the Member States can seek to accrue and to enhance their own international standing through Union diplomacy, as an EU diplomat noted, 'It was the classic French technique of coming up with a grand-sounding idea, having it changed in the process, and then claiming success at the outcome.'[116]

The six associated countries of Central and Eastern Europe were involved in Joint Action for the renewal of the NPT. France, as the President of the EU, opened the general debate at the review and extension conference, speaking not just for the Fifteen but also for the, then, six central and eastern European associates.[117]

Incurring expenditure on such operations raises the yet unresolved question of the source of finance for operational expenditure. Article J.11 of the Maastricht Treaty provides for either Community or Member State funding. The administrative expenditure for the CFSP is financed out of the Community budget.[118] The question of how operational expenditure should be financed is an intractable problem. If financing occurs under the Community budget, then the question of to what heading and/or procedure to allocate it becomes important: this is one area where the European Parliament has its greatest powers and if the budget falls under nonobligatory expenditure, Parliament would have the final say over the Council and this would take the powers of the Parliament in CFSP beyond consultation, questioning and making recommendations.[119] If financing takes place directly by the Member States then there are questions of management. The question currently remains unresolved, with the dispute being whether operational expenditure should be funded from the Commission or the Council section of the budget.

CONCLUSION

The understanding of what constitutes the EPC and CFSP framework extends to the procedures and network that have been outlined in the documents considered and decision-making process outlined above. The existent literature on EPC/CFSP judges the 'success' and 'failure' of EPC solely on the basis of those occasions on which the Member States coordinate their actions (which in itself may have little to do with EPC and more to do with coincidental interests over an issue). What is actually required is a greater understanding of the process of formulating the CFSP through a variety of sources of influence.

European Political Co-operation has been inextricably linked with the question of European Union from its earliest origins. As with the progressive moves towards European Union, the development of EPC and the CFSP has been an uneven and incremental process. Foreign policy has traditionally been an area of 'high' politics and, as is illustrated in the three-pillar structure created by the Treaty on European Union, there is an unwillingness by the Member States to relinquish direct control. EPC has operated through the existing structure of foreign ministries and embassies operated by the Member States. However, as signatories to the Treaty of Rome the Member States of the EC ceded representation of economic issues in an international context to the EC. The CFSP process has moved beyond the economic strength of the EC to back up its foreign policy decisions through the Joint Actions detailed above. As was outlined, these measures have not displaced the actions and efforts of Member States but rather are reliant upon the Members as a primary source of influence and implementation. In accompaniment with the instruments that were detailed in Chapter 2 the Union has a set of instruments through which it can give effect to its aspiration to assert its identity in the international environment. In the next chapter the standing of the Union within the contemporary international environment is explored.

NOTES AND REFERENCES

1. Council of the European Communities, Commission of the European Communities, *Treaty on European Union* (Luxembourg, Office for Official Publications of the European Communities, 1992), Article J.1.4.
2. W. Wessels, 'European Political Co-operation: A New Approach to European Foreign Policy', in D. Allen, R. Rummel and W. Wessels (eds), *European Political Co-operation: Towards a Foreign Policy for Western Europe* (London, Butterworth, 1982), p.1.
3. W. Wallace, 'Political Co-operation: Integration through Intergovernmentalism', pp.373–4 in H. Wallace, W. Wallace and C. Webb (eds), *Policy-making in the European Community*, 2nd edn (Chichester, John Wiley & Sons, 1983).
4. For a full account of the de Gasperi proposals and the factors behind the EDC, pp.212–7 and chapters 6–8 in E. Fursdon, *The European Defence Community: A History* (London, Macmillan, 1980).
5. D. Allen and W. Wallace, 'European Political Co-operation: The Historical and Contemporary Background', chapter 2 in Allen, Rummel and Wessels (eds), *op. cit.*
6. G.L. Goodwin, 'A European Community Foreign Policy', *Journal of Common Market Studies* XII 1 (September 1973): 7–27.
7. 'Communiqué of the meeting of Heads of State or Government at The Hague, 1 and 2 December 1969', Article 5. Text reproduced in S. Patijn (ed.), *Landmarks in European Unity: 22 Texts on European Integration* (Leyden, A.W. Sijthoff, 1970), pp.213–9.
8. *Ibid.*, Articles 8 and 13.
9. *Ibid.*, drawn from Articles 3, 4 and 15, respectively.
10. 'Report by the Foreign Ministers of the Member States on the Problems of Political Unification', *Bulletin of the European Communities* 11 (1970): 9–14 [hereafter *Bulletin*].
11. *Bulletin* 11 (1970: 10.
12. *Bulletin, ibid.*, Part Two.
13. There was also provision for a conference of the Heads of State or Government if 'the situation is serious enough or the subjects to be discussed are sufficiently important to warrant this.' *Bulletin, ibid.:* 11.
14. *Bulletin, ibid.:* 12.
15. *Bulletin, idem.*
16. *Bulletin, ibid.:* 13.
17. Goodwin, *op. cit.*, p.21.
18. *Bulletin* 1 (1971): 15.
19. W. Brandt, *People and Politics: The Years 1960–1975, transl. J. Maxwell Brownjohn (London, Collins, 1978), p.247.*
20. Quoted in S. Nuttall, *European Political Co-operation* (Oxford, Clarendon Press, 1992), p.86.
21. 'Statement of the Conference of the Heads of State and Government of the Member States of the European Community' (Paris, 21 October 1972), reproduced in: *European Political Co-operation*, 5th edn (Bonn, Press and Information Office of the Federal Government, 1988), pp.31–4.

22. 'Document on the European Identity published by the Nine Foreign Ministers (Copenhagen, 14 December 1973)', *ibid.*, p.48.
23. Contained within the section on 'The Unity of the Nine Member Countries of the Community', Point 1, *ibid.*, p.49.
24. *Ibid.*, Point 4, p.50.
25. *Ibid.*, Point 5, p.50.
26. *Ibid.*, Point 7, p.50.
27. *Ibid.*, Point 8, pp.50–1.
28. *Ibid.*, Point 10, pp.51–2.
29. *Ibid.*, Points 11–21, pp.52–4.
30. *Ibid.*, Point 14.
31. *Bulletin* 9 (1973): 14–21.
32. D. Allen and W. Wallace, 'European Political Co-operation: the historical and contemporary background', chapter 2 in Allen, Rummel and Wessels (eds), *op. cit.*
33. *Bulletin* 9 (1973): 15.
34. *Ibid.*, p.16.
35. *Idem.*
36. *Ibid.*, pp.16–7.
37. *Ibid.*, p.17.
38. *Ibid.*, p.18.
39. *Idem.*
40. *Idem.*
41. Crispin Tickell in I.G. John, *EEC Policy towards Eastern Europe* (Farnborough, Saxon House, 1975), p.115.
42. A. Pijpers, *The Vicissitudes of European Political Co-operation: Towards a Realist Interpretation of the EC's Collective Diplomacy* (Leiden, Proefschrift, 1990), pp.129–30.
43. A. Budd, *The EC and Foreign and Security Policy,* European Dossier Series 28 (London, University of North London Press, 1993), p.15.
44. W. Wallace, 'Political Co-operation: Integration through Intergovernmentalism', chapter 13 in Wallace, Wallace and Webb (eds), *op. cit.*
45. W. Laquer, *A Continent Astray: Europe 1970–78* (New York, 1978), p.153.
46. *Bulletin* 6 (1971): 31.
47. The following account is drawn from D. Allen, 'Political Co-operation and the Euro-Arab Dialogue', chapter 6 in D. Allen, R. Rummel and W. Wessels, *European Political Co-operation: Towards a Foreign Policy for Western Europe* (London, Butterworth, 1982).
48. 'June 1975 Cairo Joint Memorandum', reproduced in P. Ifestos, *European Political Co-operation: Towards a Framework of Supranational Diplomacy?* (Aldershot, Avebury, 1987), p.611.
49. 'The Euro-Arab Dialogue: Procedurally Innovative, Substantially Weak', chapter 4 in: G. Edwards and E. Regelsberger, *Europe's Global Links: The European Community and Inter-Regional Co-operation* (London, Pinter, 1990), p.62.
50. *Bulletin* (Supplement) 3 (1981): 14–17.
51. *Bulletin* (Supplement) 3 (1971): 15.
52. *Ibid.*, p.16.

53. *Idem.*
54. *Ibid.*, p.17.
55. *Idem.*
56. *Bulletin* 11 (1981): 87–91.
57. *Ibid.*, p.10.
58. *Ibid.*, p.89.
59. W. Wallace, 'Political Co-operation: Integration through Intergovernmentalism', pp.398–9, chapter 13 in Wallace, Wallace and Webb (eds), *op. cit.*
60. *Bulletin* 6 (1983): 24–9.
61. *Bulletin, ibid.:* 28.
62. 'Final Communiqué of the informal meeting of the Foreign Ministers of the Ten on the development of the situation in Poland (Brussels, 4 January 1982)' in *European Political Co-operation (EPC)*, 5th edn (Bonn, Press and Information Office of the Federal Government, 1988), pp.147–9.
63. Greece was exempted from the provisions of this Regulation. A. Pijpers, E. Regelsberger and W. Wessels, *European Political Co-operation in the 1980s: A Common Foreign Policy for Western Europe?* (London, Martinus Nijhoff, 1988), p.112.
64. L. Freedman and V. Gamba-Stonehouse, *Signals of War: The Falklands Conflict of 1982* (London, Faber & Faber, 1990), pp.152–3.
65. *Ibid.*, pp.347–48.
66. See M. Holland, 'Sanctions as an EPC Instrument', chapter 9 in M. Holland (ed.), *The Future of European Political Co-operation: Essays on Theory and Practice* (London, Macmillan, 1991), p.190.
67. *Treaties establishing the European Communities*, abridged edn (Luxembourg: Office for Official Publications of the European Communities, 1987), pp.563–9, [hereafter Treaties].
68. Article 30, 10(g). *Treaties, ibid.*, p.568. G. de Bassompierre, Changing the Guard in Brussels (New York, Praeger, 1988), pp.59–60, outlines the staffing of this Secretariat.
69. SEA Article 30.11; *Treaties, op. cit.*, pp.568–9.
70. Council of the European Communities, Commission of the European Communities, *Treaty on European Union* (Luxembourg: Office for Official Publications of the European Communities, 1992), pp.7–8, (hereafter TEU).
71. *Ibid.*, p.8.
72. TEU, Article C.
73. These objectives are as follows:

    to safeguard the common values, fundamental interests and independence of the Union:

    - to strengthen the security of the Union and its Member States in all ways;
    - to preserve peace and strengthen international security, in accordance with the principles of the United Nations Charter as well as the principles of the Helsinki Final Act and the objectives of the Paris Charter;
    - to promote international co-operation;
    - to develop and consolidate democracy and the rule of law, and respect for human rights and fundamental freedoms. (*Ibid.*, pp.123–4).

74. 'Speech by M. Alain Lamassoure, Minister Delegate, attached to the Minister of Foreign Affairs with responsibility for European Affairs, to the European Parliament', Brussels 26 April 1995. *Statements*, Ambassade de France á Londres, Service de Presse et d'Information SAC/95/81 – CFSP, p.1.
75. 'Declaration on Practical Arrangements in the Field of Common Foreign and Security Policy' *Treaty, op. cit.*, p.240.
76. G. Edwards and S. Nuttall, 'Common Foreign and Security Policy', in A. Duff, J. Pinder and R. Pryce, *Maastricht and Beyond: Building the European Union* (London, Routledge for the Federal Trust, 1994).
77. TEU, *op. cit.*, p.241.
78. Articles J.9 and J.8.3. For the organisational sub-division, see *Directory of the European Commission: 16 December 1993* (Luxembourg, Office for Official Publications of the European Communities, 1994).
79. The appointment created a private and public dispute between van den Broek and the other Commissioners dealing with external relations Leon Brittan and Manuel Marin. See 'Daggers Out in War for Words', *The European*, 8–11 April 1993, p.12.
80. TEU, Article J.5.1–3.
81. TEU, *op. cit.*, p.124.
82. TEU, Article J.2.1.
83. TEU, Article J.2.2.
84. TEU, Article J.2.2–3.
85. TEU, Article J.3.1.
86. TEU, *op. cit.*, p.125. A declaration attached to the Treaty 'On voting in the field of common foreign and security policy' takes this principle further; with regard to Council decisions requiring unanimity, Member States will, to the extent possible, avoid preventing unanimous decision where a qualified majority exists in favour of that decision' TEU, *ibid.*, p.239.
87. *Ibid.*, p.126.
88. Annex I, 'Conclusions of the Presidency', European Council, Lisbon 26–27 June 1992. DOC92/3, Commission of the European Communities.
89. *Ibid.*, Point 2.
90. *Ibid.*, Point 3.
91. 'This will enable the European Union to have an improved capacity to tackle problems at their roots in order to anticipate the outbreak of crises'. *Idem.*
92. *Ibid.*, Point 10.
93. *Ibid.*, Point 12.
94. *Ibid.*, Points 30 and 32.
95. *Ibid.*, Point 17.
96. *Ibid.*, Point 35.
97. 'Presidency Conclusions', European Council in Brussels, 29 October 1993, p.3.
98. EC Treaty, Article 228a.
99. For an example, see: Council Regulation (EC) No. 109/95 of 23 January 1995 amending Regulation (EC) No. 2472/94, suspending certain elements of the embargo on the Federal Republic of Yugoslavia (Serbia and Montenegro); *Official Journal*, No. L 20, 27.1.1995.
100. *Agence Europe*, 9 March 1994, pp.4–5.
101. See any European Political Co-operation Press Release; as an illustration, see 'Statement on Nigeria', Brussels, 13 July 1993, p.69/93.

102. As an illustration, see 'Declaration by the European Union on Algeria', *Common Foreign and Security Policy Press Release* 31 (January 1995) PESC/95/5.
103. 'Belgium calls for clear EU policy on Russia', *Reuters Euro Community Report*, 10 January 1995.
104. *Europe: Agence Internationale d'Information pour la Presse* (hereafter *Agence Europe*), No. 6103, 8/9 November 1993, p.3.
105. *Agence Europe*, No. 6123, 8 December 1993, p.3.
106. *Agence Europe*, No. 6164, 5 February 1994, p.3.
107. *Agence Europe*, No. 6125, 10 December 1993, p.4.
108. *Idem.*
109. *Agence Europe*, No. 6152, 20 January 1994, p.6.
110. *Agence Europe*, No. 6123, 8 December 1993, p.3.
111. 'New French pact aims to avoid "second Yugoslavia"', *Financial Times*, 10 June 1993, p.2.
112. *Agence Europe*, No. 6139, 31 December 1993, p.3.
113. Note the comments by Alain Juppé:

    > to our minds there is also a link between this exercise in preventive diplomacy and the major issue that will be on the next decade's agenda: the enlargement of the European Union...[it is] that the applicant countries also put their own affairs in order, in the same way as the Union must put its affairs in order, by solving their own problems of neighbourly co-existence. This is why the conference on stability will help facilitate future enlargement.
    >
    > 'Address by M. Alain Juppé, Minister of Foreign Affairs, at the Anglo-American press lunch', *Service de Presse et d'Information, Ambassade de France á Londres*, 2 May 1994, SS/94/89, p.15.

    See also 'Foreign Secretary to Visit Paris', Press Release, Foreign and Commonwealth Office, No. 76, 26 May 1994:

    > The EU's objective is to help nine countries (Estonia, Latvia, Lithuania, Czech Republic, Slovakia, Romania, Poland, Hungary, Bulgaria) resolve problems, especially concerning frontiers and minorities, which could be an impediment to EU membership.

114. 'Address by M. Alain Juppé, Minister of Foreign Affairs to the National Assembly (Paris, 12 April 1994)', *Speeches and Statements*, Ambassade de France á Londres, Service de Presse et d'Information, SS/94/72, p.27; and *Agence Europe*, No. 6154, 22 January 1994, p.3.
115. *Financial Times*, 21 March 1995, p.2.
116. 'Stability Pact may be Balladur's Swansong', *Reuters Euro Community Report*, 20 March 1995.
117. 'Address by M. Alain Juppé, Minister of Foreign Affairs, on behalf of the European Union and the countries of Eastern and Central Europe at the NPT Review and Extension Conference (New York, 18 April 1995)', *Statements*, Ambassade de France á Londres, Service de Presse et d'Information, SAC/95/78, p.31.
118. *Agence Europe*, No. 6141, 5 January 1994, p.5.
119. The role of the Parliament is detailed in TEU, Article J.7.

Part II
The Facets and Sources of Influence on the International Identity

4 The External Sources of Influence: The European Union in the International System

> The European Community, if it were to become politically cohesive, would have the population, resources, economic wealth, technology, and actual and potential military strength to be the preeminent power of the twenty-first century.
>
> Samuel Huntington[1]

In Part I of the text the development of the instruments of the international identity have been explored. Part II focuses on identifying sources of influence that account for the nature of the international identity and the instruments through which it is given effect. The systems approach which we are using takes the European Union as the system and a set of sources as the operational environment.

THE EXTERNAL SOURCES OF INFLUENCE

This chapter focuses on the external sources of influence on the construction and representation of the international identity of the European Union. The function of this chapter within the overall framework of the text is two-fold. Firstly, it seeks to identify the changing external context within which the European Union is operating. Secondly, it provides the bridge between the two parts of the study. The external sources of influence have not only played a key role in the creation of the international identity but the changing context has also created a situation in which the instruments available to the Union have become increasingly significant in the post-Cold War era. The crux of this chapter is to raise the question of what makes the European Union significant in international affairs and to identify further instruments at its disposal.

The contention is that changes to the international context, within which the Union has operated, have shown the commonly made distinctions within the Union between the integrative and inter-governmental dimensions of the international identity to be unhelpful. The development of the dual systems of decision-making, outlined in Chapters 2 and 3, have affected the ability of the Union to utilise its international significance fully and to use instruments available to enhance its international identity. As a French Minister has noted:

> The disadvantage is that the power authorised to represent Europe is not clearly identified. It is in fact shared between the presidency, the Council of Ministers and the Brussels Commission. This vagueness harms the effectiveness of Europe's action and image.[2]

In spite of these arrangements the Union has become a significant international actor *without* transforming itself into a nation state, the agreed significant actor in classical approaches to international relations. The reason for this state of affairs is that the international context within which the Union now operates, and the instruments available at its disposal, have converged to enhance the relative significance of the Union. The Union is in a curious position in that it is the collective capabilities of the Fifteen Member States of the Union that contribute to the international significance of the Union, yet the Union lacks 'fungibility' – that is, the ability to fully transform, and to utilise, the capabilities of the Member States and thereby to put them fully at the disposal of the Union without any loss of efficacy.[3]

In this chapter we seek to examine contemporary international relations and the Union's position within them. In Chapter 1 we examined the view that the European Union is not an internationally significant actor in terms of Realist theories of international relations. In this Chapter it is not asserted that the Union is becoming a more significant actor in international relations through the adoption of state-as-actor characteristics. Rather, we are exploring the capabilities of the Union in comparison to significant states in the international system. The coverage of international affairs is limited by identifying a set of sources of influence significant for the development of the international identity.

Using a systems approach, this set of sources provides the external sources of influence upon the decision-making system of the Union. The notion of a foreign policy-making system that orders this study suggests that the policy-making system and its operational environment are to be considered in a symbiotic relationship. Traditional approaches to the study of foreign policy-making rest upon two sets of distinctions. In considering the relationship between foreign policy and the environment within which it is made, a distinction is drawn between the *domestic* and the *international* and the *psychological* and the *operational*.[4] The distinction between the domestic and the international rests upon an understanding of the differing nature of domestic and international politics, and the international is seen to be determinate. The distinction between the psychological and the operational environment rests upon the policy-making environment as understood by policy-makers and the settings that impact upon decision-makers, and provide the sources of influence that we seek to identify in this book.

The exploration of the operational environment for the international identity of the European Union forms the focus of this and the succeeding chapters. The identity of the Union is not constructed within a vacuum but rather is constrained and organised with reference to the operational environment within which the Union finds itself. A number of points of clarification need to be made. The operational environment is not a synonym for the international system, as this constitutes only one part of the operational environment. Likewise, environment does not merely imply either the biosphere, the ecosystem or the politics of international environmental diplomacy. Again, these elements in themselves form a part of the operational environment.

The constituent elements of the operational environment of the European Union that will be explored in this chapter as external sources are as follows: the international system, the international political economy, the European context and the cultural context.[5] It is important to note that each of these elements is separated for analytical purposes and each element is both inter-related and inter-active with all of the other elements that compose the operational environment.

The hypothesis that the changing external context has contributed to the increasing international importance of the Union rests on three propositions about contemporary international relations and the empirical material to support these contentions. It is suggested that three inter-related dimensions of contemporary international relations contribute to the increased international significance of the Union: the changing balance of power in the international system, the increasing institutionalisation of international relations and the changing international political economy. Each of these propositions will be outlined briefly: we examine in depth the change they have undergone and how these changes have contributed to the international rise of the European Union. It will be suggested that each of these factors has contributed to the rise of the 'integrationist diplomacy' of the European Union.

THE OPERATIONAL ENVIRONMENT

The term 'bipolarity' has been frequently used to characterise the distribution of significant, and effective, world power in the international system that emerged in the aftermath of World War II. The widespread alignment of nation states to one or other of the two states characterised as superpowers, the United States and the Soviet Union, came to exemplify the balance of power of the international system of the post-war period. One of the characteristics of the bipolar system and the institutions and arrangements that characterised its development was its relative stability, understood as no direct war between the great powers in the system.[6] The inference is that bipolarity tended to induce stability and cautiousness rather than recklessness, which might bring about war.

The termination of World War II also coincided with the creation of the United Nations. This new institution, committed as it was to the elimination of war between nation states, did not exercise authority over and above the nation state and, therefore, did not displace the perception that nation states had ultimately to rely upon their own resources and alliances to ensure their own security. The United Nations codified the principle that nation states were equal in international law but did not eliminate the stratification of influence of the international system, with some states having greater influence over others.

The end of the Cold War raises many questions about the nature of the new international environment. Some analysts have suggested that the international system has now moved into a state of tripolarity, with economic confrontation replacing power politics as the new ordering principle of the international system.[7] Such interpretations place the European Union as one of the pre-eminent actors of the international system in the twenty-first century. The new talk is not of geopolitics but of geoeconomics.[8] The tools and instruments of commerce are viewed as replacing the accoutrements of war as measures of significant power in the international system. However, alongside all these indications of change nation states still remain the only units of governance that stretch across the international system. Indeed, the post-war period has seen an explosion in the number of nation states that can be measured by membership of the United Nations.[9]

In recent years there has also been a substantial increase in regionalism, with inter-governmental and non-governmental organisations encompassing regions of the globe and incorporating a variety of tasks.[10] The EU, as a manifestation of regionalism in the international system, has developed the institutions of governance (detailed in Chapter 2), incomplete as they are, to exercise power above the nation state. It is for this reason that a distinction can be made between Western Europe operating as a self-contained system that has profoundly transformed relations between its constituent units and the wider international system within which Western Europe remains. The distinction between these two systems serves this study as a heuristic device to facilitate the exploration of this phenomenon. Even cursory empirical attention would suggest that neither the Western European system nor the international system are hermetically sealed from one another. Rather, there has been an interplay between the two. The growth of transnationalism and interdependence, and more recently globalisation, suggest that the previously clear distinction between the domestic and the international, and the retention of sovereignty by the nation state, are under challenge.[11]

The impact of the transnational pressures of demography and accompanying environmental and technological change have raised questions about the future of the nation state as a form of political organisation and its ability to cope with a new security agenda driven by global imperatives and challenges.[12] Although the political significance of geography has been altered by advances in technology and communications narrowing the 'technological distance', the impact of the immediate environment upon the exercise of power and the conduct of foreign policy, or geopolitics, remains high.[13] Contemporary geopolitics represents an interest in the inter-relationship between population, economy and technology (questions of resource possession and their location) expressed as a political relationship between nation states.[14] It is the possession of these capabilities by the European Union and the distribution of these capabilities relative to other states that raise the question of the balance of power in the contemporary international system.

THE INTERNATIONAL SIGNIFICANCE OF THE UNION

The European Union has increasingly attracted significance as a major force in international relations, to such an extent that is increasingly suggested as one of a set of emergent powers in the international system. However, despite the well-rehearsed attempts to fit the EU into one or other of the existing categories of international actor offered by the literature of International Relations theory, explored in Chapter 1, the question remains as to why the Union should be considered internationally significant.

The view advanced in this chapter is that there are three factors of significance in assessing whether the Union should be considered one of the primary international actors. Firstly, there is the *milieu*: the geographical, demographic, economic, and technological resources of the Fifteen Members of the Union and how these contrast to the resources available to other significant actors in the international system. Secondly, there are the changes in the structure of the international system that are of particular significance to the Union because of its milieu. These encompass the decline of bipolarity and the relative decline of the United States and their impact internationally and within Europe. Thirdly, there is the creation of a network of bilateral relationships between the European Union and other states and regional groupings, the emergence of which was detailed in Chapters 2 and 3, which gives the diplomacy of the European Union a distinctive form of its own and can be called 'integrative diplomacy'.

THE MILIEU AND THE BALANCE OF POWER

The notion of the balance of power has a long and distinguished history as a means of designating and distinguishing between international systems. During the period of the Cold War the notion of the balance of power became central to the concerns of many practitioners and scholars of international relations, encompassing both its essence and as a direct guide to policy formulation and implementation.[15] As would be expected of a concept whose ancestry is traced to Thucydides, it has also generated various interpretations. The idea of the balance of power has, amongst other definitions, been used to designate a policy aimed at achieving a certain state of affairs, an objective or actual state of affairs, an approximately equal distribution of power or any distribution power including a preponderance of power. The balance of power has been offered as an ordering device of the contemporary international system.[16]

In attempts to plot the polarity of the contemporary international system it has become commonplace to identify a disjunction between economic and military power, alongside a diffusion of power through transnationalism and inter-dependence.[17] Where scholars tend to disagree is to what extent the structure of the international system and state behaviour has been modified by the latter two phenomena.[18] The consensus is that the international system has moved from the bipolar system, that emerged at the end of World War II, to a system of uncertain configuration.[19] With the termination of the 50 years of the Cold War, and the ability to assess the period in totality, there is a realisation that the confrontation era of the cold war has not yet given way to a comprehensive and enduring post-war peace settlement or an easily comprehensible international landscape, with all the uncertainties that this entails.

The more thoughtful commentators on post-Cold War international relations have not seen this situation as *back to the future* and the opportunity to continue the long-standing debate on the inherent stability or instability of bipolar or multipolar international systems.[20] Rather, the view has been advanced that we are now confronted by a new concert of 'Great Powers' encompassing the United States, Russia, the EU, Japan and China.[21] However, as will be explored below, any analogy with the nineteenth century is flawed, in the first instance, by the dissimilarities in the types of capabilities of these states.[22] Secondly, with the increasing regionalisation and institutionalisation that is the hallmark of the contemporary international system, the position of putative great powers has been transformed. Thirdly, the widespread recognition of the increasing inter-mingling of the domestic and the international through the rising inter-dependence of nation states, commonly referred to as globalisation, has called into question the viability of the exercise of state power internationally. Indeed, a concern with the 'world of states' rather than the 'state of the world' may be misplaced.[23] The emergence of a 'bifurcated' global system with a state-centric world co-existing, interacting and competing with a multicentric world of transnational, national and subnational actors is upon us.[24] It is the disaggregation of power between the Member States and the European Union and their co-existent relationship that places the EU simultaneously within the state-centric and the multicentric world of post-international politics, a characteristic that can be captured using the framework of a system.

THE EU AND THE WORLD OF STATES

Of particular importance in the world of states is the issue of the perceived decline of a US hegemony and its consequences for both world order and the functioning of the international economy. A concern for the rise and fall of the great powers in the global system, and in particular the contemporary relative decline of the United States as a great power, has been granted considerable popular attention since the publication of *The Rise and Fall of the Great Powers* in 1989.[25] The inter-relationship between economic wealth as the mainstay of military power and military power as the best guarantee for the expansion and retention of economic strength, and the measure of the economic and military strength of one nation state relative to others in the system provides a guide to the retention and elimination of great power status over the long-term. Assessment over the long term is clearly crucial for discerning trends in the changing distribution of relative capabilities of nation states. However, for the purposes of this text we are seeking to assess the contemporary international identity of the European Union and this, inevitably, requires a snapshot assessment of the EU relative to other putative great powers in the international system.

This snapshot can be attempted by an examination of the resource power available to the major powers in the international system.[26] Of the five main concentrations of economic and military power identified as the new concert of powers in the international system today, the only one that is not a sovereign nation state is the EU. The EU itself calculates and publishes the capabilities of the EU in contrast to Japan and the United States by comparison of elements of their respective resource capabilities: geographical area, population, Gross Domestic Product, and Gross Domestic Product per head. To these statistics have been added comparable statistics for China and Russia. The graphs in Table 4.1 illustrate that in the areas that the EU chooses to calculate for comparative purposes, it enjoys considerable capabilities. In themselves, these measures provide no indication as to how these capabilities translate into political power in the international system.

In preference to the notion of 'Great Power' it would be more appropriate to consider these entities as 'significant' powers, defined purely on the basis of the preponderance of the resource capabilities detailed above.

A further measure of significant power is membership of international organisations that derives from resource capabilities and involve the political and economic management of the international system. As can be seen from the table, only two of these entities gain membership of all of these limited-membership organisations (Table 4.2).

Table 4.1 The relative capabilities of the European Union

Significant power	*Geographical area* (km^2)	*Population* (millions)	*GDP* ($ bn)	*GDP per head* ($ bn)
United States	9,372,614	255.4	5,905	23,119
Japan	377,708	124.3	3,508	28,217
China	9,561,000	1,166.1	442	379
Russia	17,075,400	148.9	398	2,671
EU (15)	3,235,000	370.5	7,269	19,948

Source: Eurostat, Statistical Office of the European Communities (1994) and *The Economist* 1994

Table 4.2 The Membership of EU Member States and the Commission in selected international organisations

Organisation (membership at 30 June 1995)

Significant Power	*G-7 Founded 1975*	*OECD Founded 1961*	*UN Security Council Founded 1945*
China	Not member	Not member	permanent member
European Union	France Germany Italy United Kingdom EU Commission* EU Presidency*	15 EU Member States European Commission	France + United Kingdom + Italy ++ Germany ++
Japan	Member	Member	Not member
Russian Federation	Full participation in political G-8**	Not member	Member
United States	Member	Member	Member

* The President of the European Commission and the President of the European Union (if not a G-7 Member State) have participated since 1977

** The Russian Federation was invited to participate in the annual G-7 summit of Heads of State and Government dubbed the 'political G-8' from the Naples Summit in July 1994 onwards[27]

\+ Permanent members

++ Elected by the General Assembly to serve a two-year term from 1 January 1995

The question that is raised by the European Union's involvement in these three organisations (the OECD, the United Nations and the G-7) is how far the preponderance of EU Member States and the Commission translates into a coherent pursuit of the interests of the Union. The record across these three organisations is mixed.

Organisation for Economic Co-operation and Development

Within the OECD the Union has a somewhat interesting status, composing just under two-thirds of the total membership. The Commission has a special status within the OECD: it is not a formal member or an observer but an active participant under Article 13 of the OECD Convention and of its additional Protocol No. 1. The Permanent Representative of the European Commission to the OECD, who enjoys ambassador status[28] and members of the Permanent Representation, may speak on matters of Community competence or where the Community has a common position or in the name of the Commission.[29] The EU Members collectively contribute 40 per cent of the OECD budget and act collectively caucus within the OECD; they recently clashed directly with the United States over the most appropriate candidate for the post of OECD Secretary General.[30]

The OECD had also been used as a mechanism through which to pursue Union initiatives – for example the creation of the European Bank for Reconstruction and Development (EBRD) – and, in turn, the OECD has used the Union to administer and disburse the PHARE programme of aid to Poland, Hungary, Bulgaria, the Czech and Slovak Republics, Romania and the pre-conflict Yugoslavia. The then Twelve, the Commission and the European Investment Bank provided 51 per cent of the capital for the EBRD, 72 per cent of the grants and over 50 per cent of the loans issued through PHARE.[31]

The United Nations

Under General Assembly Resolution 3208 (XXIV) of 11 October 1974, the then EEC was invited 'to participate in the sessions and work of the General Assembly in the capacity of observer'. The UN Diplomatic List notes that the EU is represented by the Head of the Delegation of the EU Commission *and* by the Permanent Representative of the European Union Member State holding the Presidency of the Union. The double-headed or bicephalic representation is necessitated by the UN work encompassing both Community and CFSP work. The EU either on its own or in combination with one of the Member States has become the only non-state entity signatory of over 50 multilateral UN conventions and agreements, including the Vienna Convention and the Montreal Protocol.[32]

The then EC Commission established an official observer mission in New York in 1976 and its full official diplomatic status was confirmed in a letter of 4 August 1977 from then Secretary of State Kissinger to European Commissioner Soames.[33] The legal foundations of the Union's integrative diplomacy are discussed in Chapter 5 and the relevant EPC/CFSP documents were outlined in Chapter 2.

The Fifteen Member States of the European Union, which are all members of the United Nations, collectively contribute 32.65 per cent of the UN's regular budget, as against 25 per cent for the United States, 12.45 per cent for Japan, 6.71 per cent for the Russian Federation and 0.77 per cent for China.[34] The UN has provided a forum in which the EU has attempted to conduct its integrative diplomacy, as was highlighted by

Anthony Parsons in his comment, '[T]hat it had great value as a place in which to develop multilateral coalitions in pursuit of common aims – European Community coordination across virtually the whole spectrum of the UN agenda being a striking case in point'.[35]

The EU attempts to co-ordinate its work and to adopt a common standpoint prior to the meetings of the main Western caucuses operating within the General Assembly such as the Western, Vinci and Barton caucuses.[36] According to a former Commission External Relations official, the work of the EU on EPC/CFSP questions in New York and Geneva is much more reactive than elsewhere, as the EU Members are responding to an agenda not of their making and for which there is insufficient detailed guidance from central authorities.[37] The consequence is that the Member States and the Commission delegation meet frequently, ambassadors meeting weekly, and on a daily basis during the sessions of the General Assembly. The EU also uses the occasion of UN events to conduct its own bilateral diplomacy. UN General Assembly meetings are used to pursue the procedural instruments of the international identity. The most recent meeting was used for the regular contacts between the EU Foreign Ministers and the Rio Group and the Gulf Co-operation Council.[38]

The voting records of the Member States in the General Assembly have been analysed to assess to what extent European Political Co-operation has been a success in the harmonisation of the foreign policies of the Member States.[39] Figures taken across time of the voting patterns of the Member States appear to suggest that there has been a drawing together of the positions of the Member States over time (Table 4.3).

The relationship of the two permanent members of the Security Council to the European Union has altered with the coming into force of the Treaty on European Union. The CFSP provisions in the CFSP specifically dealt with the question of the responsibilities of members:

> Member States which are also members of the United Nations Security Council will concert and keep the other Member States fully informed. Member States which are permanent members of the Security Council will, in the execution of their functions, ensure the defence of the positions and the interests of the Union, without prejudice to their responsibilities under the provisions of the United Nations Charter.[40]

That this represents a substantive change has been acknowledged by former British Foreign Secretary Douglas Hurd: 'Under CFSP we commit ourselves to try to reach agreement on common positions and to abide by them once agreed. The change is a significant one: once agreed, common positions and joint actions will now be international legal obligations.'[41]

Table 4.3 The voting patterns of EU Member States in the UN General Assembly, 1981–1991*

	1981		*1991*	
	Figure	*%*	*Figure*	*%*
Number of resolutions*	182	100	206	100
EC unanimity	134	73.5	202	89.9
EC states not united	48	26.4	27	13.1
EC voting against** one another	15	8.1	2	1.0
EFTA*** in accordance with EC	159	87.4	202	98.1
EFTA states not in accordance with the EC majority	23	12.6	4	1.9
EFTA states voting against the EC majority	6	3.3	0	0.0

* The most relevant resolutions were analysed, grouped according to the *Yearbook of the United Nations*. These groups included Political and Security Questions (all), Regional Questions (all), Economic and Social Questions (Development Policy and International Economic Co-operation, Operational Activities and Human Rights), Administrative and Budgetary Questions (UN Financing and Programming)

** This figure is included in the one registering the number of times the states did not vote together. The phrase 'voting against one another' means that the states with a dissenting opinion did not abstain from voting, but took a stand against the majority

*** The states labelled 'EFTA states' are those EFTA states which were subsequently to seek EU and (with the exception of Norway) to acquire EU membership, i.e., Austria, Finland, Norway and Sweden

**** 1981 is selected as the date of publication of the London Report of the EPC process that tightened co-operation in EPC. 1991 is the last year for which the *Yearbook of the United Nations* is currently available

Source: *Yearbook of the United Nations*, 1981 and 1991****

The question of whether France and the United Kingdom should relinquish their seats on the Security Council in favour of a Union representative has been raised within the Union by both Members of the Commission and other Member States.[42] However, the mainstream of the debate revolves around enlargement, with Germany as a prospective new member.[43] The proposal to create an Economic Security Council within the UN structure would only serve to enhance further the role of the EU in the UN system.[44]

The UN Security Council demonstrates that advantages can accrue to the EU by not *formally* becoming a single actor in the international system. EU Member States currently provide over 26 per cent of the membership of the Security Council yet Western European states comprise only 12 per cent of the total UN membership.[45]

G-7

A similar advantage would appear to apply to the G-7, with EU Member States constituting five EU Members, in addition to the Commission. However, the G-7 has moved away from efforts to co-ordinate economic policy that have often ended in failure, such as the 1987 Louvre accord on exchange rates, and has developed a more informal approach at its two most recent summits in Naples and Halifax. Of the two most recent substantive initiatives of the G-7, the proposals for reform of multilateral organisations and the special ministerial conference on the Information Society, the latter was an initiative both proposed and enacted by the European Commission.[46]

Despite the active role of the Commission within the G-7, the Union itself is not an effective and cohesive entity acting within the G-7, as one commentator has noted: '[the] member-states are not even coordinated enough among themselves to advance consistent positions and, once a common policy is achieved, it is often rigid, fragile or nearly immutable in negotiations.'[47] The inclusion of the European Commission in the G-7 in 1977 reflected the increasing economic importance of the European Union, especially as the largest market and the largest trader. The G-7 itself was created in 1975 to co-ordinate the economic and monetary strategies of the major economies, faced with the inability of the United States to remain the pre-eminent actor in this task. The breakdown of the Bretton Woods system, alongside the increase in the independence and vulnerability of the major economies of nation states became manifest during the first oil crisis of 1973.

THE EUROPEAN UNION IN THE INTERNATIONAL POLITICAL ECONOMY

The question of hegemony and the status of the hegemonic power and hegemony in the international system has been defined as 'the preponderance of material resources'.[48] The elements of hegemonic power that relate to the world political economy are control over raw materials, markets and capital as well as competitive advantages in those goods which are especially valued and involve the use of new and complex technologies. From this resource power a hegemon is in a position to make and enforce the rules of the world political economy. As was illustrated above when the resource capabilities of the significant powers were contrasted, the United States does not enjoy a predominance of the resource capabilities examined but remains significant in all categories. The United States has been perceived to be in a situation of relative decline and it is this that has opened up a debate on hegemony, its loss and appropriate responses. The debate divides into three main areas.[49] Firstly, the manner in which hegemony is exercised, whether it is the provision of public goods for the international political economy or shaping the system to its own advantage: benign hegemony, hegemony by coercion or exploitative hegemony. Secondly, whether the United States has lost a position of hegemony previously exercised. And thirdly, if the United States, as the creator of regimes, is declining in hegemonic power, will they survive its relative decline?

The focus of our analysis is not the debate on the relative decline of the United States from a perceived position of hegemony but the position of the EU with respect to the other putative great powers of which the United States is among the most significant. The largely US-based debate is of interest to a discussion of the international significance of the EU in that it introduces the notion that power and its exercise can be demonstrably more than military strength. The United States may be, in the words of Joseph Nye, *Bound to Lead*, as the only state with the capacity to exercise anything like global leadership, and the expectation that it will do so, outside of its geographically circumscribed region.[50] However, the EU, although it may not be able to claim such a grand geopolitical role for itself, or even to be considered a cohesive actor in the international system, possesses both the resource capabilities to make itself significant and the instruments through which to implement. The extent of the growing influence of the EU relative to the United States is illustrated through changes in the international political economy.

The history of the post-war international economy is not just a history of the industrialised economies, of the relations among them and their relative success or failure in absolute terms; it is also a history of international economic institutions and international economic management. The story of the world economy since 1945 is one of reconstruction, recovery and growth, followed by an economic slowdown and the emergence of severe problems in many of the constituent national economies in the late 1970s and early 1980s. Through the 1960s and 1970s America's Cold War allies sheltering under the US security umbrella moved away from relations of economic dependency to economic capabilities that increased their assertiveness and independence. In the aftermath of the Cold War, the recognition of the shift of economic power towards the European Union and Japan was pushed further by some who suggested that the twenty-first century would be marked by a 'head-to-head' economic competition with the United States.[51] US observers noted that by 1988 the combined output of the then twelve European Community (EC) countries and Japan was over $950 billion greater than US output. Thirty years earlier in 1960 it did not even equal US output.[52]

The EU is currently the world's leading trader, accounting for 15 per cent of world trade in comparison to 13.8 per cent for the United States and 8.1 per cent for Japan (Figure 4.1). Trade for the Union also occupies a greater proportion of GDP than that for either the United States or Japan (Figure 4.2). However, the EU's percentage share of total world trade has fallen from 22 per cent in 1958 to 15.6 per cent in 1989.

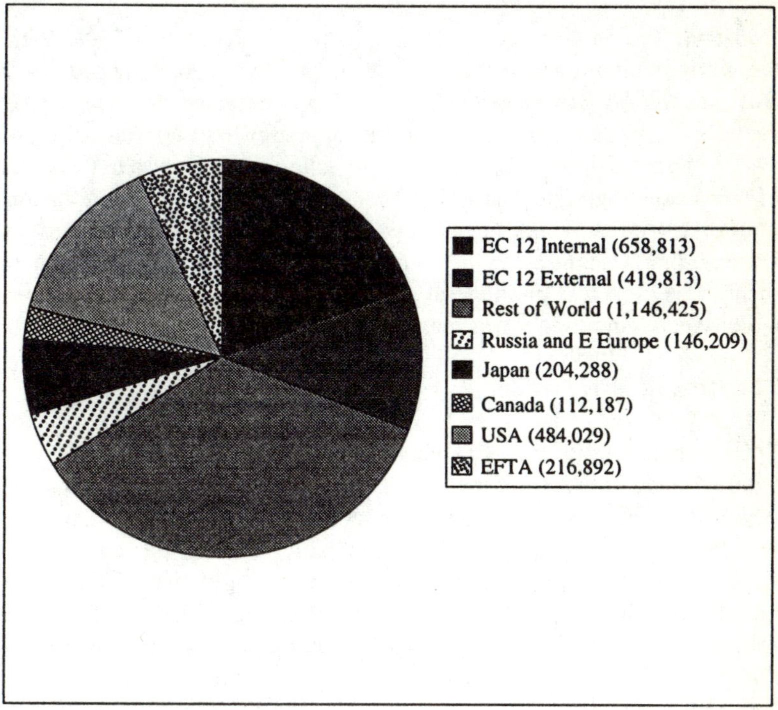

Figure 4.1 Shares of world exports
Source: Eurostat (1994)

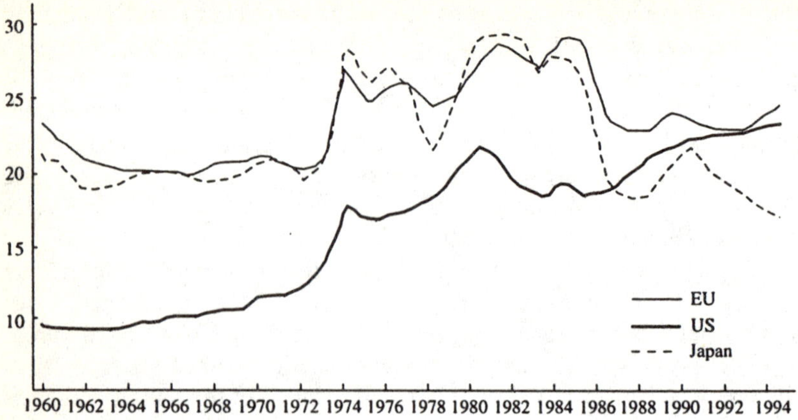

Figure 4.2 Trade in goods and services as a percentage of GDP (current prices)
Source: European Commission (1994)

Despite the relative decline of the position of the United States within the world economy the institutions of the post-war economic order – the IMF, the World Bank and the GATT – have remained in place. The US economy played a central role in the operation of the Bretton Woods system with the dollar – linked to gold – acting as numeraire in the system of fixed exchange rates, as well as being a major source of international liquidity. Bretton Woods created two regimes: a monetary a regime and a trade regime. In contrast to the monetary regime that was largely bilateral, the trade regime was multilateral and the emergence of Western Europe as a major economic trader was manifest through the GATT.

The EU and world trade

The competencies of the EC Treaty, that allow the Community to conduct external trade on behalf of the Fifteen, provide the Union with a context in which it speaks with a single voice. As the World Trade Organisation noted in a recent report 'The European Union is among the pace-setters in the multilateral system owing to its economic weight and reliance on external trade.'[53] The WTO also went further, and suggested that in the sphere of world trade the Union's policy and profile is only comprehensible within the new WTO framework.[54] In Chapter 2 it was illustrated that the GATT provided a context within which the EC was born and is therefore the offspring of multilateralism. It will also be illustrated in Chapter 5 that a commitment to multilateralism is embedded within the constitution

Imports (Total: 484.4 million ECU)

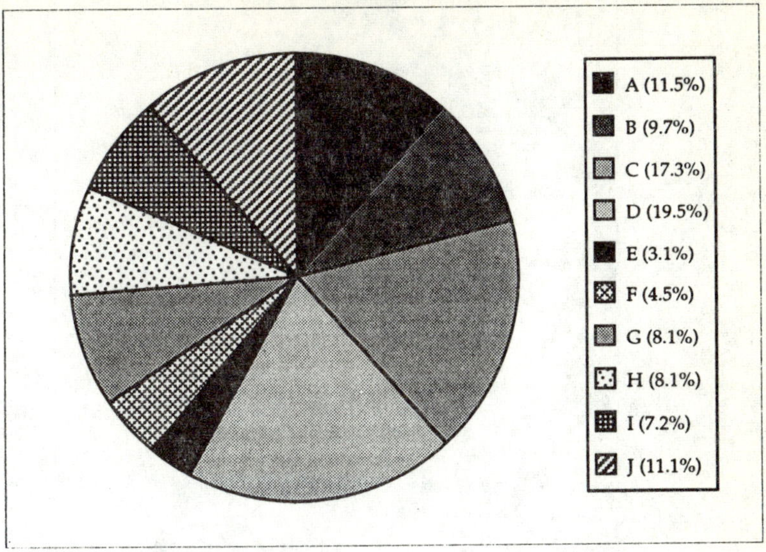

KEY: TO BOTH CHARTS

A: Austria, Finland & Sweden
B: Japan
C: United States
D: Other
E: ACP countries
F: Latin America
G: Central and Eastern Europe
H: Mediterranean States
I: Other industrialised countries
J: Other EFTA

Exports (Total: 486.9 million ECU)

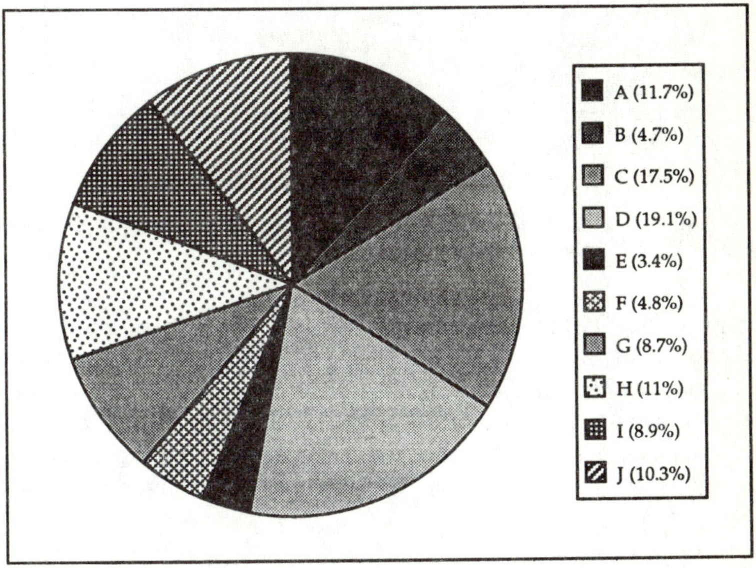

Figure 4.4 External merchandise trade by region (EU12), 1993
Source: World Trade Organisation (1995)

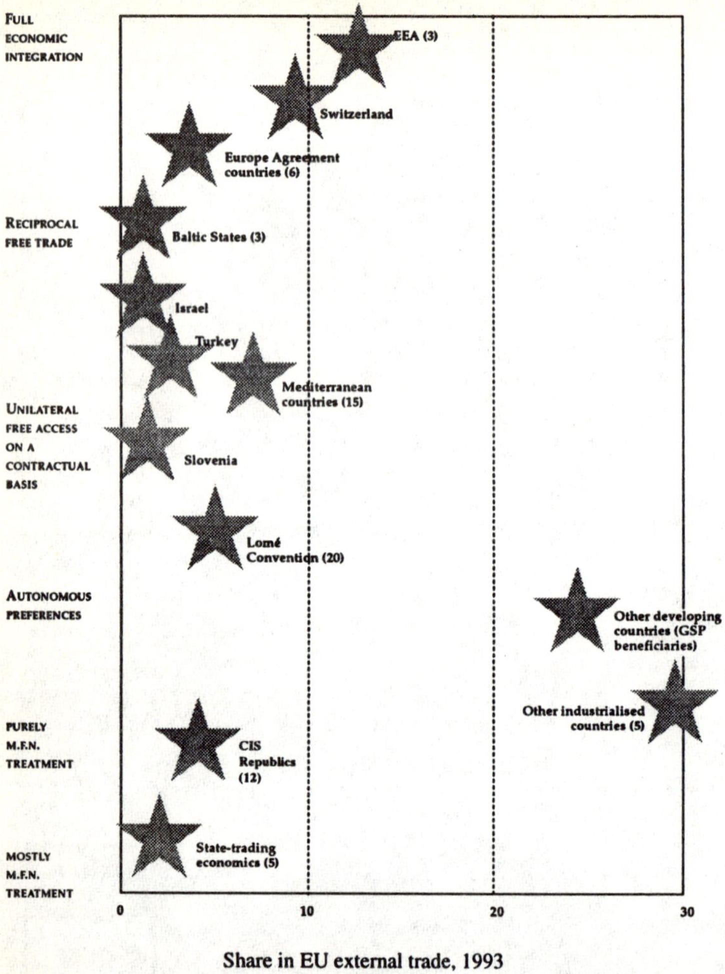

Figure 4.5 The EU preferential trade system, early 1995
Source: World Trade Organisation (1995)

parities. The larger economies moved to a system of co-ordinated, managed floating. Two consequences followed from this change: co-operation between the larger economies to co-ordinate action on exchange rates became more important – a change which reinforced the linkage with national politics. Secondly, interest rates were used to influence exchange rates and interest rates have been used for domestic economic management.

In the post-Bretton Woods monetary era the Union has sought to create a zone of monetary stability as a strategy with which to cope with the world-wide phenomenon of monetary interdependence. It has been suggested by one commentator that through these efforts, 'Western Europe now looks like an area of closer coherence within a less stable, global monetary system'.[58]

The original provisions of the EC Treaty provided no basis for either a Community macro-economic or monetary policy. Monetary policy was to take place within the confines of the Bretton Woods system. In 1970, under the Werner Plan, the Community embarked upon a project for monetary union that proved to be short-lived, as the monetary instability created by the collapse of the Bretton Woods system ended the initial stage of the project to keep Member States' currencies exchange rates within narrow margins.[59]

In 1979 the Member States created the European Monetary System (EMS), a system based upon two elements, an Exchange Rate Mechanism (ERM) and a European Currency Unit (ecu). The EMS was a part of the variable arrangements that the Member States had created alongside EPC and the European Council and was not brought within the scope of the Treaties until the Single European Act. The ERM gives each participating Member States' currency a central rate defined in ecu, and from this rate a grid of bilateral exchange rates between the Member States is created and maintained. Whereas all Member States are Members of the EMS, only ten Member States are Members of the ERM.[60] The TEU fine-detailed the expansion of the EMS into the timetable, and participating conditions, for a project of Economic and Monetary Union with the single currency envisaged in the TEU, at the latest by 1 January 1999.[61] The viability of the project, or timetable, for EMU is not within the purview of this study, but the significance of the current monetary arrangements as they impact upon the international identity are of importance.

The EU Member States are significant in the international monetary system in two important respects; firstly, because the EU Member States' currencies collectively rank foremost in the composition of official reserves and International Monetary Fund positions (Tables 4.4 and 4.5); and secondly, because of the role that the EU Member States play in global monetary management, most notably through the G-7 and the Bank of International Settlements (BIS). The EC Treaty now provides for the Member States to act, by a qualified majority vote, and to adopt a common position for use in international economic and financial institutions if any one state has recourse to such organisations because of balance-of-payments difficulties.[62] Financial and capital markets do not conform to

Table 4.4 Official gross reserves of convertible currencies and special drawing rights

Country	Convertible currencies		SDRs	
	End 1992	*End 1993*	*End 1992*	*End 1993*
EUR 12	237,674	248,186	2,483	2,945
Belgium	10,748	9,535	143	151
Denmark	8,781	8,143	77	149
Germany	71,980	68,226	705	823
Greece	3,883	5,819	0	0
Spain	37,023	34,178	154	185
France	20,496	22,556	137	394
Ireland	2,581	5,485	104	115
Italy	20,923	23,419	199	225
Luxembourg	0	0	8	9
Netherlands	16,959	26,322	464	506
Portugal	15,730	13,935	39	58
United Kingdom	28,570	30,568	453	340
Austria	9,647	10,180	286	204
Finland	4,001	3,297	91	100
Iceland	406	343	0	0
Norway	9,303	16,082	160	265
Sweden	18,403	16,726	38	49
EEA	279,434	294,814	3,058	3,563
Switzerland	27,187	26,261	13	106
Turkey	5,125	5,907	0	2
USA	33,531	36,963	7,124	7,823
Canada	7,863	7,341	871	929
Japan	51,867	75,436	917	1,298

Source: Eurostat (1994)

political boundaries, as the EU discovered during the ERM crisis in July and August 1992 and although the creation of the Single Market removed obstacles to the financial and capital markets of the Members States the Fifteen exist within the wider Euromarket of money and capital.[63] The EU Member States thereby operate within a global monetary system that impacts upon plans for their own integration, but collectively they also form an important component of any attempt to manage that system.

Table 4.5 International Monetary Fund positions, 1992–1993

Country	*Quota*		*SDR allocations*		*Reserve position in the Fund**	
	31.12.1992	*30.09.1993*	*31.12.1992*	*30.09.1993*	*31.12.1992*	*30.09.1993*
EUR 12	44,309	47,062	7,562	8,034	12,981	12,914
Belgium	3,522	3,741	551	585	675	696
Denmark	1,215	1,291	203	216	398	387
Germany	9,359	9,941	1,375	1,461	3,553	3,519
Greece	668	709	118	125	135	137
Spain	2,197	2,334	340	361	959	932
France	8,420	8,943	1,226	1,303	2,080	2,088
Ireland	596	633	99	105	198	187
Italy	5,213	5,537	797	847	2,044	2,014
Luxembourg	154	163	19	21	30	30
Netherlands	3,911	4,154	602	639	961	968
Portugal	634	673	60	64	263	272
United Kingdom	8,420	8,943	2,172	2,307	1,685	1,684

Table 4.5 (Continued)

Country	*Quota*		*SDR allocations*		*Reserve position in the Fund*[*]	
	31.12.1992	*30.09.1993*	*31.12.1992*	*30.09.1993*	*31.12.1992*	*30.09.1993*
Austria	1,349	1,450	203	217	449	476
Finland	979	1,052	162	172	277	276
Iceland	97	104	18	20	12	13
Norway	1,254	1,348	190	203	543	543
Sweden	1,833	1,970	280	297	520	544
EEA	49,821	52,986	8,415	8,943	14,782	14,765
Switzerland	2,805	3,015	0	0	670	720
Turkey	729	774	127	135	37	39
USA	30,122	31,994	5,564	5,910	9,856	10,289
Canada	4,905	5,210	885	941	847	855
Japan	9,359	9,941	1,013	1,076	7,242	7,274

[*] Unconditional drawing rights available

Source: Eurostat (1994)

INTEGRATIONIST DIPLOMACY: THE NETWORK OF RELATIONS

The Union has long held a common conception of itself and its role with the outside world which it vigorously promotes through the informational instrument of the Office for Official Publications of the European Communities (EUR-OP) established in 1969. Although set up to serve as the collective publishing house of the institutions of the Union and responsible for the production and distribution of the *Official Journal of the European Communities*, it now publishes a vast array of brochures, videos and CD-ROMs and provides on-line data services. In 1993 EUR-OP published approximately 5,000 publications and produces work in 11 EU languages.[64] EUR-OP, alongside the work of Eurostat, the statistical office of the European Communities, promotes the perception of the EU as both a single and a major international actor: 'The Community, along with the United States and Japan, represents one of the three pillars on which a global system of pluralist democracy and market economy is built.. Solutions to specific international economic and even political problems will depend on a common approach by all three.'[65]

The Union promulgates, through the instrumental instrument of EUR-OP publications, a structure to its trade policy as consisting of multilateral, regional and bilateral relationships. Bilateral relationships are divided into several categories. Firstly, those conducted with industrial partners, collectively through the OECD, the G-7, the Quadrilateral group, and bilaterally with the United States, Japan, Canada, Australia and New Zealand. Secondly, EU relations with the EFTAn states, through the European Economic Area (EEA), encompassing Norway, Liechtenstein and Iceland, and with Switzerland. Thirdly, relations with Central and Eastern Europe. These are divided between the Europe Agreements with the Czech and Slovak Republics, Poland, Hungary, Romania, Bulgaria and the Baltic states of Estonia, Latvia and Lithuania, with the confirmation that these Associate Members can eventually join the Union, and the bilateral agreements with Slovenia and Albania. All are included in the PHARE programme. Fourthly, those with Russia and the CIS through partnership and co-operation agreements, the TACIS programme and the International Energy Charter. Fifthly, Mediterranean countries through a network of co-operation and association agreements (excluding Libya), including the existing Association Agreements with Turkey, Cyprus and Malta which are intended lead to customs unions. Sixthly, the Lomé Convention, bringing together the EU and 70 states from the African, Caribbean and Pacific (ACP) areas; and seventhly, the most amorphous grouping of Asian and Latin American (ALA) states that have either signed bilateral agreements or as members of regional groupings. The Union is keen to present these relationships as both well ordered and well structured, especially through its publication efforts.[66]

The self-publicised structure of bilateral relations does hold up as a device for conceiving the geographical coverage of Union relationships and as a framework through which informational, procedural, transference and overt instruments are deployed. The content of each of these bilateral relationships has been amended and upgraded over time to include a political dialogue alongside trade matters. The legal frameworks within which bilateral agreements are constructed is explored in Chapter 5.

The development and the deepening of the region-to-region dialogue of the then pre-TEU Community has provided the basis for characterising 'a new European identity in the international system' in previous analyses.[67] These analyses have encompassed elements of the procedural and overt instruments of the identity and have illustrated the increase in scope and coverage of the procedural instrument over time, especially during the mid- and late-1980s.[68] The extent of the coverage of the bilateral relationships conducted by the Union is now such that it has been characterised by a former Director of the external relations directorate of the Union as 'a global network of partnerships and responsibilities'.[69]

The recognition of the increasing international significance of the Union is reflected in the number of states which are now accredited to the European Union. The EU now has 147 missions accredited to it. This contrasts to with 169 accredited to the United States in Washington, the major centre of bilateral accreditation.[70]

The Union has also gone further to create its own overt instrument through its own network of external delegations accredited to 112 countries. The accreditation of these delegations takes place at the Head of State level and, as a Commission official noted in interview on the position of these delegations: 'we do occupy a place in the diplomatic register that is unique, and we are not a sovereign state, nor are we an international organisation...in the pecking order, we normally figure just after the sovereign states but before the international organisations'.[71]

The Union delegations were previously divided into two main types; those that reported to DG1, the external relations directorate of the Commission, or those that reported to DG8, the directorate responsible for development. The responsibility for the management and inspection of both sets of delegations was transferred to the new DG1A for external political relations, created as the Commission's response to the TEU, and with the commitment to assert the international identity of the Union. The delegations report on political matters direct to Hans van den Broek, the

Commissioner responsible for external political relations, and seek instructions and report on economic or development matters to DG1 or DG8.[72] The functions of the delegations are dependent upon the nature of the procedural instrument that the Union has deployed in its relations with the third country. Delegations accredited to Associate Members manage and monitor the implementation of the Agreements and their financial protocols; Delegations in co-operation agreement countries monitor the trade provisions and implementation of the financial protocols, those in ACP states apply the provisions of the Lomé Convention.

The relationship between the delegations and the Member States' embassies in third countries which, as was noted in Chapter 3, are involved in the implementation of the CFSP, is close and meetings are timetabled on a monthly basis, hosted by the Presidency. The delegations are associated within any *démarche* presented to the host government.[73] However, the relationship between the delegations and the Member State missions in third countries may not always run smoothly:

> It is true that in one place or another you may find that the *amour propre* of a particular ambassador is aroused by some imagined solecism or other. The fact is that there are still quite a few Member State ambassadors out there – let's say veterans of their systems – which have really no familiarity with the Community, and no great love for it either, and to whom the Head of Commission Delegation is very much the new boy in town and should know his place and there are imagined snubs and slights and put-downs which can happen. But in my experience, they are limited and of no significance.[74]

As is outlined in Chapter 6, the delegations are not replacing the Member State sources but are another manifestation of the Union co-existing, and drawing upon, the capabilities of the Member States. In this respect the delegations could be viewed alongside the missions of the Member States as the sixteenth mission that the Union can utilise in third countries.

TOWARDS A PAX BRUXELLANA?

The emergence of transnationalism and interdependence suggests that the emergence of a *Pax Americana* to a *Pax Nipponica*, *Pax Bruxellana* or *Pax Sinoana*, is unlikely. The European Union is not a superpower in the making despite its resource capabilities and its position in the international political economy. However, the Union has moved beyond being a civilian power in two important respects. Firstly, it has recently broken a taboo in contemplating questions of defence and military security. Secondly, it both defines its interests and conducts its diplomacy on a global basis. We will explore each of these questions in turn.

Breaking the taboo

In an annually published, comprehensive, quantitative assessment of military forces and defence expenditures, the European Union does not warrant an entry on its capabilities. The absence of a European Union military capability, commensurate with the economic strength of the Union, gives rise to popular commentaries describing the Union as a 'strange superpower'.[75] The contrast between its weakness in military capability with its economic strength is curious in that the Union derives its economic significance from aggregated measurements of its Member States yet such calculations are rarely made of the aggregated military capabilities of the Member States.

Table 4.6 illustrates a quantitative comparison of the defence budget and active armed forces for the EU Member States, the United States, Japan, China and Russia. The presentation of such data represents no comment upon the capabilities, force posture or defence policy of those under comparison. The figures place the combined active armed forces of the EU Member States second to the figure claimed for China, and the combined defence expenditure of the Fifteen second to the figure claimed for the United States.

The armed forces of the Member States are brought together in four main structures; the North Atlantic Treaty Organisation (NATO), NATO's Partnership for Peace, the Western European Union (WEU) and Eurocorps. Through these organisations the Member States have a variable geometry of defence relationships and obligations. Of the Fifteen only Ireland remains outside any of these institutional arrangements. The strongest relationships exist in the NATO structure with the 11 Member States who are committed, alongside other members of NATO, to a common defence under the Washington Treaty. This defence burden is shared with the other four members of NATO outside the Union and, of course, of greatest significance is the commitment of the United States to the defence of these members and the existence of a pluralist security community binding these NATO members together. The Partnership for Peace draws Finland, Sweden and Austria into a bilateral co-operative relationship with the NATO members and operationally, 'for the purpose of joint planning, training and exercises in order to strengthen their ability to undertake missions in the fields of peacekeeping, search and

Table 4.6 The defence budget and active armed forces of the EU (15) in contrast to the United States, Japan, China and Russia

Country	*Defence budget $ bn*	*Active armed forces*
United States	271.1	1,650,500
Japan	42.1	237,700
China	6.7	2,930,000
Russia	79.0	1,714,000*
EU (15)	145.9	2,413,450
NATO members		
Belgium	2.6	63,000
Denmark	2.6	27,000
France	35.6	409,600
Germany	28.6	367,300
Greece	3.3	159,300
Italy	16.1	322,300
Luxembourg	0.1	800
Netherlands	7.2	70,900
Portugal	1.5*	50,700
Spain	5.8	206,500
United Kingdom	34.0	254,300
Non-NATO members		
Austria	1.6*	51,250
Finland	1.6	31,200
Ireland	0.5*	13,000
Sweden	4.8	64,000

* Estimated

Source: International Institute for Strategic Studies (1995)

rescue, humanitarian operations, and others as may be subsequently agreed'.[76]

The TEU, in establishing the CFSP, widened the extent of the Member States' efforts at foreign policy harmonisation to 'include all questions related to the security of the Union, including the eventual framing of a common defence policy, which might in time lead to a common defence' and designated the WEU 'to elaborate and implement decisions and actions of the Union which have defence implications'.[77]

Under the TEU the Union had signalled the intent of the Member States of the Union to move beyond a civilian power Europe and to develop a defence dimension to the international identity of the Union. In a declaration attached to the TEU the then nine members of the WEU spelled out their proposals for the role of the WEU and the relationship of the WEU and NATO, pledging that the 'WEU will be developed as the defence component of the European Union and as a means to strengthen the European pillar of the Atlantic Alliance. To this end, it will formulate common European defence policy and carry forward its concrete implementation through the further development of its own operational role.'[78] As well as setting out a list of practical measures to enhance relations with the EU and a strengthening of the European pillar of the Atlantic Alliance and its own operational role, the Declaration offered either accession to the WEU or observer status to any member of the Union. Other European members of NATO were offered an Associate Membership status.

The WEU, under Article V of the founding Brussels Treaty signed in 1948, offers a collective defence guarantee to any of the signatories subject to armed attack in Europe.[79] The WEU, reactivated in 1984 as a forum in which to pursue closer European collaboration within NATO, permitted the Western European members to act collectively outside the NATO area of operations, as in the Persian Gulf from 1985.[80] In the aftermath of the Gulf War and the outbreak of conflict in Yugoslavia[81] the Council of Ministers of the WEU, in the Petersberg Declaration of 19 June 1992, signalled their intent to expand the operations of the WEU to encompass 'humanitarian and rescue tasks, peacekeeping tasks and tasks of combat forces in crisis management' and now known as 'Petersberg tasks'.[82]

To facilitate the realisation of these objectives a Planning Cell was established and located with the WEU Council, recently moved from London to Brussels, thereby indicating symbolically the new status with respect to the Union and the practical benefits of proximity. Within the Planning Cell the WEU has recently added an Intelligence Section, alongside a Situation Centre and a politico-military group in support of the Council, these as parts of its commitment to enhance its operational development

The development of capabilities by the WEU to match its aspirations was given a boost by the NATO summit of January 1994 and the endorsement of the principle that NATO assets and capabilities could be made available for WEU operations – in particular, through the concept of Combined Joint Task Forces (CJTF). Alongside this endorsement, the WEU Planning Cell developed an inventory of Forces Answerable to WEU (FAWEU) to identify those available to carry out WEU tasks and a framework for the development of a WEU Maritime Force. The WEU has also made a commitment to create an independent European satellite system and to develop further the WEU capability to use satellite imagery for security purposes by enhancing the WEU Satellite Centre at Torrejon, Spain.[83] The WEU was also offered Russian satellite intelligence data by Andrei Kozyrev in a speech to the WEU Parliamentary Assembly in December 1994.[84] In the future a WEU strategic transport capability may be enhanced through the Future Large Aircraft project.[85]

The WEU has already produced a preliminary document outlining the objectives, scope and means of a common European defence policy (CEDP) and described by the Minister of Foreign Affairs of the Netherlands as 'the *acquis*, as it were – which have already been developed in the WEU, in the European Union and in NATO'.[86] The preliminary work details four levels of responsibilities and interests:

- WEU governments have a direct responsibility for the security and defence of their own peoples and territories.
- WEU governments have a responsibility to project the security and stability presently enjoyed in the West throughout the whole of Europe.
- WEU governments have an interest, in order to reinforce European security, in fostering stability in the southern Mediterranean countries.
- WEU governments are ready to take on their share of the responsibilities for the promotion of security, stability and the values of democracy in the wider world, including through the execution of peacekeeping and other crisis management measures under the authority of the UN Security Council or the CSCE, acting either independently or through WEU or NATO. They are also ready to address new security challenges such as humanitarian emergencies; proliferation; terrorism; international crime and environmental risks including those related to disarmament and the destruction of nuclear and chemical weapons.[87]

The proposal was also made that the CEDP required a greater strengthening of operational capabilities, in particular, exercising, preparation and inter-operability of forces; generic and contingency planning; strategic mobility; anti-missile defences and defence intelligence in Europe; and a mechanism for the sharing and burdens and the pooling of resources.[88] The importance of creating a European armaments policy, as a part of a CEDP, was acknowledged as taking place through the Western European Armaments Group (WEAG) and with the eventual aim of a European armaments agency.

The Union, through the WEU, has, tentatively, created a defence force and an embryonic defence policy intended to be compatible with the

Atlantic Alliance and to strengthen its European pillar based upon the principle of separable but not separate military capabilities. However, the disjuncture between WEU and EU membership remains. Only 10 members of the Union are currently full members of the WEU and enjoy the defence guarantee of Article V, Ireland, Denmark, Austria, Sweden and Finland being currently confined to observer status within the WEU.

The defence identity of the Union therefore excludes one-third of the Membership of Union but at the same time encompasses another 17 states through different forms of membership of the WEU. Alongside an observer status the WEU created, through the *Document on Associate Membership* agreed at the WEU Ministerial Council in Rome on 20 November 1992, an Associate Member status open to European members of NATO, which has been granted to Turkey, Norway and Iceland. These Associate Members, by their nomination of assets to FAWEU, now participate in WEU operations on same basis as full members. The Associate Members are also integrated into WEU planning through the nominating of officers to the Planning Cell and connection to the WEUCOM communications network.[89]

The WEU has also created an Associate Partner status offered to the nine Central European and Baltic countries that have Europe Agreements with the EU. The Associate Partner status offers involvement in the meetings of the WEU Council, liaison arrangements with the Planning Cell, participation in exercises and association with the WEU operations involving Petersberg tasks. In any involvement in WEU operations a right to involvement in the Council's decision-making process and command structures is granted.[90] The development of these arrangements has not been without its critics, and is characterised by one group of expert commentators as 'an approach which simply serves to blur the concepts of a common defence policy and common defence'.[91]

The future of the WEU and its relationship with the European Union was programmed as a subject for discussion at the forthcoming Intergovernmental Conference of the Union in 1996 and with the added context of the expiry of the Brussels Treaty due in 1998.[92] Proposals currently include the full integration of the WEU with the EU, the creation of a new pillar of the Union containing a European intervention force based upon Eurocorps with the WEU preserved for collective defence, or leaving matters as they currently exist with the addition of a WEU summit.[93] The possibility has also been raised by a French European Affairs minister that the British and French nuclear deterrents should contribute to a common defence policy.[94]

The individual Member States of the Union currently have varying degrees of military deployment outside Europe. France, the Netherlands, Spain and the United Kingdom have combat forces abroad, aside from those engaged in UN peacekeeping or NATO duties. Fourteen of the Fifteen Member States currently have personnel deployed on UN peace-keeping duties (the state without troops deployed being Luxembourg) and 11 of the Member States, nine of the WEU members (Luxembourg has committed no troops), Denmark and Norway have forces deployed in Operation Sharp Guard, enforcing UN imposed embargoes on the territories of the former Yugoslavia, under a combined WEU/NATO task force. Alongside Operation Sharp Guard the WEU is involved in a WEU police and customs operation enforcing UN sanctions on the Danube, and the WEU provides the police deployment for the EU-administered town of Mostar. The latter is the first occasion in which the WEU is implementing a decision of the EU, as envisaged under Article J (4)2 of the TEU. The WEU Presidency, Secretariat and Planning Cell has also met with a troika of EU Consular Affairs experts to make preparations for the WEU's role in evacuation operations overseas.[95]

The question of deepening the defence identity through a common European army is raised by Eurocorps, an entity with German, French, Spanish, Luxembourg and Belgian forces. Eurocorps was formed by an expansion of a previously existing Franco-German brigade on 5 November 1993, four days after the TEU came into effect. Based in Strasbourg and with an emblem containing a map of Europe, the 12 stars of the Union's flag and a broadsword, the Eurocorps has signed an accord with NATO to come under its command as a unit in times of crisis.[96] Eurocorps was intended to be fully operational by 1995. By that time it would consist of 40,000 troops.[97]

Alongside Eurocorps the Member States have a number of bilateral arrangements which have been placed at the disposal of the WEU. These include an Anglo-Dutch amphibious force that Portugal has indicated a commitment to join[98] and a Franco-British Euro Air Group to co-ordinate RAF–French Air Force joint operations, either in support of peacekeeping, or offensive activities.[99] France, Italy and Spain have organised EUROFOR, a land force, and EUROMARFOR, a maritime force, open to all WEU members, which has been declared 'forces answerable to WEU'.[100]

The EU through the WEU and its associates, and through bilateral arrangements between the Member States, has a developing defence profile, both in potential capabilities and policy. Alongside the EU emergent-defence identity the Member States, taken collectively, retain considerable numbers of armed forces personnel and defence expenditure and provision for defence. However, clearly all of these capabilities of the Member States are not at the direct disposal of the Union. In particular there remains a disjuncture between the willingness of all the Member States to commit military personnel to UN peacekeeping across the globe and a reluctance of some to commit to a credible EU collective defence on account of neutrality, derived either from constitution, recent history or Atlanticism.[101]

THE DOMINANT BILATERAL: ATLANTICISM

With the foundation and organisation of NATO alongside the Marshall Plan, Western Europe made a political commitment to align itself with the United States and thereby contributed to the formation of the US camp. What is important for our purposes is that Western Europe committed itself to a political and economic alignment with one of the two significant powers in the post-war system. The shared geography and common history of the European continent were subordinated to other concerns. In the aftermath of the Cold War, the period of the 'long hostilities' in Europe, dating from 1914, has given way to the 1990s as the rediscovery of the perception of a new Europe, a Europe defined as wider than its western half but centred upon the European Union as the core institution. The anticipation of this rediscovery can be seen in the distinctive European strand of *détente* and the initiation of the CSCE process and the differences between Western Europe and the United States in the period designated as the Second Cold War.

The story of the early Cold War is well rehearsed and should not detain us here. However, of interest is the economic and political change that took place under the overlain conflict of the Cold War which witnessed a relative increase in European economic power and a relative economic decline of the United States. The end of the Cold War has created a major challenge for the continuation of a conflict-free relationship between the United States and the European Union. The end of the Cold War threw into stark contrast the underlying changes in the international economic and political system that marked a relative decline of the standing of the United States in the relationship. The United States moved from being the primary source of influence upon the international identity to a second-order influence.

As has been charted in the previous sections of this chapter, the global economic significance of the European Union has increased alongside the rise of Japan and the relative decline of the United States. With the end of the Cold War, the EU has become less reliant upon the United States for its defence and has been able to pursue its own diplomacy unencumbered by Cold War concerns. This is not to suggest that the two sides no longer share mutual interests but rather that the EU is no longer under such severe constraints to subsume its interests to the wider interests of the Western Alliance.

Of specific interest here is not the US response to the wider changes in Europe but its response to the EU. The complex nature of the transatlantic relationship is best encapsulated as 'a fundamental fact about US–EC relations is that EC members, individually and as a single entity, are both allies of *and* competitors with the US'.[102] This means that there are inevitably elements of both deep co-operation and conflict in the relationship.

Although this is the dominant bilateral relationship, it remains substantially underdeveloped. Whether the United States is becoming a more 'ordinary country' in the international system is, perhaps a moot point.[103] The Member States of the European Union and the United States remain deeply inter-dependent in the areas of security and economics. The United States is the EU-15's biggest trading partner, accounting for 6.5 per cent of EU exports (73,917 million ecu) and 7.2 per cent of EU imports (86,776 million) in 1992.[104] For the United States the EU is the destination of 23 per cent of US exports, and the EU counts as the source of 17.6 per cent of the imports to the United States.[105] The EU currently enjoys an 64,577 million ecu trade surplus with the United States, the continuation of the trend of the last 10 years.[106]

Alongside this inter-dependence of the respective economies, the trade of the two adds up to more than half of world trade. Clearly, the actions of one side in the sphere of trade and investment will impact directly upon the other. The mutual inter-dependence of the relations between the United States and the EU occurs in a context in which the EU is most able to deploy its capabilities in totality. The Common Commercial Policy gives the EU a unity of purpose and identity that it does not enjoy in the realm of military security.

The relationship between the United States and the EU has undergone a profound change in the last two decades: 'Up to 1970, the EC–US relationship resembled that of patron and client: the EC responded to US pressures and nothing else. The EC has since grown increasingly independent of US tutelage'[107] In December 1989 the United States publicly declared its desire to develop a strengthened set of institutional and consultative links in a speech delivered by the then Secretary of State, James Baker.[108] The US action was prompted by the process of preparation of the Delors

Report on economic and monetary union which generated a direct response from the Bush Administration and ultimately culminated in the Transatlantic Declaration of November 1990.[109] The Declaration established for the first time a formal framework for a structured dialogue directly between the EU and the United States. The Declaration formally de-coupled US–EC contacts which had taken place on the fringes of NATO ministerial meetings and set out a set of common goals and challenges and proposed co-operation in economic, education, scientific and cultural co-operation. The Declaration also set out an institutional framework for consultation, to include bi-annual summits between the US President and the Presidents of the European Council and the Commission, the same frequency of meetings between the US Secretary of State and the EC Foreign Ministers and Commission; *ad hoc* meetings between the EC Presidency, troika and the US Secretary of State; and briefings to US representatives on EPC Ministerial meetings.

The framework established by the Transatlantic Declaration is not to the exclusion of bilateral contacts between the Member States and the United States Nor, of course, has the framework displaced consultations that take place either through NATO or through multilateral organisations such as the WTO. Indeed, the US–EU framework is subordinated to these other contacts. The bilateral relationship remains dominant in terms of military security and trade but of second order importance when the use of the deployment of the instruments of the Union is in question.

The US mission to the EU was the only mission subject to a significant increase in staffing. The US response to a proposed single currency and the forthcoming Single Market appears to be an instance confirming an element of the *externalisation hypothesis*, that internal integration generates an external implication and/or a response from actors outside.[110]

The challenge now being faced by each side is to maintain the EU–US bilateral relationship amidst a plethora of competing multilateral concerns. Indeed, the contact of the two sides in multilateral institutions vastly outweighs the institutionalised bilateral contact and has generated calls for a reinvigorated relationship. It is through the joint NATO–WEU operation Sharp Guard that differences have appeared in the relationship between the European pillar and the transatlantic pillar.[111] The soul-searching on the future of NATO contrasts with discussions of the WEU.[112] Clearly, it would be implausible to suggest that the EU is manoeuvring to engage in a series of military deployments to challenge those of the United States. Likewise its relationships with Japan and China suggest that the Union does not contemplate its involvement in an emergent multipolar balance of power. Rather, relations between the United States, Japan and China are played out predominantly through multilateral fora, an emergent inter-regional dialogue and a weak bilateral context. The Union's primary focus and the region with which it is most engaged is Europe, and relations with Russia are to be comprehended as a part of a regional dialogue that we will explore as the European subsystem.

THE EUROPEAN SUBSYSTEM

The European subsystem currently incorporates four components, each of which is defined by the Union's relationship with each of them. The first is the notion of Europe and the part that the Union plays in defining Europe. Secondly, there is the war in the former Yugoslavia which has been both detrimental to the Union but is also defining new instruments for the Union. Thirdly, there is the institutional complexity of Europe. Fourthly, there is the network of relationships that have been created by the Union through membership, association, and partnership and co-operation.

Defining Europe is a problematic and perilous exercise. 'Europe' can be explored from many perspectives and through divergent methodologies.[113] The definition and identity of Europe have been explored, for example, through the *mythology* of Europa, defined through the *process* of historical expansion of Europe's frontiers across the continent and beyond, from the *otherness* to the Orientalism immediately beyond Europe, or the manner in which Europe has been represented through language or cartography.[114] In short, the western peninsula of Asia has generated a particular resonance and distinctiveness whilst its essence remains uncertain.

Questions of European identity are central to the self-definition of the European Union. Article O of the TEU states: 'Any European State may apply to become a member of the Union.' Taken together with the assertion in the TEU that the Member States' governments are 'founded on the principles of democracy' and the acceptance of the *acquis communitaire*, the primary conditions for consideration as a member are only rendered problematic by the definition of a 'European' state.

The emergence of the 'New Europe' with the end of the Cold War in Europe has seen the enlargement of the Union to encompass three former EFTAns and created a substantial increase in the possible membership of the Union. Former Warsaw Pact countries look for the earliest possible entry to the Union and Western European states which remain outside the Union contemplate membership. The challenge for the Union in the near future is to cultivate and structure relationships with nation states which will remain outside the Union in the foreseeable future.

The legacy of colonialism takes the territories encompassed by the European Union beyond the geographical extent of Europe. There are three forms of relationship that exist with territories beyond Europe. Firstly, the Treaty of Rome extends the Community to the French overseas departments of Réunion, Guadeloupe, Guiana and Martinique, which are all integral parts of the Union.[115] Secondly, the non-European countries and territories which currently enjoy special relations with Belgium, Denmark, France, Italy, the Netherlands and the United Kingdom are associated in a relationship with the Union that varies in intensity.[116] The Faeroe Islands and the Sovereign Base Areas of the United Kingdom in Cyprus are explicitly excluded.[117] Thirdly, autonomous or semi-autonomous regions with special relations with Spain (the Canary Islands, Ceuta and Melilla on the Mediterranean coast of Morocco), Portugal (the Azores and Madeira) and the United Kingdom (the Channel Islands, Gibraltar and the Isle of Man) each have varying degrees of relationship with the Union, in accordance with relevant provisions in respective Acts of Accession to the Community.[118] Independent countries also exist within the boundaries of the Member States: Andorra, Monaco, San Marino and the Vatican City. None of these states is a member of the Union.

The post-war division of Europe into competing blocs within an international bipolar division of power introduced a degree of rigidity and predictability into European diplomatic relationships. The events of 1989–1991 demolished the post-World War II two-bloc architecture in Europe, and beyond Europe reinforced an already apparent demise of the bipolar international system that was explored above. The demise of a two-bloc Europe removed the primary constraint upon the development of the European Union understood as a civilian power and transformed the European Union into *the* primary political entity in Europe and one of an emergent set of principal actors in the international system.

For some commentators the transformation of Europe at the end of the Cold War weakened stability.[119] The conflict in the former Yugoslavia would appear to encourage such a supposition. Indeed, a majority of the United Nations peacekeepers in action across the world are now deployed in Europe.[120] In addition to the UN peacekeeping missions, the OSCE has deployed missions in the territories of the former Yugoslavia, CIS and Baltic states.

The conflict in the territories of the former Yugoslavia demonstrated both the inability of the Union to cope with a conflict of such magnitude through its own efforts and instruments and also with problems of decision-making in a system in which the Member States are a substantive source of influence. The EU can take little comfort from its involvement in the region and has been a secondary actor in the attempts at conflict resolution since the UN involvement at the end of 1991. A paradox exists in which the EU is the political actor of greatest significance in Europe yet is effectively marginalised in the resolution or the management of the conflict. The Yugoslav crisis has proved a salutary lesson in the development of the international identity of the Union and significantly closed the gap between the realisation of the capabilities of the Union and expectations made of it.[121]

Inevitably the Yugoslav conflict has generated calls for the strengthening of the Common Foreign and Security Policy; in short, attempts to make the European Union perform more like a single actor in the international system.[122] It has also generated a more piecemeal reaction with the development of a number of new overt instruments, all contributing to the definition of the international identity of the Union. These new instruments illustrate the impact of external sources of influence upon the construction and representation of the international identity of the Union and in particular the piecemeal development of instruments of crisis management.

The European Community Monitor Mission (ECMM), established in July 1991 to monitor the withdrawal of the Yugoslav army from Slovenia, is now deployed in Croatia and Bosnia-Herzegovina, assisting with mediation and confidence-building measures. The unarmed mission operating under the auspices of the OSCE from August 1992, and headed by the rotating EU Presidency, deploys 200 unarmed monitors and an equal number of support staff, with three Italian helicopters.[123] Dressed in white and wearing EU insignia, members of the ECMM mission represented the first deployment of EU monitors. Monitors have subsequently been deployed in the Russian and South African elections, as detailed in Chapter 3. The European Union also embarked, in July 1994, upon a two-year mandate to administer the town of Mostar in Bosnia, headed by a UN appointed mayor and including an EU police force.[124]

There are also elements of stabilisation in Europe which can be explored through its institutionalisation. The chief characteristic of the international relations of the European subsystem is its institutionalisation, which forms a large part of both the operational and the psychological environment of policy-making in Europe. The significance of the European Union is that it encompasses or seeks to encompass the remit of many of the existing organisations in Europe by its coverage of economic, political and now security matters. In the latter instance, as the European Union slowly feels its way forward on questions of defence, matters of security, encompassing military security, are being redefined on to territory that is much more favourable to the Union.

The Union has rendered the role of some existing organisations, such as EFTA, increasingly insignificant. The EU has also co-opted both the anthem and flag of the Council of Europe and made it the Union's own. The European Union itself has directly contributed to the institutionalisation of Europe through the creation of the Europe Agreements, and has also pursued its own policies through existing organisations such as the OSCE and the Council of Europe. These institutions both constrain and characterise the European subsystem of which the EU is a part.

OSCE

The membership of the European subsystem of the international system is delineated by the membership of the Organisation for Security and Co-operation in Europe (OSCE). The OSCE, formerly the Conference on Security and Co-operation in Europe (CSCE), was re-launched under its new name at the Budapest Conference in December 1994 and encompasses 53 nation states of the wider Europe, including North America, and the states formerly of the Soviet Union.

The 1990 Charter of Paris and the 1992 Helsinki Document re-orientated the then CSCE from a system of maintaining dialogue and negotiation to a more operational structure. This was reflected in the creation of the first permanent body for the CSCE, the permanent committee meeting on a weekly basis and the increasing importance of the Chairman-in-Office, the Foreign Minister of the country which hosted the last Council of Ministers meeting.[125]

The Helsinki Summit endorsed the idea that the CSCE could call upon 'existing organizations such as the EC, NATO and the WEU' to make their resources available for CSCE peacekeeping activities. As was noted above, the Union sought the endorsement for the role of the ECMM in the former Yugoslavia. It has also placed the Stability Pact in the hands of the OSCE. The Union has also operated in partnership with the OSCE; it did, for instance, appoint a joint CSCE-EU Sanctions Co-ordinator in February 1993 for sanctions imposed on Serbia and Montenegro.[126]

In July 1992 the OSCE created the first High Commissioner on National Minorities, and this reflects the notion that such matters are no longer questions of internal affairs but impact upon the wider states.[127] This is a position the Union has recognised and sought to promote through the stability pact.

COUNCIL OF EUROPE

The Council of Europe, with a statute signed in May 1949, predates the Union. The 34 Members of the Council encompass the EU Fifteen and the nine European Agreement States. The Parliamentary Assembly of the Council of Europe defined the European states to which the organisation is open as those existing Members, those states whose legislative assemblies enjoy special guest status, Albania, Belarus, Bosnia-Herzegovina, Croatia, Latvia, the former Yugoslav Republic of Macedonia, Moldova, Russia and the Ukraine. Membership is open to the Socialist Republic of Yugoslavia, Montenegro and Serbia and in view of their cultural links with Europe, Armenia, Azerbaijan and Georgia have the possibility of applying for membership.[128] The Council of Europe has one strong advantage over the Union in only having two official languages, French and English.

The EU is not a member of the Council of Europe, although the prospect of Union membership has been mooted by the EU's external affairs commissioner who was in attendance at the first Council of Europe summit meeting of Heads of State and Government in Vienna in October 1993.[129] Opinion appears to be divided within the Union as to whether membership of the Council of Europe is 'a democratic finishing school, enabling countries from the east to deepen their democratic roots' prior to membership of the Union or, as the French ambassador to the Council of Europe has insisted, 'an end in itself, not a transit point'.[130]

The Commission participates in the committee work of the Committee of Ministers and in the drafting of agreements on the basis of an exchange of letters between the Commission and the Council of Europe Secretariat. As a consequence, the Commission has signed a number of the Council of Europe's Conventions.[131] There is also a regular programme of meetings between the President of the Commission, the President of the Council of Ministers and the Secretary General of the Council of Europe and the Chairman of the Committee of Ministers.[132]

The Council deals neither with military or economic matters, but the European Human Rights Convention and its Court and the Commission on Human Rights play a special part in the constitution of the Union, as will be explored in the next chapter. The United Kingdom, whilst jointly holding the Presidency of the EU and the Council of Europe, attempted to co-ordinate the Council of Europe's and the EU's aid programmes to Eastern and Central Europe and thereby built upon previous co-ordination between the two organisations in the areas of drug-trafficking, money-laundering and refugees.[133]

The Council of Europe plays a role as an organisation that is a part of the variable geometry of membership and has special interest in the rule of law, democracy and cultural affairs. However, the progressive enlargements of the Union and the lengthening queue of prospective applicants to the Union suggest that it is the EU which is becoming increasingly the predominant actor in the continent of Europe, with a full and associate membership straddling West, Central and Eastern Europe. The boundaries of the Union are no longer determined by the geopolitics of the Cold War.

CONCLUSION

The European Union can be considered to be a power of international significance in the international system through the capabilities of both the Union and its Member States. Furthermore, its economic strength and the network of relationships that it has created in the international political economy encompass an area that is undergoing substantive change as a consequence of the relative decline of the United States.

The international significance of the EU is not that it should be measured as a nation state writ large. The collective geographical, demographic, economic and diplomatic resources of the Member States illustrate that the Union has a substantial international identity. This identity has been enhanced by both the relative decline of the United States and the demise of the Cold War. However, the enhancement of the international identity of the Union has not taken place solely because of changes in the international context within which the Union operates. The Union has actively sought to enhance its international identity through the instruments that it has at its disposal.

Within the European subsystem of the international system the EU is undoubtedly the most significant actor: its membership is sought after and it is able to use a variety of instruments – procedural, overt, transference, declaratory, informational – in pursuit of a continental order. Although the Union is enmeshed within an institutionalisation in Europe, and is part of a wider informal integrative process in Europe, it stands apart from the other institutions of the European subsystem. This is for two substantive reasons: firstly, because of the unique legal arrangements of the Union; secondly, because of the processes of integration that have taken place within the Union itself. These two factors act as the most important influences upon the Union, and in identifying such influences form the focus of the next two chapters.

NOTES AND REFERENCES

1. S.P. Huntington, 'The U.S. Decline or Renewal?' *Foreign Affairs* 67, 2 (Winter 1988–89): 93–4.
2. M. Lamassoure, then Minister Delegate, attached to the Minister of Foreign Affairs, with responsibility for European Affairs, published in *Quest France* (Paris, 2 February 1994). *Speeches and Statements*, Ambassade de France á Londres, Service de Presse et d'Information.
3. For a discussion of the notion of fungibility, see: R.O. Keohane, 'Theory of World Politics: Structural Realism and Beyond', *NeoRealism and its Critics* (New York, Columbia University Press, 1986).
4. The two-fold distinction is outlined by Christopher Farrands: 'The Context of Foreign Policy Systems: Environment and Structure', chapter 4 in M. Clarke and B. White, *Understanding Foreign Policy: The Foreign Policy Systems Approach* (Edward Elgar, Aldershot, 1992).
5. As will become apparent, these represent a modification of operational environments outlined elsewhere. See, for example, the categories of social structure and culture, physical environment, economic environment, structure of the international system, knowledge structure outlined by Farrands, *op. cit.*

   Also see the operational environment offered by Brecher in his study of the foreign-policy-making system of Israel; external setting, Middle East subordinate system, military capability, economic capability, political structure, advocacy: interest groups and competing elites and communication network – M. Brecher, *Foreign Policy System of Israel: Settings, Images, Process* (Yale University Press, New Haven, Conn., 1972).
6. See the argument of John Lewis Gaddis in J.L. Gaddis, 'The Long Peace: Elements of Stability in the Postwar International System', *International Security* 10, 4 (Spring 1986): 99–142; J.L. Gaddis, *The Long Peace: Inquiries into the History of the Cold War* (Oxford, Oxford University Press, 1987).
7. See, for example, L. Thurow, *Head to Head: The Coming Economic Battle among Japan, Europe and America* (London, Nicholas Brealey, 1993).
8. Edward Luttwak, 'From Geo-Politics to Geo-economics', *National Interest* 20 (Summer 1990): 17–23.
9. From 50 founding members the UN has expanded to 184, the last entrant being Andorra on 28 July 1993, in A. Roberts and B. Kingsbury, *United Nations, Divided World: The UN's Roles in International Relations*, 2nd edn (Oxford, Clarendon Press, 1993), Appendix C.
10. For a discussion and supporting empirical material, see P. Taylor, 'Regionalism: The Thought and the Deed', chapter 11 in: A.J.R. Groom and P. Taylor, *Frameworks for International Co-operation* (London, Pinter, 1990).
11. See the special issue of *Government and Opposition* 28, 2 (Spring 1993), 'Globalisation: The Interweaving of Foreign and Domestic Policy-Making'.
12. For a succinct summary of contemporary geo-political concerns and possible future scenarios, see P. Kennedy, *Preparing for the Twenty-First Century* (London, Harper Collins, 1993).

13. Quincy Wright quoted in J.E. Dougherty and R.L. Pfaltzgraff, Jr, *Contending Theories of International Relations: A Comprehensive Survey*, 3rd edn (Harper & Row, New York, 1990), p.55.
14. For a brief historical account of the development of ideas of geo-politics, see: Dougherty and Pfaltzgraff, *op. cit.*, chapter 2; W.C. Olson and A.J.R. Groom, *International Relations Then and Now: Origins and Trends in Interpretation* (London, Harper Collins, 1991), pp.252–7.
15. See the opening remarks of John Chipman in J. Chipman, 'The future of strategic studies: beyond even grand strategy', *Survival* 34, 1 (Spring 1992): 109–31.
16. See, for example, H. Bull, *The Anarchical Society: A Study of Order in World Politics* (London, Macmillan, 1977), chapter 5.
17. As illustrative and exemplary in combining these themes, see: J.S. Nye, 'What New World Order?' *Foreign Affairs* 71, 2 (Spring 1992): 88.
18. See the debate between neo-realists and neo-liberals: D.A. Baldwin (ed.), *Neorealism and Neoliberalism: The Contemporary Debate* (New York, Columbia University Press, 1993).
19. For the notion of a system change to polarity, see: A. Deporte, *Europe Between the Superpowers* (New Haven, Conn., 1979).
20. For coverage/a sample of the literature on this debate, see: J.L. Gaddis, *The Long Peace: Inquiries in the History of the Cold War* (Oxford, Oxford University Press, 1987), especially chapter 8; Dougherty and Pfaltzgraff, *op. cit.*, chapter 4.
21. R. Rosencrance, 'A New Concept of Powers', *Foreign Affairs* 71, 2 (1992): 65.
22. Nye, *op. cit.*: 86.
23. For the designation, see: P.A. Reynolds, 'The World of States or the State of the World', *Review of International Studies* 18 (1992): 261–9.
24. For the notion of a bifurcated global system and that of post-international politics, see: J.N. Rosenau, 'The Relocation of Authority in a Shrinking World', *Comparative Politics* 24, 3 (1992): 253–72; J.N. Rosenau, *Turbulence in World Politics: A Theory of Change and Continuity* (Hemel Hempstead, Harvester Wheatsheaf, 1990).
25. P. Kennedy, *The Rise and Fall of the Great Powers: Economic Change and Military Conflict from 1500 to 2000* (London, Fontana Press, 1989).
26. Questions of resource power were raised in Chapter 1 as a method of calculating the power of the EC as a putative power.
27. 'G-7 Leaders Welcome Russia as Full Partner', *Financial Times*, 11 July 1994, p.1.
28. 'New European Commission Representative to the OECD', *Organisation for Economic Co-operation and Development Press Release*, 95/9 7 February 1995.
29. L. Fielding, *Europe as a Global Partner*, UACES Occasional Papers 7 (London, UACES, 1991), p.33.
30. See respectively: 'EU Tries to Break OECD Deadlock', *The European*, 9–15 September 1994, p.17; 'US and EU Remain Split on OECD Chief', *Financial Times*, 22 September 1994, p.2.
31. J. Pinder, *The European Community and Eastern Europe* (London, Pinter for RIIA, 1991), chapter 7.

32. Fielding, *op. cit.*, p.35.
33. Detailed in P. Bruckner, 'The European Community and the United Nations', *European Journal of International Law* 1, 1/2 (1990): 177.
34. Based upon the assessed contributions agreed by the General Assembly in 1993. Information extracted from 'Member States of the United Nations', Appendix C, in A. Roberts and B. Kingsbury (eds), *United Nations, Divided World: The UN's Roles in International Relations*, 2nd edn (Oxford, Clarendon, 1993), pp.530–6.
35. Roberts and Kingsbury, *op. cit.*, p.115.
36. Bruckner, *op. cit.*, p.188.
37. S.J. Nuttall, *European Political Co-operation* (Oxford, Oxford University Press, 1992), pp.27–8.
38. 'Secretary of State to Visit UN General Assembly and Canada', *FCO Press Release*, No. 129, 21 September 1994.
39. See: L. Hurwitz, 'The EEC in the United Nations: The Voting Behaviour of Eight Countries 1948–1973', *Journal of Common Market Studies* 13 (1975): 224–32; R. Foot, 'The European Community's Voting Behaviour at the United Nations General Assembly', *Journal of Common Market Studies* XVII, 4 (June 1979): 350–60; B. Lindemann, 'European Political Co-operation: A Challenge for the Nine', in D. Allen, R. Rummel and W. Wessels (eds), *European Political Co-operation: Towards a Foreign Policy for Western Europe* (London, Butterworth, 1982).
40. TEU, Article J.5.2.
41. Douglas Hurd, 'Developing the Common Foreign and Security Policy', *International Affairs* 70, 3 (July 1994): 425.
42. 'EC Puts its Weight Behind Security Council Revamp', *Guardian*, 27 January 1993, p.8.
43. For a summary of the debates, see: 'Reform of the UN Security Council: Changing the Seats at the Top Table', *Briefing Paper* No. 15 RIIA International Security Programme (December 1994).
44. For this proposal, see: *Our Global Neighbourhood: The Report of the Commission on Global Governance* (Oxford, Oxford University Press, 1995).
45. For the expression of the geographical distribution of UN membership expressed as a percentage, see: P. Baehr and L. Gordenker, *The United Nations in the 1990s*, 2nd edn, p.42.
46. For details, see: *Network Europe and the Information Society* (London, Federal Trust for Education and Research, 1995).
47. G.J. Ikenbury, 'Salvaging the G-7', *Foreign Affairs* 72, 2 (Spring 1993): 132–9, 135.
48. R.O. Keohane, *After Hegemony: Co-operation and Discord in the World Political Economy* (Princeton, Princeton University Press, 1984).
49. For a summary of these areas, see: A. Payne, 'US Hegemony and the Reconfiguration of the Caribbean', *Review of International Studies* 20, 2 (April 1994): 150–2.
50. J. Nye, *Bound to Lead: The Changing Nature of American Power* (New York, Basic Books, 1990).
51. Thurow, *op. cit.*
52. C.W. Kegley and E.R. Wittkopf, *American Foreign Policy: Pattern and Process*, 4th edn (New York, St Martin's Press, 1991).

53. World Trade Organisation, *Trade Policy Review European Union: Report by the Secretariat*, WT/TPR/S/3, 30 June 1995, p.xi.
54. WTO, *ibid.*, p.xvi.
55. Commission of the European Communities, *Europe in a Changing World: The External Relations of the European Community* (Luxembourg, Office for Official Publications of the European Communities, 1993), p.20.
56. J.H. Jackson, 'Regional Trade Blocs and the GATT', *The World Economy* 16, 2 (March 1993): 121–31.
57. See: R.N. Gardner, *Sterling-Dollar Diplomacy in Current Perspective: The Origins and Prospects of our International Economic Order* (New York, Columbia University Press, 1980).
58. E. Thiel, 'Changing Patterns of Monetary Interdependence', chapter 4 in W. Wallace (ed.), *The Dynamics of European Integration* (London, Pinter, 1992).
59. For a discussion of the history of this project, see: J. Pinder, *European Community: The Building of a Union* (Oxford, Oxford University Press, 1995).
60. Greece, Austria, Sweden and Finland have not yet joined the system. The UK withdrew from the ERM after turbulence in the foreign exchange markets in July–August 1992. Intervention obligations on the Italian lira were suspended at the same time.
61. TEU, Article G.
62. *EC Treaty*, Article 109.2.
63. E. Israel, 'Position of the European Community in the Global Capital Market', in A. Clesse and R. Vernon, *The European Community after 1992: A New Role in World Politics?* (Baden-Baden, Nomos Verlagsgessellschaft, 1991).
64. 'A Publisher for Europe. Twenty five years of EUR-OP (Office for Official Publications of the European Communities)' *European Access* (1 February 1995): 23.
65. Commission of the European Communities, *Europe in a Changing World: The External Relations of the European Community* (Luxembourg, Office for Official Publications of the European Communities, 1993), p.4.
66. See, for example, the 'Europe on the Move' series of publications: *The European Economic Area, The Community and the Third World, The Community and its Eastern Neighbours, The European Community and Mediterranean Countries, The European Community and Latin America* (Luxembourg, Office for the Official Publications of the European Communities, various years).
67. E. Regelsberger, 'The Dialogue of the EC/Twelve with Other Regional Groups: A New European Identity in the International System?' chapter 1 in G. Edwards and E. Regelsberger (eds), *Europe's Global Links: The European Community and Inter-Regional Co-operation* (London, Pinter, 1990); E. Regelsberger, 'The Dialogue of the EC/Twelve with Other Groups of States', *The International Spectator* XXIII, 4 (October–December 1988).
68. Regelsberger 'The dialogue of the EC/Twelve', Table 1.1, p.6.
69. Sir Leslie Fielding, KCMG, *Europe as a Global Partner*, UACES Occasional Papers 7 (London, UACES, 1991), p.13.

70. Extracted from *The World Directory of Diplomatic Representation* (London, Europa, 1992).
71. Interview: Head of Unit, Inspection of Delegations, DG1(A), Commission of the European Communities, Brussels, 15 July 1993.
72. *Idem.*
73. *Idem.*
74. Interview: Commission Official, DG1(A), Commission of the European Communities, Brussels, 9 July 1993.
75. D. Buchan, *Europe the Strange Superpower* (Aldershot, Dartmouth, 1993).
76. 'Partnership for Peace: Framework Document', *NATO Review*, February 1994, p.29.
77. TEU, Articles J.4.1 and J.4.2.
78. TEU Declaration No. 30 on Western European Union.
79. Brussels Treaty as amended by the Protocol modifying and completing the Brussels Treaty, signed at Paris on 23 October 1954. Article V states:

    If any of the High Contracting Parties should be the object of an armed attack in Europe, the other High Contracting Parties will, in accordance with the provisions of Article 51 of the Charter of the United Nations, afford the Party so attacked all the military and other aid and assistance in their power.

80. P. Tsakaloyannis, *The Reactivation of the Western European Union and its Effects on the European Community and its Institutions* (Brussels, EIPA, 1985).
81. For an account of the history of the WEU from 1985–1992, see: T. Salmon, 'Testing Times for European Political Co-operation: The Gulf and Yugoslavia, 1990–1992', *International Affairs* 68, 2 (1992): 233–53.
82. Western European Union Council of Ministers, *Petersberg Declaration*, Bonn, 19 June 1992, II.4.
83. Western European Union Council of Ministers, *Kirchberg Declaration*, 9 May 1994, I.6.
84. *The Economist*, 10 December 1994, p.40.
85. The UK government disputes that proposed aircraft is large enough to be considered strategic. 'Britain Relents on Common Defence', *Financial Times*, 15 May 1995, p.2.
86. Hans van Mierlo, *Nato Review*, March 1995, p.8.
87. *Preliminary Conclusions on the Formulation of a Common European Defence Policy*. The document was endorsed by the WEU Council of Ministers under the Noordwijk Declaration, 14 November 1994.
88. *Preliminary Conclusions on the Formulation of a Common Defence Policy*, Part B II.25.
89. Noordwijk Declaration, 14 November 1994.
90. WEU, Kirchberg Declaration, II, 'Document on a Status of Association with WEU for the Republic of Bulgaria, the Czech Republic, the Republic of Estonia, The Republic of Hungary, The Republic of Latvia, The Republic of Lithuania, The Republic of Poland, Romania and the Slovak Republic'.

91. High Level Group of Experts on the CFSP, *European Security Policy Towards 2000: Ways and Means to Establish Credibility*, Brussels, 19 December 1994, p.4.
92. TEU, Declaration No. 30 on Western European Union, I.6.
93. See respectively: 'A European Union capable of more effective action in the field of foreign and security policy', *Discussion Paper of the Executive Committee of the CDU/CSU Parliamentary Group for the Intergovernmental Conference in 1996*; High Level Group of Experts, *op. cit.*, p. 13.

    The position of the UK government: 'PM Outlines Plan for European Defence Pact', *Financial Times*, 2 March 1995, p.10.
94. Alain Lamassoure in 'French Minister Seeks EU Defence Pact in 1996', *Reuters Euro Community Report*, 10 January 1995.
95. Lisbon Declaration, 29 and 31.
96. 'Nato Blessing for the Euro-corps', *Financial Times*, 22 January 1993, p.2.
97. 'Europe Presents Arms', *The European*, 12–18 November 1993, p.6. Eurocorps currently consists of the 4,200 strong Franco-German brigade, three armoured divisions (one from France, Belgium and German respectively). Spain has contributed a mechanised brigade and Luxembourg was due to assign an infantry battalion on 1 January 1995.

    For the latter, see: IISS, *The Military Balance*, 1994–1995 (London, Brassey's for IISS, 1994), p.36.
98. 'Portugal Proposes WEU Intelligence Organisation' *Reuters Euro Community Report*, 4 January 1995.
99. 'Air Forces Link Paves the Way to a New European Alliance', *Guardian*, 19 November 1994, p.11.
100. WEU Council of Ministers, Lisbon Declaration, 15 May 1995, 5.
101. For a recent discussion on the shifting concept of neutrality and its different foundations in EU Member States, see: P. Calvocoressi, 'Neutrality Now', chapter 5 in S. Harden, *Neutral States and the European Community* (London, Brassey's, 1994).
102. M. Ougaard, 'Dealing with the Community: The Bush Administration's Response to Western European Integration', in O. Norgaard, T. Pedersen and N. Petersen, *The European Community in World Politics* (London, Pinter, 1993), p.186.
103. R. Rosencrance (ed.) *America as an Ordinary Country: US Foreign Policy and the Future* (Ithaca, Cornell University Press, NY, 1976).
104. Eurostat, *Basic Statistics of the Community*, 31st edn (Office for Official Publications of the European Communities, 1994).
105. Eurostat, p.320.
106. Eurostat, pp.304–5.
107. R. Ginsberg, *Foreign Policy Actions of the European Community: The Politics of Scale* (London, Adamantine Press, 1989). For an account of this period as a turning point, see: J. Robert Schaetzel, *The Unhinged Alliance: America and the European Community* (New York, Harper & Row, 1975).
108. James Baker, Speech to the Berlin Press Club, 12 December 1989, *Europa Archiv* 45/4 (1990): 77–84.
109. United States Information Service (USIS), 'Declaration on US-EC Relations' (23 November 1990) US Embassy, London.

110. P.C. Schmitter, 'Three Neo-functional Hypotheses about International Integration'. International Organisation, 23 (1969), pp.161–166.
111. 'Cracks are Appearing in the Alliance's Cohesion', *Financial Times*, 2 December 1994.
112. See, for example: Martin Woollacott, 'Nato – The Club that Soon No Nation will Want to Join', *Guardian*, 7 December 1994, p.22; 'A Neutered Nato Caught in the Firing Line', *The European*, 9–15 December 1994, p. 11; Edward Mortimer, 'In Search of a Unifying Threat', *Financial Times*, 7 December 1994, p.21.
113. For some recent attempts to define Europe, see: *What is Europe?* Book 1 *The History of the Idea of Europe*, K. Wilson and J. van der Dussen (eds); Book 2 *Aspects of European Cultural Diversity* Book 3 *European Democratic Culture* Book 4 *Europe and the Wider World*, B. Waites (ed.) (Milton Keynes, Open University Press, 1995).
114. For differing accounts, see respectively: George Steiner, 'Modernity, Mythology and Magic', *Guardian*, 6 August 1994, p.27; R. Bartlett, *The Making of Europe: Conquest, Colonisation and Cultural Change 950–1350* (Harmondsworth, Penguin, 1993); E. Said, *Orientalism* (Harmondsworth, Penguin, 1994); I.B. Neumann and J.M. Welsh, 'The Other in European Self-definition: An Addendum to the Literature on International Society', *Review of International Studies* 17, 2 (1991): 327–48.
115. Article 227.2.
116. Part Four, Treaty of Rome.

    Mayotte
    New Caledonia and dependencies
    Overseas Territory of French Polynesia
    Overseas Territory of the Wallis and Futuna Islands
    French Southern and Antarctic Territories
    Overseas countries of the Kingdom of the Netherlands
    Anguilla
    Cayman Islands
    Falkland Islands, South Georgia, South Sandwich Islands
    Turks and Caicos Islands
    British Virgin Islands
    Montserrat
    Pitcairn
    St Helena and dependencies
    British Antarctic Territory
    British Indian Ocean Territory
    Greenland

    As per Council Decision 86/283/EEC 30 June 1986
    Official Journal of the European Communities L 175, 1.7.1986.
    This list of colonies has expanded and contracted according to the vagaries of enlargement, decolonization and withdrawal from the Union (Greenland).
117. *EC Treaty*, Article 227.5.
118. For further details, see: 'The European Community's Relations to French Overseas Departments, European Autonomous Regions, Overseas Countries and Territories and Independent Countries within EC Boundaries', *Background Report*, ISEC/B33/92, 10 December 1992.

119. J. Mearsheimer, 'Back to the Future: Instability After the Cold War', *International Security* 15, 1: 5–56.
120. S. Tharoor, 'United Nations Peacekeeping in Europe', *Survival* 37, 2 (Summer 1995): 121–34. The UN has three peacekeeping missions in Europe: UNFICYP in Cyprus, UNPROFOR in Yugoslavia and UNOMIG in Georgia.
121. For the capabilities/expectations gap, see: C. Hill, 'The Capability-Expectations Gap, or Conceptualising Europe's International Role' chapter 4, S. Bulmer and A. Scott (eds), *Economic and Political Integration in Europe: Internal Dynamics and Global Context* (Blackwell, Oxford, 1994).
122. See, for example: High-level group of experts on the CFSP, *European Security policy towards 2000: ways and means to establish genuine credibility*, Brussels, 19 December 1994.
123. The International Institute for Strategic Studies, *The Military Balance 1994–1995* (London, Brassey's for IISS, 1994), pp.276–7.

    Since the endorsement of the deployment by the then CSCE non-EU states have joined the mission. Canada, Czech and Slovak Republics, Poland.

    Swedish monitors were also involved prior to Sweden's accession to the EU. See *NATO Review* (April 1994): 11.
124. 'EU Sees Long Mission to Resurrect Mostar', *Reuters Euro Community Report*, 28 April 1995.
125. Wilhem Hoynck, 'CSCE Works to Develop its Conflict Prevention Potential', *Nato Review* (April 1994): 16.
126. Hoynck, *ibid.:* 20.
127. *Financial Times*, 16 December 1992, p.21.
128. D. Tarschys, 'The Council of Europe: Towards a Vast Area of Democratic Security', *NATO Review* (Dec. 94–Jan. 95): 9.
129. 'Building Bridges for the Future', *The European*, 14–17 October 1993, p. 12.
130. *The European, ibid.*
131. Exchange of Letters between the Council of Europe and the European Community, *Official Journal of the European Communities*, L 273/35–37, 26 September 1989.
132. B. Laffan, *Integration and Co-operation in Europe* (London, Routledge, 1992), p.46.
133. *The European*, 12–15 November 1992, p.7.

5 The Legal Dimension as a Source of Influence

In considering the legal sources of influence that impact upon the construction and representation of the international identity of the Union we have to go beyond a purely institutional focus upon the European Court of Justice (ECJ). The sources relevant to an understanding of the construction and representation of the European Union are significant in two regards. Firstly, they contribute, from an external perspective, to one facet of the international identity of the Union. Secondly, from an internal perspective, understood as falling within the system used to organise this study, they act as a source of influence upon the formation of policy and the development of instruments available at the disposal of the Union.

This chapter seeks to explore the legal sources of identity by examining four sets of issues. Firstly, it seeks to illustrate how the legal order of the Union has contributed a distinctive facet to its international identity. Secondly, it will look at how the treaties and other legal arrangements have created a distinctive legal order that governs and facilitates the conduct of the international relations of the Union. Thirdly, we look at the ECJ as an actor in a decision-making process concerning external relations. Lastly, we consider the role of the law of the Union in both clarifying and modifying the competencies of the Union to conduct external relations with reference to the Common Commercial Policy (CCP).

LAW AND THE CREATION OF IDENTITY

The legal order of the Union has contributed a distinctive facet to the international identity by distinguishing the Union from other actors in international society. An examination of the legal basis of the Union illustrates that it has transcended the commonplace understanding of the form and function of an international organisation (IO) but does not conform to the classification in international law of a state.

The legal order of the European Union represents the single most important factor in illustrating the inadequacy of classifying the European Union as an IO. In this chapter the starting point is to provide a definition of IOs and to illustrate the degree to which the EU has moved beyond existent notions of IOs. International organisations are to be understood in this study as being concerned with 'the more concrete manifestation of regularised international relations as in international organisations with their formal and material existence separate from, though for the most part dependent on, states and groups within states.'[1]

The notion that an IO can be conceived as separate from its components has been the guiding framework for this study of the European Union. The EU conforms to the definition of an IO, with 'a formal continuous structure established by agreement between members...with the aim of pursuing the common interest of the membership'.[2] The European Union conforms to these definitions of IOs, and more particularly its membership, constituting nation states, designates it as an inter-governmental organisation (IGO).

However, the EU has moved beyond classification with other IOs, IGOs or classification as an international regime because of its unique legal foundation and legal order. As two distinguished commentators have noted: 'No other international organization enjoys such reliably effective supremacy of its law over the laws of member governments, with a recognized Court of Justice to adjudicate disputes. The Community legal process has a dynamic of its own.'[3]

The reason for adherence to the law of the Union will be reflected upon below. The EU shares a similarity with other IOs by virtue of being established by treaties that are enacted under international law. However, the content of these treaties also provides the point of departure from other IOs. The treaties upon which the EU rests establish independent Communities endowed with their own sovereign rights and competencies. The Member State signatories have pooled parts of their own legislative powers and have placed them in the hands of institutions in which, however, the Member States retain substantial rights of participation. This form of relationship separate from, yet also composed of the Member States has created a relationships between states distinctive enough to warrant its designation as a distinctive legal order.

The EU occupies a distinctive place among the legal systems of nation states and in international law. EC law enjoys a symbiotic relationship with the legal systems of the Member States and with international law, as will be explored below, yet it remains distinguishable from both systems and is a truly unique legal phenomenon. However, any attempt to characterise this unique legal arrangement is complicated by continuing uncertainty as to the final form of the Union. Typologies of supranationalism that were explored in Chapter 2 highlighted the importance of the development of legal arrangements that challenge the exclusive legal competence of the state within its own frontiers. Using this formulation, the legal system of the Union is undoubtedly supranational.[4] The Union is endowed with independent authority, with distinctive sovereign rights and a legal order independent of the Member States to which both the Member States and, importantly, their citizens are subject in matters in which the Community has been granted competence. This grant of competence is important because, as will be outlined below, powers have been conferred on the Community institutions only in limited spheres and the institutions have not been given any power to increase their competencies merely by their own action. Therefore in this important respect the Community lacks the universal jurisdiction characteristic of a state with the power to create new fields of competence.

The hybrid nature of the legal arrangements of the Union – more than those of an IO, less than those of a state – can be illustrated by an exposition of the legal order of the Union and within this focus by drawing out the legal sources of influence that impact upon the construction and representation of the international identity of the Union.

THE POLITICAL CONSTITUTION OF THE EUROPEAN UNION

The starting point in considering the legal order of the EU is to seek to identity whether the EU possesses what is normally understood as a constitution. It is posited here that the EU has a constitution, and further, from that constitution we can draw certain inferences about the form and functioning of the legal order of the Union and provide another distinctive facet to the international identity.

The understanding of what constitutes a constitution for the purposes of this study is that it refers to 'the institutions, practices, and principles that define and structure a system of government and to the written document that articulates such a system'.[5] It is conjectured that not only does the EU possess a constitution but that this constitution is of a two-fold nature. The EU possesses both a written legal constitution and a written political constitution. Both of these dimensions are identifiable, and indeed, provide a particular character to the Treaty on European Union.[6]

The delineation between the written legal and the written political constitution of the EU extends directly to the framework of the foreign relations of the Union. The substance of Chapter 3 was to detail the codification of EPC through to CFSP, and Chapter 2 outlined the relevant articles of the treaties that govern external relations. Taken in totality, Chapters 2 and 3 outlined the elements of the political constitution that govern both the conduct and the form of the external relations of the European Union. In seeking to distinguish between these two elements as separate decision-making processes, the role and jurisdiction of the ECJ is of defining importance. The three-pillar structure, used as a means of visualising the European Union, reflects the total political constitution but also distinguishes between those elements covered by the jurisdiction of the ECJ.

In outline, those elements that fall solely within the political constitution of the Union, and are not subject to the ECJ are the following components of the Treaty on European Union: Title I, The Common provisions; Title V, Provisions on a common foreign and security policy; Title VI, Provisions on co-operation in the fields of justice and home affairs – excluding the third paragraph of Article 3(2)(c)) and the Declarations attached to the Treaty.[7]

The Common provisions have three main purposes. Firstly, to clarify the intended relationship of the European Union established by the Treaty to existing Communities:

> By this Treaty, the High Contracting Parties establish among themselves a European Union, hereafter called 'the Union'.
>
> This Treaty marks a new stage in the process of creating an ever closer union among the peoples of Europe, in which the decisions are taken as closely as possible to the citizen.
>
> The Union shall be founded on the European Communities, supplemented by the policies and forms of co-operation established by this Treaty. Its task shall be to organise, in a manner demonstrating consistency and solidarity, relations between the Member States and between their peoples.[8]

The intention of the drafters was, therefore, that the European Union was not to supplant the existing Communities but to enjoy a complementary relationship. This intention is reinforced by Articles C–E of the Common provisions that cover institutional matters. As Article C states: 'The Union shall be served by a single institutional framework which shall ensure the consistency and the continuity of the activities carried out in order to attain its objectives while respecting and building upon the *acquis communautaire*.'[9] However, despite the commitment to a single institutional framework, the roles and functions of the European Parliament, the Council, the Commission and the Court of Justice are flagged as being different when use is being made of the provisions excluded from the written legal constitution.[10] The only explicitly Union institution not a part of the written legal constitution is the European Council composed of the Heads of State or Government of the Member States and the President of the Commission.[11]

The Common provisions also outline the five-fold objectives of the Union:

- to promote economic and social progress which is balanced and sustainable, in particular through the creation of an area without internal frontiers, through the strengthening of economic and social cohesion and through the establishment of economic and monetary union, ultimately including a single currency in accordance with the provisions of this Treaty;
- to assert its identity on the international scene, in particular through the implementation of a common foreign and security policy including the eventual framing of a common defence policy, which might in time lead to a common defence;
- to strengthen the protection of the rights and interests of the nationals of its Member States through the introduction of a citizenship of the Union;
- to develop close co-operation on justice and home affairs;
- to maintain in full the *acquis communautaire* and build on it.

The objectives of the EU, as articulated in the written political constitution, illustrate that the remit of the Union is to traverse activities normally considered part of both the domestic and the international spheres. However, the intention is not to supplant the core role and functions of the state in the domestic sphere. The elements of the written political constitution dealing with co-operation in the fields of justice and home affairs merely designate areas of common interest and establish mechanisms to co-ordinate action.[12] The intended method of operation replicates the other pillar of the Union, the CFSP, covered in Chapter 3.

The three-pillar structure of the European Union established by the Treaty on European Union encompasses, alongside the pillars dealing with justice and home affairs and the CFSP, the three Communities of the ECSC, EAEC and the EC (changed under the TEU from the EEC). It is to these as elements of the written legal constitution that we now turn.

THE LEGAL CONSTITUTION OF THE EUROPEAN UNION

It can be said as a starting point that the notion of a legal constitution of the Union is a nonsense in that the Union does not enjoy legal personality.[13] Therefore, for the purpose of discussing the written legal constitution we will refer to EC law, and this expression is intended to include the law of all three Communities.

As has been indicated above, the Union constitution is not laid down in a single document encompassing a single legal order. Indeed the content of the constitution can be drawn very much more widely, '[and]...arises from the totality of rules and fundamental values by which those in authority regard themselves as bound. These rules are to be found partly in the founding treaties or in the legal instruments produced by the Community institutions, but they also rest partly on custom.'[14]

If we focus upon the written legal constitution we must, therefore, go beyond the founding treaties, and their amendments, to clarify those legal instruments that make up the legal constitution: the treaties, Community legislation, international law and principles of law. The starting point is to turn to an exposition of the framework of the EC Treaty. The European Court of Justice (ECJ) itself has taken the view that the EC Treaty is the 'constitutional charter of the Community based on the rule of law'.[15] As will immediately become apparent, EC law does not range as widely as the law of its member nation states. For example, EC law is not directly concerned with matters of criminal law or family law.

The treaties

The first component of the written legal constitution are the founding treaties and their successive amendments. These are also often called the primary law of the EC.[16] The treaty-element of the legal constitution can be explored by examining the framework of the EC Treaty. If we focus upon the content of the treaties (and the EC Treaty is illustrative), it becomes apparent that a large part of the contents of the treaties concern the details of policy providing both general principles and policy sectors for development. Placed alongside the written constitution of one of the Member States, such as the Basic Law for the Federal Republic of Germany, it appears cluttered with policy matters rather than just providing for the means of its enactment.[17] As with any constitutional document, the EC Treaty also specifies the allocation of powers for the conduct of foreign policy.

The EC Treaty text is divided into six parts: Principles; Citizenship of the Union; Community Policies; Association of the Overseas Countries and Territories; Institutions of the Community; General and Final Provisions.

Part One, Principles, establishes that the Community's primary concern is with economic activity:

> The Community shall have as its task, by establishing a common market and an economic and monetary union and by implementing the common policies or activities referred to in Articles 3 and 3a, to promote throughout the Community a harmonious and balanced development of economic activities, sustainable and non-inflationary growth respecting the environment, a high degree of convergence of economic importance, a high level of employment and of social protection, the raising of the standard of living and the quality of life, and economic and social cohesion and solidarity among Member States.[18]

The activities of the Community intended to give effect to these objectives are established in Article 3 of the Treaty. The Article conveys differing levels of commitment to 20 differing activities. Aside from the creation of a customs union and an internal market, and matters concerned with their regulation such as competition policy, the strongest commitment is to common policies. These are designated in the fields of commercial policy, agriculture and fisheries and transport. Areas designated as policy areas, as distinctive from common policies, are in the social sphere, environment and development co-operation. Economic and social cohesion and the competitiveness of Community industry activities are subject to 'strengthening'; 'measures' are to be taken in the spheres of energy, civil protection and tourism. Research and technical development are subject to 'promotion'; 'encouragement' for the establishment of trans-European networks; and 'contribution' in the activities of consumer protection, health protection, education and training and 'the flowering of the cultures of the Member States'.[19] The Association of Overseas Countries and Territories, also enshrined as an activity, was covered in Chapter 4.

In none of these areas is the Community granted exclusive competence to exercise power (except the Common Commercial Policy, to which we will return). Exclusive competence is of importance because of the principle of subsidiarity introduced to the EC Treaty by the TEU.

> The Community shall act within the limits of the powers conferred upon it by this Treaty and of the objectives assigned to it therein.
>
> In areas which do not fall within its exclusive competence, the Community shall take action, in accordance with the principle of subsidiarity, only if and so far as the objectives of the proposed action cannot be sufficiently achieved by Member States and can therefore, by reason of the scale or the effects of the proposed action, be better achieved by the Community.
>
> Any action of the Community shall not go beyond what is necessary to achieve the objectives of this Treaty.[20]

The division of powers between the Member States is perhaps obscured rather than clarified by the principle. It has always been clear that the Community can only act where it has a legal basis to do so and through the Council the Member States retain both legislative and executive power. Indeed, the extension of the competencies of the Community in pursuit of the objectives of the EC beyond those areas explicitly provided for in the treaties requires unanimous agreement by the Council.[21] Likewise, it is only the governments of the Union, convened as an intergovernmental conference, which have the powers both to amend and to ratify any amendments to the treaties.[22] Therefore the principle of subsidiarity, which comes under the jurisdiction of the ECJ, applies to the exercise of existing powers and does not confer a division of powers, which is a matter of decision for the Member States. Therefore, any extension of the powers enshrined in the EC Treaty that concern the construction or representation of the international identity require unanimous agreement among the Member States.

Part Two of the Union, also introduced by the TEU, created a citizenship of the Union. The attainment of citizenship of the Union is through nationality of a member state. Under Article 8 of the EC Treaty:

1 Citizenship of the Union is hereby established. Every person holding the nationality of a Member State shall be a citizen of the Union.
2 Citizens of the Union shall enjoy the rights conferred by this Treaty and shall be subject to the duties imposed thereby.[23]

The Citizenship is intended to complement, rather than to displace, citizenship of a Member State. The Citizenship establishes a set of transnational citizenship rights:[24]

- the right to move and reside freely within the territory of the Member States;
- the right to vote and stand as a candidate in municipal elections in the EU state of one's residence;
- the right to vote and stand as a candidate of the European Parliament in whatever Member State one resides;
- the right to petition the European Parliament;
- the right to raise any case of alleged maladministration by any EC institution with an ombudsman;
- entitlement to diplomatic and consular protection in a third country by any of the other states when one's own state does not have representation.

This last right can be expected to have a future impact upon the diplomatic practices of the Member States. At present there are only four countries in which all the Member States are represented – China, the United States, Japan and Russia.[25] Furthermore, there are 17 countries in which only two Member States are represented.[26] However, the Member States have yet to agree guidelines among themselves governing the practical implementation of these citizenship entitlements.[27]

Part Three of the EC Treaty sets out the Community policies as outlined above. The importance of these policies for the international identity is that they represent a codification of the measures for formal integration agreed among the Member States. The importance of this codification and the way that the ECJ has issued rulings that impact upon the conduct of external relations is detailed below. Of especial importance is that this part of the Treaty seeks to establish the four freedoms of the Community of the movement of goods, persons, services and capital. The policies outlined above and the common market established sit behind a Common External Tariff and a Common Commercial Policy that will be examined below.

The impact that the depth of internal integration has upon the conduct of the international identity is detailed in Chapter 6. However, in a number of the policy areas, aside from the common policies, there is a recognition, and a requirement, for the Community and the Member States to share the conduct of certain aspects of external relations in the areas of education and vocational training, culture, public health, trans-European networks, research and development and the environment.

The TEU introduced 'development co-operation' as a new title. The intention of the this new area with an explicitly outward focus is as follows:

> The Community and the Member States shall co-ordinate their policies on development co-operation and shall consult each other on their aid programmes, including in international organizations and during international conferences. They may undertake joint action.[28]

An attempt was made to co-ordinate the development programmes conducted through the Lomé Convention and other Community agreements with developing countries with the individual policies of the Member States. The view of the Commission is that it has not resulted in a discernible convergence: 'co-ordination still falls short of the ideal. Indeed it works very much in one direction. More precisely, the Member States rarely set out their own bilateral aid policies at meetings in Council bodies.'[29]

The substance of Part Four of the Treaty on the Association of the Overseas Countries and Territories was covered in Chapter 4. Part Five, on the Institutions of the Community, deals with the decision-making processes and we will turn to the role of the institutions in the legislative process below. With respect to Part Six of the Treaty, certain provisions have been touched upon in Chapter 2, covering Treaty-based external relations. The intention here is to provide the relevant Treaty articles in detail.

Article 210 grants the Community legal personality, which was not extended to the European Union. Articles 223 and 224 encompass matters undertaken to protect the national security of the Member States. Article 223 places no obligation on a Member State to disclose information which is considered contrary to the essential interests of its own security. Article 224 states:

> Member States shall consult each other with a view to taking together the steps needed to prevent the functioning of the common market being affected by measures which a Member State may be called upon to take in the event of serious internal disturbances affecting the maintenance of law and order, in the event of war, serious international tension constituting a threat of war, or in order to carry out obligations it has accepted for the purpose of maintaining peace and international security.[30]

Article 224 provided the basis on which the United Kingdom requested the other Member States of the EC to undertake economic sanctions against Argentina, following the invasion of the Falkland Islands in 1982.[31] The General and Final Provisions also contain Article 227, which sets out the elements of the treaties applying to the overseas territories for which some states are responsible, and were detailed in Chapter 4, and Article 228a, on the use of economic sanctions under a joint action, was covered in Chapter 3. If any Member State believes improper use is made of these Articles, then under Article 225 of the Treaty it is able to refer the matter to the Court of Justice.

Article 228 sets out the procedure whereby the Council both empowers the Commission to undertake negotiations for agreements with single states, groups of states, or IOs and oversees their negotiations by Council committees. Various voting procedures apply at different stages of this process and these are detailed below.

The Council is required to consult the Parliament, unless the agreement is conducted under Article 113(3) of the EC Treaty. The TEU introduced an amendment which requires that any Association agreements (created under Article 238) or 'other agreements establishing a specific institutional framework by organising co-operation procedures, agreements having important budgetary arrangements for the Community...shall be concluded after the assent of the European Parliament has been obtained'.[32]

Article 228a, authorising sanctions under joint actions, was covered in Chapter 3 and the provisions in Articles 229–231 on relations with other international organisations were detailed in Chapter 2.

The Treaty of Rome originally contained an Article 218 governing the diplomatic privileges and immunities of the then EEC. This Article was repealed and replaced by Article 28 of the Merger Treaty that established a single Council and a single Commission for all three Communities in 1967.[33] The Merger Treaty Article 28, which is still in force, states:

> The European Communities shall enjoy in the territories of the Member States such privileges and immunities as are necessary for the performance of their tasks, under the conditions laid down in the Protocol annexed to this Treaty. The same shall apply to the European Investment Bank.[34]

Article 28, in replacing similar provisions existing in the EEC, EAEC and ECSC treaties, extended full diplomatic privileges and immunities to the Communities as governed by the Vienna Convention. Full privileges and immunities were also extended to the representative of the Member States taking part in the work of the Communities. Officials and other servants of the Community irrespective of their nationality, enjoy personal immunities, in the operation of their duties and exemptions from national income taxes and travel under *laissez-passer*, both between Member States and third countries. Diplomatic missions accredited to the Community from third countries enjoy full privileges and immunities.

International law

The Agreements that are conducted under the above Articles are agreements concluded in international law. As we have noted throughout this text these agreements with non-member countries and with other IOs range from treaties providing for extensive co-operation in trade or in the industrial, technical and social fields to agreements on trade in particular products. As was outlined in Chapter 2, there are two substantive forms of these agreements. Firstly, Association Agreements that go beyond the mere regulation of trade and involve close economic co-operation and financial assistance. As was noted, a distinction can be drawn between two different types of Association Agreement: Agreements that maintain special links between certain Member States and non-member countries (for example, former colonies of the Member States) and Agreements as preparation for accession to the Community or for the establishment of a customs union. The second substantive form are Co-operation Agreements, which are not as far-reaching as Association Agreements and are aimed at intensive economic co-operation.

The ECJ has progressively established in its judgments that, as the EU has increasingly developed its international role and taken over powers from the states, the same rules of international law that apply to the Member States also apply to the Community. In two cases, the *International Fruit Company* case and *Nederlandsche Spoorwegen*, the ECJ ruled that the Community is bound by the GATT and the Community has succeeded to the rights and obligations that the Member States entered into as signatories of the agreements.[35] This is most clearly illustrated with regard to treaty law and the privileges and immunities of international organisations. When the EU signs an international agreement, it is implemented by a legislative acts and therefore these acts can be viewed as constituting EU legislation. This both embeds the Union within international law but also places the Union in the role as a substantive generator of international law as part of its integrative diplomacy.

European Community Legislation

The agreements conducted as part of the external relations having force in international law require a legislative process within the EU to ensure their implementation. Laws adopted by the EU institutions acting under the treaties contribute to the written legal constitution of the European Union and also constitute secondary legislation. The legislative action of the Community institutions converts the general principles articulated in the treaties into specific rules. As was asserted above, the Community institutions lack the capacity to extend the competencies of the Community, and are reliant upon an inter-governmental bargain being cast among the Member States, then codified in the treaties, for such extensions to take place.

Part Five of the EC Treaty, as was noted above, covers the Institutions of the Community, and more especially for our purposes here outlines the different types of legislation provided for by the treaties (regulations, directives, decisions, recommendations and opinions) and the legislative process. As was noted above, clarity about the differing types of legislation and forms of the legislative process is important because matters relevant to the conduct of external relations can take the form of each distinctive piece of legislation and be enacted under one of a number of differing processes. For example, decisions are the form used when the Union is seeking to enact measures to counter cases of suspected dumping. Likewise, the Union adopts a regulation when it wishes to impose economic sanctions. Of the differing forms of legislation, recommendations and opinions do not carry the force of law.

The law made by the Community institutions in the exercise of the powers conferred on them under Part Five of the EC Treaty is often referred to as secondary legislation and is the second source of the legal constitution. The Community's range of legal tools differs across the three Communities. The differences in the ECSC and EAEC treaties will be outlined before turning to the EC. The ECSC Treaty makes provision for only three types of legal act – decisions, recommendations and opinions.[36] The EEC and EAEC treaties provide for five forms – regulations, directives, decisions, recommendations and opinions.[37] The changes in the pattern arose because it was recognised that the forms developed for the ECSC would not adequately meet the needs of the EC and Euratom.

The legal acts that enable the Community institutions to encroach furthest on the domestic legal systems are regulations in the EC and EAEC treaties, and the general decisions in the ECSC Treaty. Two features unique in international law mark them out. Firstly, their Community character, which means that they lay down the same law throughout the Community, and apply in full in all Member States. Secondly, their direct applicability, which means that they do not have to be transformed into the domestic law of the Member States, but confer rights or impose duties directly on the citizens of the Community in the same way as domestic law. The Member States and their governing institutions are directly bound directly by Community law and compliance is as with domestic law.

The second form of binding Community legislation is the directive, which appears in the ECSC Treaty as the recommendation. Directives are addressed to Member States, sometimes to all Member States and sometimes only to specified ones; ECSC recommendations may also be addressed to firms in the Community. Unlike the regulation, or general ECSC decision, this form does not create new, uniform Community law binding throughout the whole Community: it requires the addressees to take such measures as may be necessary in order to achieve an aim desired by the Community. The directive or ECSC recommendation states an objective which the addressee must realise within a stated period. How this is to be done is a matter for the addressee.

When they implement a directive or an ECSC recommendation, the Member States have to introduce new domestic law, or recast or repeal their existing domestic statutory and administrative rules so as to bring them into line with the objectives set out in the directive or recommendation. Apart from cases in which an ECSC recommendation is addressed directly to a Community firm, directives and ECSC recommendations do not confer direct rights and duties on Community citizens, as they are addressed solely to the Member States. Citizens acquire the relevant rights and duties only when the directive or recommendation is incorporated into domestic law by the Member States.

A third category of Community legal acts consists of EC or EAEC decisions (or individual ECSC decisions). The individual decision is the means normally available to the Community institutions to order something to be done in an individual case. Lastly, there are opinions and (and under the EC and EAEC treaties) recommendations. This category of legal measures is the last one explicitly provided for in the treaties; it enables the Community institutions to express a view to Member States, and in some cases to individual citizens, which is not binding and does not place any legal obligations on the addressees. To confuse matters, under the ECSC a 'recommendation' is a binding legal act, corresponding to the directive in the EC and EAEC treaties. While EC and EAEC recommendations urge the addressees to adopt a particular form of behaviour, opinions are used where the Community institutions are called upon to state a view on a current situation or particular event in the Community or the Member States.

The real significance of these recommendations and opinions is political and moral. They are non-binding legal acts not adopted by the legislative procedure described below, but are simply issued by a single Community institution.

The question of which one of these acts is available for use is dependent upon the provision of the Treaty under which the institutions of the Community are acting and, in turn, impacts upon the role of the institutions in the process. For example, the process of negotiating an Agreement with a state, group of states or international organisations requires the Commission to make a recommendation to the Council on the need to negotiate an Agreement. The Council authorises the negotiations through a directive, requiring either a qualified majority or unanimity, and the Council then acts again on the basis of the Agreement proposed by the Commission. The adoption of the eventual legislative act and its implementation is undertaken through one of 22 different procedures under the EC Treaty. Four of these procedures are used under the EC Treaty for the purposes of concluding international Agreements. The substantive difference in each of these procedures is the manner in which the Council takes a decision which is either by unanimity or by a qualified majority. A total of 87 votes are distributed across the Fifteen Member States. The number of votes required for the passage of legislation when voting under qualified majority is 62.[38] The other main difference across these procedures is the role of the European Parliament in the process: the Parliament is involved either in procedures of consultation, co-operation or assent. Another procedure, entitled 'co-decision', exists, but no articles dealing with international Agreements come under this procedure. The relevant roles of the institutions in these processes are detailed below.

Assent and unanimity

The assent procedure (Figure 5.1), with the Council voting unanimously, is required for Agreements for new membership to the Union, Association Agreements between the Union and other states, and for any international Agreement that covers internal rules which the Council has to enact unanimously.[39] The assent procedure also covers any international Agreement

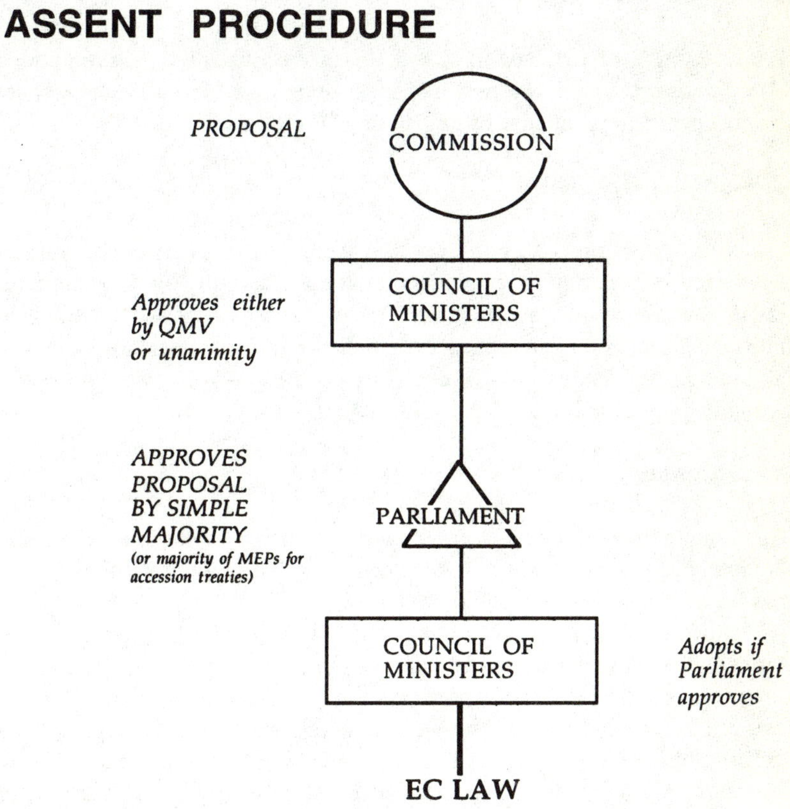

Figure 5.1 The assent legislative procedure for international Agreements
Source: Author

which establishes an institutional framework by means of a co-operation procedure, which has budgetary implications for the Union or which involves the amendment of an act which has previously been adopted under the co-decision system of legislation.[40]

Since the extension of the assent procedure under the TEU to international Agreements other than Treaties of Accession and Association Agreements, the procedure has been used on international agreements on five occasions: the Agreements resulting from the Uruguay round of the GATT; the Accession Agreements for the membership of Austria, Finland and Sweden; twice on elements to enact the European Economic Area; and the conclusion of a protocol on financial and technical co-operation between the EC and the Syrian Arab Republic.[41]

Co-operation procedure

The enactment of acts under Title XVII of the EC Treaty, Development Co-operation requires the use, and involvement of the Parliament under the co-operation procedure for legislating (Figure 5.2).

Consultation procedure

The consultation procedure (Figure 5.3) accounts for two different ways of legislating international Agreements: firstly, the consultation procedure requiring unanimity in the Council.[42] This procedure is used when an international Agreement encompasses a field of internal legislation that is adopted either under the co-decision or the co-operation processes. Secondly, the Council acts by a qualified majority.[43]

No consultation

The conclusion of trade Agreements conducted under the Common Commercial Policy does not involve any consultation with the Parliament, and the Council acts by a qualified majority.[44]

The detailing of these different systems of legislation for international Agreements illustrates a number of important sources of influence on the processes required to enact Agreements to enhance the international identity. Firstly, the role of the Commission in its role of negotiating, drafting and implementing international Agreements. Secondly, the centrality of the Council of Ministers, and thereby the Member States, as a source of influence in the oversight and the enactment of international Agreements.

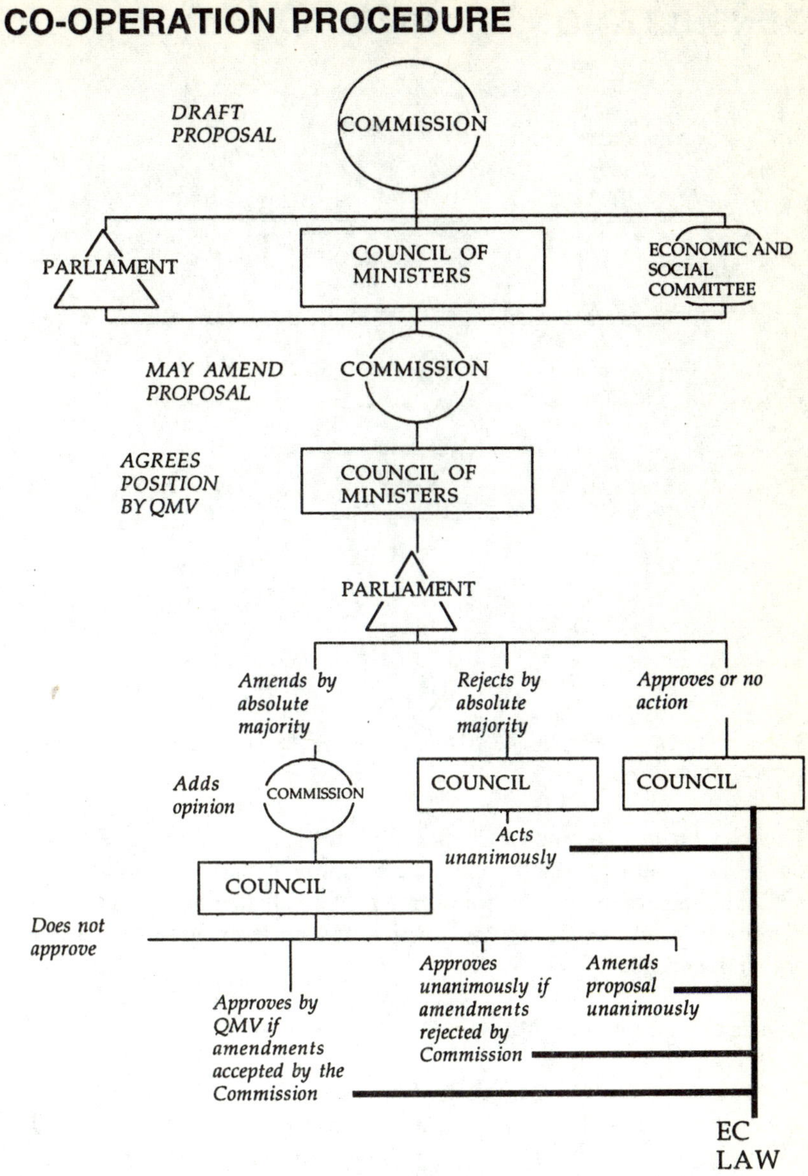

Figure 5.2 The co-operation legislative procedure
Source: Author

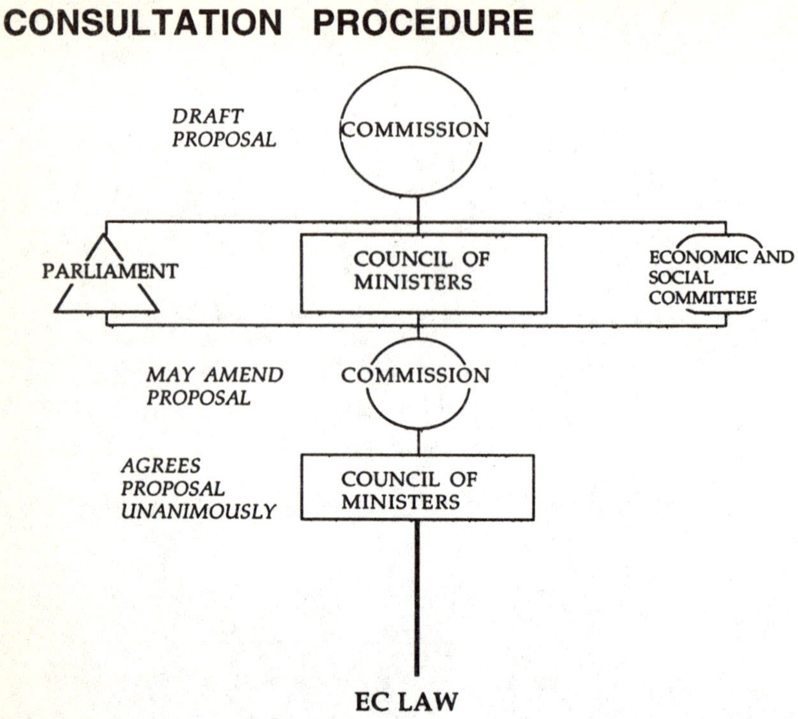

Figure 5.3 The consultation legislative procedure for international Agreements
Source: Author

This is a factor explored in Chapter 6. Thirdly, the role of the European Parliament, and importantly under the assent procedure, its ability to veto any enlargement or Association Agreement conducted by the Union, and thereby to influence in the construction and representation of the international identity.

The general principles of law

The fourth facet of the legal constitution is not enshrined as specific Community law. The ECJ also has a much wider source of law to consider when making judgments by having recourse to the general principles of law. All three Community treaties charge the Court of Justice with the task of ensuring 'that in the interpretation and application of this Treaty the law is observed.'[45] The implication of this, and of certain other Treaty articles, is that the Court has the right of regard over general principles of law, including proportionality, non-discrimination, adherence to legality and respect for procedural rights.[46] Fundamental rights are not part of the written legal constitution but the Court has referred to them on several occasions: so, for example, in *Hauer* v. *Land Rheinland-Pfalz* the Court ruled that fundamental rights are an integral part of the general principles of law and the Court must ensure their observance.[47]

THE ECJ AND ITS RULINGS

The rulings of the ECJ have played an important part in shaping and making EC law. This stems from the fact that EC statute law is unclear or incomplete. The ECJ has increasingly come to cite its own case law. The Court is, in effect, extending the written legal constitution through its interpretations and judgments.

The ECJ has two main functions: it is responsible for directly applying the law in certain types of cases; and it has a general responsibility for interpreting the provisions of EU law and ensuring that the application of the law (by national Courts) is consistent and uniform.[48] The Court has also played a role in law-making by creating judicial law in four respects:[49] the Court has clarified and strengthened the status of EC law; EC policy competence has been strengthened and extended by Court judgments; Court judgments have saved the EC the need to make law in existing areas of competence; the powers and functioning of the institutions have been clarified and affected by rulings of the Court.

However, the Court cannot initiate actions: it must wait for cases to be referred to it and this can happen in a number of ways. Under EC Treaty Articles 169 and 170, the Court rules on whether Member States have failed to fulfil obligations under the Treaty. Actions under this article can be brought by the Member States or the Commission. Under Article 173 the ECJ has the power to review (and under Article 174 to annul) acts. An increasingly important aspect of this work is the Treaty base under which the EU legislation is proposed and adopted. In certain limited spheres the Commission is empowered to impose financial penalties to ensure compliance with EU regulations. The TEU gave power to the Court powers to impose such penalties on Member States. Under Article 175 there are provisions for the institutions to be taken to the Court for failure to act in an area designated as Community policy. Lastly, the Court can act to establish the grounds on which the Community is subject to liability. The ECJ also plays a role in giving judgments in law for cases that are being heard by national Courts.[50] The right to refer a case is a prerogative of the national Courts. Preliminary rulings now constitute the largest category of cases brought before the ECJ. Increasingly, national Courts are looking to the ECJ to perform the role of a supreme Court in the competencies covered by the treaties.

The ECJ plays a particular role under Article 228 in delivering opinions on whether any Agreement that is envisaged is compatible with the provisions of the Treaty. If the Court rules this is not the case, then an Agreement can only be entered into if the Treaty is amended first through an inter-governmental conference.[51]

A recent example that has impacted upon external relations is the ECJ ruling that Uruguay round Agreement of the GATT includes shared competencies between the Community and the Member States in the areas of services and intellectual property. This has been complicated by a recent ruling by the ECJ on the ratification of the GATT Uruguay round, giving exclusive competence to the Community to conclude international Agreements relating to goods but sharing competence in the areas of services and intellectual property with the Member States.[52]

WHY ADHERENCE TO EC LAW?

The question must be raised as to why the Member States adhere to Community law. If this is considered form a legal perspective, then a set of issues significant to the status of EC law become significant. The ECJ ruled in *Costa* v. *ENEL* that the EC constitutes an autonomous legal system imposing obligations and rights on both individuals and Member States and limiting the sovereignty of Member States.[53] Three main pillars can be identified as maintaining this legal order: direct applicability, direct effect and primacy.

The direct applicability of Community law means that the latter confers rights and imposes obligations directly not only on the institutions and the Member States but also on the Community's citizens. The ECJ has enforced the direct applicability of the provisions of Community law established with the *Van Gend en Loos* case.[54] In this the Court ruled that the legal order includes individuals as well as states. EC law is directly applicable where there is no need for the law to have binding force within the Member States: other legal acts beyond regulations are therefore directly applicable under certain circumstances.

Direct effect is the principle whereby certain provisions of EU law may confer rights or obligations on individuals which national Courts are bound to recognise and enforce. There is no explicit reference in the treaties to the primacy or supremacy of EU law over national law. The Court from an early stage took an active role in establishing the primacy of EU law. It has been consistently asserted that national Courts must apply EU law in the event of any conflict, even if the domestic law is part of the national constitution. In this regard the ENEL case made two important observations on the relationship between Community law and national law. Firstly, the Member States have definitively transferred sovereign rights to a Community created by them. They cannot reverse this process unilaterally. Secondly, it is the principle of the Treaty that no Member State can call into question the status of Community law as a system uniformly and generally applicable throughout the Community.

THE LEGAL SYSTEM AND THE PURSUIT OF EXTERNAL RELATIONS: THE CCP AND THE CCT

As was noted in Chapter 2, the Common Customs Tariff is one of the main tools of an external trade policy which is based on the basic principle of uniformity of treatment vis-à-vis third countries, rather than the abolition of barriers and integration of markets. However, the Community is committed to the furtherance of global free trade. Article 18 EC states:

> The Member States declare their readiness to contribute to the development of international trade and the lowering of barriers to trade by entering into Agreements designed, on a basis of reciprocity and mutual advantage, to reduce customs duties below the general level of which they could avail themselves as a result of the establishment of a customs union between them.[55]

Article 110 EC further links together the customs union, the CCP and the pursuit of free trade:

> By establishing a customs union between themselves the Member States aim to contribute, in the common interest, to the harmonious development of world trade, the progressive abolition of restrictions on internal trade and the lowering of customs barriers.
>
> The common commercial policy shall take into account the favourable effect which the abolition of customs duties between Member States may have on the increase in the competitive strength of undertakings in those states.[56]

These Articles do not create juristicable duties on the part of the Member States as a Community to lower their customs barriers towards third countries, but at the most articulate a duty to negotiate for the achievement of free trade within organisations such as the GATT. The objective is to ensure that the customs union does not undermine the GATT system. The policies, as formulated unilaterally by the Community or in negotiation with other countries, are primarily concerned with ensuring that external conditions do not distort competition between the Member States and thus with preventing external factors from damaging the fabric of integration within the Community.

The closer the internal market has come to resembling a national market writ large the greater has been the required degree of uniform rules applying to products originating in third countries imported into the common market. This is why internal integration is explored in Chapter 6 as a source of influence upon the international identity.

In order to maximise the level of uniformity of protection and thus to permit the removal of internal frontiers, the work of the Community within the context of the internal market programme was extended to the external frontiers. The Commission's White Paper on *Completing the Internal Market* recognised the link between the internal and external frontiers.[57] The Community has formulated a single Community customs code which is intended in future to provide clear and transparent rules for customs administrations and businesses.[58] The code came into force on 1 January 1994.

The Common Commercial Tariff has been in place since 1 July 1968; this was 18 months before the target date set by the Treaty of Rome itself. The CCT comprises three main elements:

- a nomenclature for the classification of goods;
- rules on the valuation of goods;
- rules on the origin of goods.

A definition of the customs territory is also necessary for the operation of the CCT, and this is based on the countries which are from time to time the Member States of the Community.[59] The customs territory changed most recently in 1990 when the unification of Germany led to the incorporation of the GDR into the Community, and in January 1995, when Austria, Finland and Sweden acceded to the Union.

The customs union is implemented by the customs officials of the Member States but the Commission acts in a supervisory capacity. For example, under Article 169 it can take an enforcement action when a Member State fails to apply the customs rules or fails to pay over customs duties belonging to the Community's own resources.

Until 1988, the CCT nomenclature was based on the 1950 Customs Co-operation Council Nomenclature Convention. This was the nomenclature used by the Member States before the establishment of the Community, and the Community succeeded to the rights and duties of the Member States.[60] This has been replaced by the International Convention on the Harmonised Commodity and Description and Coding System which the European Community was involved in negotiating.[61] This Convention is given effect within the Community legal order by a Council Decision and a Council Regulation.[62] A new nomenclature was needed in order to achieve a common world-wide approach to problems of classification, to develop a more sophisticated system which could be used for statistical as well as customs purposes, and to adapt the earlier classification to technological progress. A Council Regulation provided for customs rules on customs valuation and is based on the GATT Customs Valuation Code.[63]

In contrast to the position on nomenclature and valuation, the rules governing the origin of goods are those put in place when the CCT was first set up in 1968.[64] This is in part because the Community legislation here is autonomous, there having been no international Agreement on this matter in 1968. The Regulation applies to the free movement of goods within the Community, and to non-preferential external trade.

The CCT provides for uniform tariffs in all Fifteen Member States. Consequently, it would be contrary to the system established by the CCT for the Member States to be permitted unilaterally to impose additional tariffs, or charges having equivalent effect to customs duties ('CEEs') on imported products. The Council has powers under Article 28 (unilateral measures) and Article 113 (bilateral or multilateral measures) to establish exemptions from or reductions of the CCT.

CONCLUSION

In summary, the pursuing of policy under the Articles of the Treaties requires legislative acts to give effect to Community aspirations. The decision-making process of the Union, as was noted in Chapters 2 and 3, is a crucial source of influence in both the matters covered under the written legal constitution and the political constitution of the Union.

The legal framework described in the previous pages constitutes the single most important feature distinguishing the EU from other international organisations. The claim to legal supremacy in the interpretation, application and adjudication of these laws constitutes a central element of the supranational character of the EU. The Community is a legal order, since it is not merely a creation of law but also pursues its objectives purely by means of law. To put it briefly, it is a Community based on law.

Community law lays down the procedure for decision-making by the Community institutions and regulates their relationship to one another. It provides the institutions with the means – in the shape of regulations, general ECSC decisions, directives, ECSC recommendations and individual decisions – of enacting legal instruments binding on the Member States and their citizens.

Community law must not be conceived of as a mere collection of international Agreements, nor can it be viewed as a part or appendage of national legal systems. On the contrary, through the establishment of the Community, the Member States have limited their legislative sovereignty and in so going have created a self-sufficient body of law that is binding on them and on their subjects. Yet at the same time the Community legal order and the national legal orders are interlocked and mutually dependent on each other. The legal dimension of the identity of the Union is both separable but not separate from the Member States. It is the maintenance of the Member States as distinctive sources of influence on the construction and representation of the international identity of the Union alongside an integration process that forms the basis of the next chapter.

NOTES AND REFERENCES

1. C. Archer, *International Organisations*, 2nd edn (London, Routledge, 1992), p.3.
2. Archer, *ibid.*, p.38.
3. R.O. Keohane and S. Hoffmann (eds), *The New European Community: Decision Making and Institutional Change* (Oxford, Westview, 1991).
4. For the inclusion of legal competencies in a definition of 'supranational', see: P. Taylor, 'Supranationalism', in A.J.R. Groom and P. Taylor (eds), *Frameworks for International Co-operation* (London, Pinter, 1990).
5. S. Hemberger, in J. Krieger (ed.), *The Oxford Companion to Politics of the World* (Oxford, Oxford University Press, 1993), p.189.
6. For this distinction, see: N. Nugent, *The Government and Politics of the European Union*, 3rd edn (London, Macmillan, 1994).
7. Article L of Treaty on European Union outlines those items of the Treaty covered by the Provisions of three founding treaties concerning those areas subject to the jurisdiction of the Court of Justice. *Treaty on European Union* (hereafter TEU) (Luxembourg, Office for Official Publications of the European Communities, 1992).
8. TEU, Article A.
9. TEU, Article C.
10. TEU, Article E.
11. TEU, Article D.
12. Under TEU Title VI Article K.1, the following areas of common interest are designated:

1 asylum policy;
2 rules governing the crossing by persons of the external borders of the Member States and the exercise of controls thereon;
3 immigration policy and policy on nationals of third countries;
4 combating drug addition;
5 combating international fraud;
6 judicial co-operation in civil matters;
7 judicial co-operation in criminal matters;
8 customs co-operation;
9 police co-operation; involves the creation of Europol (a European Police Office).

13. Legal personality is granted to the EC under Article 210 EC Treaty. *Treaty Establishing the European Community* (hereafter *EC Treaty*) (Luxembourg, Office for Official Publications of the European Communities, 1993).
14. K. Borchardt, The *ABC of Community Law*, 3rd edn, European Documentation Series (Luxembourg, Office for Official Publications of the European Communities, 1991).
15. Opinion 1/91, Opinion on the Draft Agreement on a European Economic Area [1992] 1, *Common Market Law Review* 245.
16. Nugent, *op. cit.*, p.209.
17. For this exercise, see: S.E. Finer, V. Bogdanor and B. Rudden, *Comparing Constitutions* (Oxford, Clarendon Press, 1995).
18. *EC Treaty*, Article 2.
19. *EC Treaty*, Article 3.
20. *EC Treaty*, Article 3b.
21. Article 235 of the EU Treaty states: If action by the Community should prove necessary to attain, in the course of the operation of the common market, one of the objectives of the Community and this Treaty has not provided the necessary powers, the Council shall, acting unanimously on a proposal from the Commission and after consulting the European Parliament, take the appropriate measures.
22. TEU, Article N.
23. *EC Treaty*, Article 8.
24. *EC Treaty*, Articles 8a–8d.
25. Commission of the European Communities, *Report on the Operation of the Treaty on European Union*, SEC (95) 731 final, Brussels, 10 May 1995, p. 9.
26. *Idem.*
27. 'Report on the Council of Ministers on the Functioning of the Treaty on European Union', *European Report Document*, supplement to European Report No. 2032, 12 April 1995, p.5.
28. *EC Treaty*, Article 130x.
29. Commission of the European Communities, *Report on the Operation of the Treaty on European Union*, SEC (95) 731 final, Brussels, 10 May 1995, p. 55.
30. *EC Treaty*, Article 224.
31. S. Nuttall, *European Political Co-operation* (Oxford, Clarendon Press, 1992), p.208.
32. *EC Treaty*, Article 228.3.

33. 'Treaty Establishing a Single Council and a Single Commission of the European Communities', in *EC Treaty*.
34. *Ibid.*
35. Cases 21-4/72 [1972] *European Court Reports* 1219; Case 38/75 [1975] *European Court Reports* 1439.
36. *ECSC Treaty*, Article 14.
37. *EC Treaty*, 189; EAEC Treaty, Article 161.
38. The votes of the Members are weighted as follows:

Austria	4
Belgium	5
Denmark	3
Finland	3
Germany	10
Greece	5
France	10
Ireland	3
Italy	10
Luxembourg	2
Netherlands.	5
Portugal	5
Spain	8
Sweden	4
United Kingdom	10

(*EC Treaty*, Article 148.2)

39. *EC Treaty*, Article 228(2), second sentence.
40. *EC Treaty*, Article 228(3), second subparagraph.
41. 'Report of the Council of Ministers on the Functioning of the Treaty on European Union', *op. cit.*, Annex V(e).
42. Articles 228(2), second sentence, and 228(3), first subparagraph.
43. *EC Treaty* 228(2), first sentence, and 228(3), first subparagraph.
44. *EC Treaty*, Article 113(3) through Article 228(3).
45. *EC Treaty*, Article 164; *EAEC* Treaty, Article 136; *ECSC* Treaty, Article 31.
46. *EC Treaty*, Articles 173 and 215.
47. Case 44/79 *Hauer* v. *Land Rheinland-Pfaltz* [1979], *European Court Reports* 3727.
48. Nugent, *op. cit.* The Court is composed of one justice from each Member State plus an extra judge when the number of Member States is even. Each judge is appointed for 6 years with a staggered turnover of three-yearly cycles. A President is elected among their number for a three-year term; assisting the judges are 6 advocates general. These numbers increase to 17 judges and 8 advocates if the full EFTA enlargement takes place.
49. Nugent, *op. cit.*
50. *EC Treaty*, Article 177.
51. *EC Treaty*, Article 228.6. Corresponding Articles exist in the ECSC Treaty, Article 95, and Article 103 of the Euratom Treaty.
52. 'Ruling on EU's Competence', Opinion 1/94; *Financial Times*, 22 November 1994.

53. Case 6/64 *Costa* v. *ENEL* [1964] *European Court Reports* 585.
54. Case 26/62 *Van Gend en Loos* v. *Nederlandse Administratie der Belastingen* [1963] *European Court Reports* 1.
55. *EC Treaty*, Article 18.
56. *EC Treaty*, Article 110.
57. Paragraphs 35–37.
58. Regulation 2913/92 establishing the Community Customs Code, *Official Journal of the European Communities* (hereafter *Official Journal*) 1992 L302/1.
59. *EC Treaty*, Article 227.
60. Case 38/75 *European Court Reports* 1439.
61. *Official Journal*, 1987 L198/3.
62. Council Decision 87/369 (*Official Journal*, 1987 L198/1) and a Council Regulation 2658/87 (*Official Journal*, 1987 L256/1).
63. Council Regulation 1224/80 (*Official Journal*, 1980 L124/1).
64. Regulation 802/68 (*Official Journal*, 1968 L148/1).

6 The Integrative and Member State Sources

The credibility and success of the European Union has long been judged by a perception of the degree, or extent, of formal integration undertaken, planned or in progress.[1] As an example, the 1970s are often viewed as a period of Euro-sclerosis or Euro-pessimism, because of the lack of substantive, formal integrative developments for the Union. In contrast, the period encompassing the construction of the Single Market, from 1985 until the completion of the negotiations for the Treaty on European Union, can be viewed as a period of re-invigoration of the Community method.[2] Inevitably, any consideration of integration requires us to reflect upon the nature of the integrative process, the extent of integration and methods of comprehending and measuring integration. Undertaking any of these projects would, in themselves, require considerable exposition. Fortunately, the interest in the integrative process in this study is confined to an assessment of the extent the integrative process has contributed to the construction and representation of the international identity of the European Union.

The presenting of the process of integration as one contributing factor, among others, in comprehending the Union suggests a rejection of the idea that a comprehensive account of the international identity of the Union can be written from a purely integrationist standpoint. Rather, a more multifarious account is required. The point made in this chapter is not that the logic of integration, or the methods of conceptualising integration, are flawed but rather, from the stand-point of seeking to assess the international presence of the Union, that a focus upon a *process* of integration can only provide a partial account of the Union's international significance. Of at least equal importance is the disintegrative counterpoint to any process of integration[3] together with the international and regional *context* within which integration takes place, and which provided our focus in Chapter 4.

The structure of this chapter is as follows. Firstly, it explores the notion of formal integration, and argues that formal integration has a significant, but not determining, impact upon the international identity of the European Union. Secondly, it explores integration as an ideology, and asserts that it has a minimal contemporary influence upon the international identity and only functions marginally as an ideology motivating European Union forcign policy. Thirdly, the chapter maintains that processes of informal integration, and their institutionalisation, cast an integrative 'shadow' beyond the Europe of the European Union and create a wider European system that acts as an influence upon the international identity, a development of the theme explored in Chapter 4. The chapter then moves to detail a schematic assessment of the impact of the Member States as a source of influence upon the construction and representation of the international identity.

FORMAL INTEGRATION

Charting the history of and inherent tensions within the European Union, between integration/federalism and inter-governmentalism/Member State sovereignty has long been a favoured device in accounting for the development of the European Union.[4] As has already been made clear elsewhere in this text, drawing such a dichotomous distinction obscures the complexity of the policy-making process in the European Union and the interaction of a much more complex set of sources of influences.

The first section of this chapter does two things: firstly, it clarifies the nature and form of formal integration; and secondly, it assesses how this impacts upon the form and function of the international identity of the EU.

Defining and explaining formal integration

The integration process in the immediate post-war period in Western Europe encouraged the development of theories of integration that themselves, in turn, assisted in the promotion of the notion of an integrative process. Therefore it is impossible to have an understanding of the integrative process without an understanding of the theory that sought to capture and account for that process.

When the European integration process was perceived to have faltered, integration theories declined in fashion. However, the integration process only faltered in what has been called the 'formal integrative' process,[5] this being integration undertaken through the framework of institutions and the consequential rules, regulations and policies created under the auspices of the Treaty of Paris and reinforced and extended by the Treaties of Rome and the successive revision of these three treaties. The essence of the formal integration process is deliberative but at the same time discontinuous.[6]

The formal integrative project has proceeded at a variegated pace; there was a period of high formal integration until the challenge to the notion of supranationalism in the 1960s manifested through the Charles de Gaulle period; there was the aftermath of the period of challenge with the establishment of different but interconnected forms of co-operation; the Hague summit in 1969 marked the start of the development of interconnected forms of co-operation, such as the European Council and EPC. However, alongside these new structures Community co-operation continued, with the consolidation of the Community budget system, the launch of proposals for EMU and the successive enlargements of the Union. The 1970s was to lay the foundations of the multidimensional forms of co-operation that characterise the contemporary Union and are built around a core of formal integration.

The apogee of this multidimensional co-operation was the Treaty on European Union, taking forward the blend of simultaneous strengthening the Community method of integration whilst codifying other associated forms of co-operation that were apparent in the earlier Single European Act.[7] The combination of formal integrative developments within the Community context alongside these other multidimensional forms of co-operation raises a question about how the integrative process is conceived and whether traditional forms of accounting for integration are deficient.

Neo-functionalism

During the early period of high formal integration, the European Community provided the inspiration for a middle-range theory that sought to account for the creation and development of the integrative process in Europe. E.B. Haas, in *The Uniting of Europe: Political, Social and Economical Forces 1950–1957*, offered a thesis on an emergent European integration. Haas's work remains a definitive approach to the study of European integration which has been subsequently rewritten without the blend of rigorous empirical work and theoretical reflection that is the hallmark of *The Uniting of Europe*. In particular, Haas was aware of three elements of the European integration process that remain crucial to an understanding of contemporary European integration and provide partial inspiration for this chapter: firstly, an understanding of integration as an ideology; secondly, integration as a set of institutions and institutional practices; and thirdly, integration as a process, and importantly, a process that has both a national and a supranational dimension.

Haas's study, published in 1958, focused upon the European Coal and Steel Community, and specifically upon those groups and countries accepting rather than rejecting European integration. Hence, the voices and attitudes of those states beyond the founding Six, and those opposed within the founding states, are absent from the study. Clearly, any attempt to understand the *contemporary* dynamics of European Union integration processes needs to move beyond a focus upon supporters of integration if it is to capture the full richness of the European Union.

Haas also concluded that the model of the integration process outlined was germane only to the socio-political landscape of Western Europe.[8] A focus upon the Western component of the continent is no longer either feasible or desirable in the aftermath of the Cold War and most especially with the commitment to enlarge the Union given at the Copenhagen European Council in 1993. As was highlighted in Chapter 1 in exploring the notion of civilian power Europe, the changing European geopolitical landscape of Europe has removed the certainties upon which earlier conceptualisations of the Union were founded.

One of Haas's key assertions was that the ECSC as a scheme of political unification does not require absolute majority support or an identical set of aims shared by the participants.[9] Haas was explicitly clear that the process he was examining was one of 'political integration' leading to the formation of a political community, understood as 'a condition in which specific groups and individuals show more loyalty to their central political institutions than to any other political authority, in a specific period of time and in a definable geographic space'.[10] The assumption was that group conflict was an integral part of the policy-making process of the existent nation-states and would be a characteristic of the emergent European political community. Groups, based on shared interests or political parties, affinity or rejection of any emergent transnational ideology, were viewed as crucial to the integration process. Alongside group conflict, the identification of a body of belief is also viewed as a central characteristic of a political community. Therefore there is a sufficient reservoir of consensus on the means of conducting any conflict to limit its depth. Our examination of the decision-making process of the Union in Chapters 2, 3 and 5 illustrates that, in the area of the construction and representation of the international identity, it is no longer possible to account for decision-making in terms of either an inter-governmentalist or a supranationalist explanatory approach.

The notion of an emergent political community identified by Haas is of especial interest in considering the development of the international identity of the Union. The notion of a European Union political community raises two questions about the international identity. First, how do we identify this political community and secondly, what influence does it have upon the creation and representation of the international identity of the European Union?

Identifying a political community

It must be clear that in seeking to identify a political community the focus is not upon the creation of a social or cultural homogeneity embraced by the populace of the European Union. The interest of this text is whether there are any indications of a shared conception of being part of a European political community that are identifiable across the peoples of the Union. These shared conceptions do not imply a replacement of the nation state as the locus of the political community but rather co-exist and overlap such sentiments.

There would appear to be two possible approaches to the examination of communities relevant to the study of the Union.[11] The first approach is to view communities as ethnically defined. The perspective points to the absence of an specifically European symbols likely to act as the foundation for a Europeanness that would replace the ties that bind nation states. From this perspective the European 'community' is remarkable for its absence, a view best captured in the words of Raymond Aron:

> the name Europe distinguishes a continent or a civilisation, not an economic or political unit....The European idea is empty; it has neither the transcendence of Messianic ideologies nor the immanence of concrete patriotism. It was created by intellectuals, and that fact accounts at once for its genuine appeal to the mind and its feeble echo in the heart.[12]

An alternative perspective on community and community-building is that of transactionalism. In this perspective institutions encourage the development of the idea of community because they create flows of contacts and communication.[13] The insight provided by both of these perspectives provide some fragmentary evidence of a political community but without the displacement of the primacy of the national political community. The existence, or sentiments, of this community can be examined through opinion-polling, which has been undertaken since the early 1960s (Tables 6.1 and 6.2). There is a paradox in that support for the integration of Western Europe (Table 6.1) appears to be contradicted by the indifference towards the scrapping of the Union (Table 6.2). In contrast, support for a common defence policy and a common foreign policy are more unequivocal (Table 6.3).

The 'new national consciousness' at a European level which Haas was searching for as an essential attribute of emergent political community has

Table 6.1 Public attitudes towards the unification of Western Europe

In general, are you for or against efforts being made to unify Western Europe? If FOR, are you very much for this, or only to some extent? If AGAINST, are you only to some extent against or very much against?

Year (mth)	*% For very much*	*% For to some extent*	*% Against to some extent*	*% Against very much*	*% No reply*	*Total*	*No. of Sample*
1962 (II–III)	40	32	4	1	23	100	6,334
1970 (II–III)	34	40	4	2	20	100	8,752
1973 (IX)	35	36	3	2	24	100	9,153
1975 (X)	33	41	2	2	22	100	5,691
1978 (X–XI)	33	47	4	2	14	100	5,442
1979 (X)	34	46	6	2	12	100	5,583
1980 (X–XI)	32	44	7	2	15	100	5,538
1981 (X–XI)	34	44	8	2	12	100	5,522
1982 (X)	28	47	8	3	14	100	5,352
1983 (X)	32	46	6	2	14	100	5,440
1984 (X–XI)	32	50	7	1	10	100	5,508
1985 (X–XI)	30	50	8	2	10	100	5,460
1986 (X–XI)	39	45	6	2	8	100	5,501
1987 (X–XI)	34	48	6	2	10	100	5,258
1988 (X–XI)	32	52	7	2	7	100	5,441
1989 (X–XI)	38	44	7	2	9	100	10,599
1990 (X–XI)	33	49	8	2	8	100	5,300
1991 (X–XI)	32	50	8	2	8	100	5,500
1992 (X–XI)	27	49	12	5	7	100	5,500
1993 (X–XI)	26	50	11	5	8	100	5,500

Source: Eurobarometer (1962–1993)

Table 6.2 Public attitudes towards the scrapping of the European Community

From November 1975: If you were to be told tomorrow that the European Community (Common Market) had been scrapped, would you...In 1974 and May 1975: If you were to be told tomorrow that (your country) was leaving the Common Market...From 1971 to 1973: If you were to be told tomorrow that the Common Market had been scrapped...

Year (mth)	*% Would be very sorry*	*% Indifferent*	*% Relieved*	*% No reply*	*Total*	*No. of sample*
1971 (VII)	40	40	5	15	100	8,670
1973 (IX)	41	36	10	13	100	9,153
1975 (X)	49	35	3	13	100	5,691
1977 (X–XI)	50	33	5	12	100	5,596
1981 (X–XI)	44	39	4	13	100	5,522
1982 (X)	43	38	6	13	100	5,352
1983 (X)	44	37	5	14	100	5,440
1984 (X–XI)	44	42	4	10	100	5,508
1985 (X–XI)	50	36	4	10	100	5,460
1986 (X–XI)	47	38	4	11	100	5,501
1987 (X–XI)	51	35	4	10	100	5,258
1988 (X–XI)	48	35	5	12	100	5,441
1989 (X–XI)	53	31	5	11	100	10,599
1990 (X–XI)	54	31	4	11	100	5,300
1991 (X–XI)	52	31	5	12	100	5,500
1992 (X–XI)	50	31	9	10	100	5,500
1993 (X–XI)	44	36	9	11	100	5,500

Source: Eurobarometer (1971–1993)

Table 6.3 Attitudes towards a common defence policy and a common foreign policy

What is your opinion on each of the following proposals? Please tell me for each proposal, whether you are for it or against it:
- The Member States of the European Community should have one common foreign policy towards countries outside the European Community (Foreign Policy)
- The EC member states should work towards a common defence policy (Common Defence)

	Foreign policy		Common defence	
Country	*% For**	*% Against*	*% For**	*% Against*
Belgium	70	15	78	12
Denmark	63	30	71	18
Germany	72	17	81	13
West Germany	71	18	81	14
East Germany	77	14	84	12
Greece	71	17	71	19
Spain	64	15	71	13
France	73	15	79	13
Ireland	65	16	52	26
Italy	73	9	75	13
Luxembourg	75	15	75	13
Netherlands	77	13	83	11
Portugal	58	18	67	16
United Kingdom	55	28	70	20
EU 12	68	17	75	15
EU 12+	68	17	75	15

* The difference between 'for' and 'against' and 100 is the percentage of 'don't know' (not shown)

Source: Eurobarometer 41 (1994)

not materialised.[14] The existence of a 'European consciousness' is apparent from opinion polling conducted over time by Eurobarometer, but it is apparent that such a consciousness has not displaced the primacy of the national consciousness. The idea that a political community analogous to that of the nation state was an essential prerequisite for actor capability for the Union is not supported by evidence about the actual international significance of the Union. Studies of foreign policy-making have long focused upon societal sources of influence and more specifically upon the impact of public opinion and the means of its transmission. In the absence of a strong European consciousness, the *primary* input of public opinion into the policy-making process is through the Member States as a source of influence. The relationship of the European Union citizens to foreign policy-making is expressed primarily through the Member States and to a lesser extent through the European Parliament, as covered in Chapter 7.

It can be suggested that the creation of a political community is not dependent upon the creation of a particular set of constitutional arrangements; for example, the creation of a federal United States of Europe. As was noted in Chapter 5, the Union has a written legal and political constitution and a particular kind of decision-making system. In the view of one commentator, the existence of both of these elements is sufficient to class the EU as a *sui generis* political community:

> A structure could emerge, however, in which a compulsory and binding judicial system is combined with a majoritarian legislative device, supervising the work of a central administration of restricted powers but with direct jurisdiction over groups and individuals, while many major decisions are still made at the level of inter-governmental negotiations. If in such a system governments negotiate and compromise so that one or several severely modify their position in the effort to arrive at a binding common agreement of profound consequence, the resulting habitual pattern of reaching consensus could well fit into the definition of political community, though representing neither the typical unitary nor federal categories of constitutions.[15]

Adopting the *sui generis* definition, the EU is indeed an existent political community without displacing the existing forms of identification with the nation state, albeit one, if the opinion poll data are correct, whose disappearance might go unmourned.[16]

The European Union has sought to create its own symbols of identification, citizenship of the Union, the now-ubiquitous twelve-starred flag, an anthem in *Ode to Joy*, and a Treaty commitment to 'the improvement of the knowledge and dissemination of the culture and history of the European peoples; conservation and safeguarding of cultural heritage of European significance'.[17] The Union has sought to pursue its own cultural diplomacy beyond the Union and has included sections on cultural cooperation in the Lomé IV Agreement, the Europe Agreements and bilateral agreements with Australia, and states in Latin America, Asia, and North America.[18]

The European Union's cultural dimension has come to global prominence through the audio-visual sector. The conflict between the United States and the European Union imperilled the successful conclusion of the Uruguay round of the GATT. The EU audio-visual policy consists of two main elements. Firstly, there is the MEDIA programme for the support of the EU programming industry in its competition in the EU and internationally with US-origin media products. This programme of support is set to double of its budget from 1996.[19] The second element of audio-visual policy is the *Television without Frontiers* directive, recently amended rather than discarded by the Union,. The provision within the directive by which European producers retain 51 per cent of programming has been at the heart of a bilateral dispute between the EU and the United States since 1991 and was responsible for holding up the GATT agreement until 40 hours before the deadline for negotiations.[20] The US–EU audio-visual dispute illustrates *externalisation*; the impact of internal integration, in this case regulations concerning culture and the creation of the internal market, having external consequences and creating a crisis point in the EU's cultural diplomacy.

The EU has also sought to promote an alternative to CNN International with the subsidisation of a 24-hour television news service called Euronews. Broadcasting via Eutelsat in six languages to Europe and the Mediterranean basin, without presenters, Euronews includes programming on the EU and coverage of European Parliament sessions.[21] Euronews claims a larger audience share than the entire CNN International audience outside of the United States but has not yet attracted the claims made for CNN International's impact upon foreign policy-making.[22]

The original concern of the neo-functionalist project was with political elites and their actions and reactions to integration and the *process* of integration clarified by the notion of 'spill-over', defined as characterising the expansion of sectoral integration on to other areas.[23] It was suggested that sectoral integration has its own expansive logic separate and separable from the development from any group-ordered demands or ideology.

The middle-range theory that was neo-functionalism underwent subsequent developments, modifications and refutation, most especially because of a perceived decline in its predictive power. The central hypotheses was taken further in a study of the formative years of the EEC.[24] However, the predictions of the theory were falsified by developments within the Community. Both the logic of functional spillover and political spillover were refuted between the 1965 crisis until the momentum generated under the first Delors Commission in 1985. The impact of Delors as President of the Commission illustrates the influence that force of personality and political leadership can have upon the integrationist process.[25] Subsequent revisions of neo-functionalism sought to amend the notion of an automatic spillover, with one commentator suggesting a variety of alternative options: spill around, build up, muddle about, retrenchment, encapsulation and spill back.[26]

The current status of the idea of functional spillover as applied to the EU is that such a process is neither automatic nor inevitable, but can be identified as a fragmented process at work across the policy agenda and in the development of some new policy areas.[27] However, instances of spillover cannot be detached from inter-governmental bargaining processes. The distinction between supranational and inter-governmental processes is blurred. Returning to our theme of Chapter 2, the historical development from the EPC through to the CFSP could not be conceived of as an instance of spillover; however, spillover has exerted a gravitational pull upon the development of foreign policy development. Participation in EPC was conditional upon Community membership, and although extensive measures were taken to ensure that there should be no 'contamination' from the Community system, our historical outline in Chapter 2 illustrated that there was a gradual drawing together over time. Indeed, the successive revisions of the founding treaties through the SEA and the TEU strengthened the interconnections. Turning to the latter instance, the two inter-governmental conferences negotiating the Maastricht Treaty were subject to a variety of influences, eventually generating a document that undoubtedly deepens formal integration whilst simultaneously creating a new geometry of institutional arrangements, issue areas and decision-making processes not amenable to a single theoretical approach.[28] Deepening formal integration was one part of an overall political package deal whereby the Member States, the Commission and the European Parliament all agreed to a spillover that was neither gradual nor non-political.[29] A similar political process can be anticipated for the 1996 inter-governmental conference timetabled in the Maastricht Treaty. In summary, spillover remains an important aid in providing a *partial* explanation for macro-level constitutional developments in formal integration. Identifying spillover as a source of influence in the daily process of EU foreign policy decision-making remains problematic.

In the original neo-functionalist formulation, concern focused on the measurement of elite views on integration.[30] Elite attitudes may provide an indication of integration but they cannot provide either a comprehensive or a consistent picture of the contemporary status of the integrative project or the primary source of influence upon the developing international identity of the Union.

INTEGRATION AS AN IDEOLOGY

The assertion of this chapter is also that a focus upon the end-point of a European integrative process, although not fully articulated, has functioned as an identifiable ideology seeking to enhance the full utilisation of the international instruments available to the European Union.[31] Integration has functioned as a ideology underpinning the development of the international identity. It is, of course, an ideology in tension with the doctrine of national sovereignty. In short, advocating a federal United States of Europe and stressing the development of instruments and policies normally associated with a nation state in the international system has influenced the development of the international identity.

It is necessary, only in passing, to mention how different the Union of the mid-1990s is from the ECSC of the early 1950s. On just one measure, membership, the enlargements of the Union from six to fifteen states clearly provide a different context for thinking and theorising about the Union. A general consensus exists that characterises the European integration process as uneven and fragmented, and depending upon the viewpoint of the commentator, it provides support for competing theses of a *Europe des Patries* or ammunition for proponents of a United States of Europe. Indeed, accounts of the history of the Union written as a struggle between inter-governmentalism and integrationism remain popular. Much of the thinking on the desired end-point for European integration remains the same: a United States of Europe.[32]

In contemplating the integration process it is worth reflecting upon the intended outcome of integration in Europe and the contending approaches for its realisation. Firstly, there is the maximalist approach most closely identified with Altiero Spinelli to establish a constituent assembly to draft a European constitution. The Spinelli route, although not adopted in the 1950s, was to re-emerge with the European Parliament Draft Treaty in 1979 and eventually resulted in the SEA.

The alternative approach that underpinned the foundation of the ECSC, and was subsequently adopted as the Community method, was a gradualist one, focusing upon decisive points to further a federation. However, the ethos of the Monnetist approach, although gradualist in respect of strategy, was intended to be federalist, and the institutional structure created was pre-federalist.[33] The gradualist route was re-affirmed with the failure of the European Defence Community and its attendant European Political Community.[34] As was noted above, theories of integration developed in parallel with the integration process itself.

The philosophy that has underpinned the Community institutions, and was exemplified by Jean Monnet, no longer provides a clear guide to the processes at work. The Community institutions were part of a strategy to create an elite constituency to be followed, gradually, by a process of social integration to surpass the nation states with a political union.

If we look back at the stated aims of those promoting European integration in the last half of the twentieth century, three descriptors have been applied. Firstly, the 'United States of Europe'; secondly, 'European Federation'; and thirdly, 'European Union'. Although each of these terms has a different history in terms of its origin and application, each has acted as the descriptor for a desired end-point of Europe united along the principles of federalism.

Essentially, two routes have been proposed for the end-point of a federal Europe: either the starting point of creating a European federal government or moving towards a federal government by a gradual convergence of the policies of different nation states. These two approaches can be characterised as follows:

> The first solution (which Altiero Spinelli fought for supported to some extent by the Italian government) puts federation at the beginning, conceiving it as the goal of a constitutional struggle. The second solution (followed by Jean Monnet and in fact adopted by European governments) places federal power at the end of a gradual process, and could be conducted by an inter-governmental mechanism mobilising the national forces interested in European solutions.[35]

The development of the variable institutional arrangements that have reached their apogee with the Treaty on European Union have re-orientated the Monnet-inspired institutional arrangements and created alternative institutional models. Monnet's heirs, advocates of a federalist vision for the Union organised at a European level, remain active in transnational organisations such as the European Movement and the Union of European Federalists but do not provide the primary source of influence upon the construction and representation of the international identity.

Integration as an ideology has influenced the international identity of the Union in one important respect: the institutionalised conduct of external relations. From the inception of the conduct of external relations the Union has favoured the creation of institutional arrangements through which to conduct dialogue. As was outlined in Chapters 2 and 4, the Union has created a network of institutionalised relations that encompass the globe. The Union, through this network, is committed to political dialogue alongside trade relations. The Union has sought to conduct international relations in its own image through 'civilian' forms of relations, and more recently has tentatively embarked upon military arrangements.

INFORMAL INTEGRATION

Consideration of integration as a source of influence illustrates that in the same way that the European Union has created a variable network of institutions to co-ordinate its activities there needs to be more developed ways of assessing the foreign policy of the Union. Integration should be viewed as only one of a series of influences that underpin the international identity rather than the primary influence.

During the period in which formal integration faltered, a series of parallel structures developed. The creation of these parallel structures resulted from the formal integrative process. Such structures were variegated in their form and functions and enjoyed differing degrees of relationship with the Community institutions. The development of European Political Co-operation and the European Council both illustrate this more pluralistic approach.

The institutional landscape of Europe has broadened beyond the Community framework, and the revolutions of 1989, whilst unlocking the previously excluded eastern half of the continent, have created a new European context. The final form of any European integration project within an unreconstructed Community institutional structure appears unlikely. The European Union has contributed to a network of overlapping, variable geometry in Europe by creating, and participating within, a collection of arrangements; for example, EU Agreements, Partnership and Co-operation arrangements and the Western European Union. The integration process can no longer be understood within the confines of the Community, and likewise integration as a source of influence requires consideration of sources beyond the confines of the Community but which enjoy an integrated relationship with the Union.

As was noted in Chapter 4, the United States provided an external source of influence in creating, and encouraging, a context in which integration could occur in the western half of the European continent under US economic and political leadership. Security and economic integration drew, and continues to draw, all the states of Europe into a distinctive and identifiable region that has now spread from Western Europe to Central and Eastern Europe. These transnational interconnections render distinctions between EU Europe and non-EU Europe less significant and require an understanding of the broader European economic, institutional, security and political landscape.

The varied nature of this process suggests that the theoretical accompaniment to integration, neo-functionalism, no longer appears able to account for the integrative project. Doubts about neo-functionalism have led to the development of alternative ways of conceptualising the wider European process. Wallace, drawing upon the approach of Deutsch originally developed in the 1950s and 1960s in an attempt to map the wider Europe, offers a frame of reference that extends beyond the western half of the continent the locus for the earlier integrative project and its theoretical nemesis: neo-functionalism.

In this conception of the wider Europe, Western Europe is core Europe with the dynamics of European integration in the 1990s operating under the impact of an integration or re-integration into a Western European order that has developed since the 1950s. Alongside, and predating, this re-integration there has developed a regional European economy that extends beyond the European Union but places all of the nation states within the region into a single economic space. This has created economic opportunity but also constrains the micro- and macro-economic policy of the constituent states.

The argument advanced elsewhere is that since the foundation of the ECSC there has been an economic and social transformation of Europe representing a very different context in which the largely unchanged institutional structure of the Union continues to operate. The preoccupations of the founders of the Community of coal and steel and then atomic power act as a yardstick to illustrate such change. As we illustrated in Chapter 4, the changed economic strength of Europe has also had implications for relations outside the Union, most notably with the United States.

MEMBER STATE SOURCES

The relationship of the Member States to the EU has been explored throughout the text thus far, and the focus is now upon a more systematic assessment of the role of the Member States as a source of influence. The role of the Member States within the decision-making process of the construction and representation of the international identity was noted in Chapters 2 and 3. It has also been suggested that the Union has not displaced the Member States, but a relationship exists between the Member States and the Union in which the Union is of international significance as a consequence of the capabilities of its Member States (Chapter 4). The instruments that the Union deploys to further its interests are also largely drawn from the Member States and placed at the disposal of the Union.

The influence of the Member States in the construction and representation of the international identity of the Union can be characterised through four main areas: the Presidency of the Union; foreign policy traditions; aberrant behaviour; and attitudes to integration.

PRESIDENCY OF THE UNION

The rise of the importance of the Presidency is a part of the story of the emergence of the structure that reached its apogee with the TEU and was detailed in Chapter 2. The role of the Presidency has evolved from the modest number of clauses in which it was mentioned in the EC Treaty to become a central actor in both the CFSP and the Community processes.[36] It is in the office of the Presidency that the CFSP and the Community structures are drawn together. The six-monthly term of office rotated between the Member States places each Member State in a position through which to exercise direct influence on the construction and representation of the Union.[37] The Presidency simultaneously rotates at the levels of the European Council; Council of Ministers; COREPER and the Political Committee and their attendant working groups; and between the Heads of EU Member State missions in third countries. The Presidency-in-Office thereby occupies a position of considerable influence but this also places considerable burdens upon the Ministers and the diplomatic service of the country holding the Presidency. During its last term, the UK Presidency chaired two European Council meetings, 44 meetings of the Council of Ministers, 67 meetings of COREPER and over 1,000 working-group meetings.[38] In its work the Presidency is assisted by the General Secretariat of the Council, a bureaucracy that has grown to support the enhanced role of the Council in the decision-making process.

The Presidency carries out four main functions: administering and managing the Council's business in conjunction with the Council Secretariat; an initiative function in collaboration with the Commission; a co-ordination function and mediation function to ensure agreement; a representational role both intra-EU, representing the Council's position to the Commission and the European Parliament, and extra-EU vis-à-vis third countries.[39]

In terms of the extra-EU representation of the Union the role of the Presidency, assisted by the troika, in political dialogue was detailed in Chapter 3. Interest in the Presidency as one element of the Member State sources of influence focuses on the programme of international action and agreements that each Presidency attempts to enact as part of its programme whilst in office. Three Presidencies have completed a full term of office since the foundation of the Union on 1 November 1993 – those of

Greece, Germany and France. The first of these Presidencies illustrates how the Member State holding the office can seek to pursue its own foreign policy priorities through the Union. It also shows how actions of the Presidency in international affairs can act to the detriment of the international identity of the Union.

The Greek Presidency, in office from 1 January 1994, made the completion of enlargement negotiations with Austria, Finland, Norway and Sweden a priority, alongside the continuing search for a resolution of the conflict in the former Yugoslavia.[40] It was notable more for the outspokenness of Greek Deputy Foreign Minister, Theodoras Pangalos, and Greece's public opposition to the recognition by other Member States of the former Yugoslav Republic of Macedonia (FYROM).[41] The imposition of a blockade of FYROM by Greece during February 1994 resulted in shuttle diplomacy by the Commissioner for External Political Relations, Hans van den Broek, between Greece and FYROM in an attempt to mediate in the dispute over FYROM's name and flag.[42] Eventually, the Commission decided to refer the embargo to the ECJ as an alleged infringement of EU trade rules.[43] Greece also became simultaneously embroiled in diplomatic disputes with both Albania and Turkey.[44] The ECJ refused to issue an emergency ruling on the trade embargo, thereby extending the period in which it would issue a judgment to 18 months beyond the end of the Greek Presidency.

Although the Greek Presidency was somewhat overshadowed by the FYROM dispute, it did succeed in guiding through the conclusion of the accession agreements with their signature at its Corfu European Council Meeting. The Corfu meeting, dominated as it was by the failure to choose Jean-Luc Dehaene as the successor to Jacques Delors as President of the Commission, also initiated a Joint Action on the preparation of the NPT review treaty (outlined in Chapter 3).[45]

The German Presidency, in office for the second half of 1994, focused attention on Asia, seeking to upgrade the Union relations with the region and to ensure that during its Presidency a dialogue was created with APEC; Co-operation Agreements were made with Nepal, Sri Lanka, Vietnam and the Republic of Korea; a Co-operation Agreement with India was upgraded; and political dialogue with ASEAN, China and Japan was intensified.[46] Although concluding these Agreements is the remit of the Commission, the Presidency is crucial in pushing such matters through the Council, to give the Commission a mandate and to ensure their ratification. However, the promotion of policy of the Union during the German Presidency was also being used to further German foreign policy: in stating the targets of its Presidency it was also noted: 'Greater commitment in Asia on a wide front and an active, outgoing Asian policy are of fundamental significance for Germany's future. Germany seeks to be, and will be, a good, reliable and useful partner for the countries of Asia.'[47]

FOREIGN POLICY TRADITIONS

The Member States can be grouped together to examine how their foreign policy traditions impact upon the construction and representation of the international identity of the Union. We have previously noted that different institutional arrangements exist amongst the Member States with respect to defence and the issue of neutrality.

The first group of Member States are those who have substantive interests beyond the Union and define their involvement in the Union as one component of their foreign policy. The foreign policy traditions of both the United Kingdom and France fall into this category. These countries differ from the other Member States in that both have retained institutionalised international relations that extend to former colonies through, respectively, the Commonwealth and the Francophonie. These relationships have directly impacted upon the Union and resulted first in creation of Association in the Treaty of Rome, to accommodate French colonies, and later, through the Yaoundé and Lomé Conventions, to accommodate the newly independent colonies and members of the British Commonwealth. The role of both the United Kingdom and France as permanent members of the Security Council and their disproportionate involvement in UN operations was noted in Chapter 4. Thereby both states maintain substantive alternative outlets for their own diplomacy.

At the other extreme are those states, notably Luxembourg and Belgium, which by virtue of size constraints have utilised the Union as the primary mechanism for pursuing their foreign policy. Constraints imposed by history have ensured that Union has remained the favoured avenue through which the Federal Republic of Germany has conducted policy.

In between these two positions are states which have extra-Union relations that they privilege. Spain's relationship with Latin America was used to promote a peace settlement in Central America in the 1980s both before and after its entry into the Union in 1986, through the San José grouping that brings together Central American, Contradora Group and EU Member States.[48] Portugal privileges its extra-Union relations in the cases of Brazil, Angola, Mozambique, and on the issue of East Timor.[49] Greece, in its promotion of Cyprus, and more detrimentally in its relationship with Turkey, is the most tense of the bilateral relationships conducted by the Member States. Denmark, Sweden and Finland all possess the link of the Nordic Union. With the accession of Finland the implication for the Union is that the Union has gained a border with Russia.

Italy, Spain, Portugal, and on occasion France, all constitute a Mediterranean sub-grouping engendered by geographical proximity and have collectively promoted Mediterranean issues. There is also a grouping identified as the 'moralists', encompassing Ireland, Denmark and the Netherlands.[50] The full impact of the membership of Austria, Sweden and Finland extends beyond the scope of this study, with their very recent accession to the Union.

ABERRANT BEHAVIOUR

The behaviour that most impacts publicly upon the Union is aberrant behaviour. These are instances in which one Member State's actions illustrate a clear rupture in the positions of other states in the conduct of the international identity. An example has been given above under the Greek Presidency, but there have also been others since the foundation of the Union. Italy has vetoed attempts to conclude an association with Slovenia pending a settlement of disputed property on the Istrian peninsula, previously a part of Italy prior to the end of World War II. Greece has vetoed 35 million ecu in EU aid to Albania in a dispute on the treatment of ethnic Greeks in Albania.[51] Aberrant behaviour can in fact enhance or promote the development of Union policy in a particular area, as was instanced with Greece's promotion of membership negotiations with Cyprus.

ATTITUDES TO INTEGRATION

At the crux of the attitude to integration among the Member States is the perception of sovereignty. In Chapter 5 the legal source of influence was detailed and the importance of the legal structure of the Union as a characteristic distinguishing the Union from other international organisations was noted. Integration is a multidimensional phenomena and, as has been suggested in Chapter 2, the Union requires unanimous inter-governmental bargains, through the inter-governmental conference process, to advance formal integrative projects.

The international context within which the Union operates has also complicated notions of sovereignty through such a process of integration, yet, as will be noted below, the Member States have retained the formal structure of their diplomatic relations. The content of the Union's competencies heavily overlaps domestic and international preserves yet the Member States retain their legal, political, cultural and economic distinctiveness. In the international system, faced with increasing interdependence, states have banded together in regimes which have acquired authority, as was noted in Chapter 4.

Whatever the objective realities of sovereignty, the *perception* of the loss of sovereignty represents a significant factor in Member States' calculations. These attitudes are most acute in the areas of foreign policy, and were the rationale for retaining the distinction between EPC/CFSP and external relations and the tight control that the member States retain over the latter. The importance of symbols of sovereignty can be seen by the unwillingness of the Member States to contemplate the creation of common embassies: they have only proceeded as far as co-locating embassies. The United Kingdom and Germany have opened joint-buildings for their embassies in Kazakhstan and Belarus; Germany, the United Kingdom, the Netherlands and the Commission delegation are to share premises in Azerbaijan, Ecuador, Tanzania and Iceland; the Netherlands and the United Kingdom are to co-locate in Bulgaria; and the British and French are to share premises in Albania.[52] A French proposal to create a joint embassy with Germany in Ulan Bator in the mid-1980s was struck down by a French court ruling that only a French citizen could represent the French President.[53] An attempt to ensure that the EU flag always hung alongside the Member States' missions was vetoed by the United Kingdom, but it has engaged in an exchange of diplomats programme with both the French and German Foreign Ministries and the Commission.[54]

A contemporary measure of the attitude to integration are arrangements that exist formally outside the Union but indicate a willingness to contemplate integrative measures deeper than the *acquis communautaire*. These measures encompass Eurocorps, detailed in Chapter 4, and membership of the Schengen Agreement. Schengen provides for the gradual suppression of border controls between the Member States of Schengen, which currently excludes the three new members of the Union and the United Kingdom, Ireland and Denmark. There are also the opt-in/opt-out arrangements that the United Kingdom and Denmark have negotiated for involvement in the third stage of economic and monetary union, the move to a single currency. The case of the United Kingdom deserves special attention because of its opt-out from the social chapter and its opposition to both the appointment of Jean-Luc Dehaene as President of the Union and to the changes in qualified majority voting associated with the enlargement of the Union. These measures are essentially intra-Union developments and, although they have an external implication in highlighting divisions between the Member States, they make for an evolving, multi-speed, intra-EU relationship. The UK position also demonstrates the impact of domestic politics upon the EU process. The impact of public opinion on the EU is expressed through both the European Parliament and the Member States themselves. The nearest instance to a commonly experienced EU political event was the ratification process of Maastricht itself, although each ratification was coloured by domestic circumstances.[55]

CONCLUSION

The thrust of this chapter is, therefore, that processes of integration, theories of integration and its counterpart, an ideology of integration, have acted, at best, as a source of influence upon the international identity of the Union. This perspective represents a departure from the norms of the conventional commentaries on the European Union and provides the starting point for this chapter. The focus then shifted to the conceptualisation of the formal integrative process that has been central to an understanding of the European Union, before we finally turned to the importance of informal integration for an understanding of the regional and international significance of the Union.

Integration impacts upon the creation and representation of the international identity in three ways: formal integration; informal integration; and integration as ideology. In Chapter 4 we considered integration at the international and global level as a source of influence that has impacted upon the international identity. In this chapter the focus is on integration measured within our system. As with all of the other sources of influence that have been identified, integration provides another facet of the international identity as well as providing a source of influence upon the international identity.

The Member States are intimately involved in the construction and representation of the international identity of the Union through the decision-making process. However, they also represent substantive sources of influence through holding the office of the Presidency and through the foreign policy traditions that they bring to the Union. When the behaviour of these states is seen to be at variance with that of the other Member States this both restrains the Union in its actions and acts to enforce an impression of disunity rather than unity amongst the Member States. The Member States themselves have used the Union as an instrument through which to pursue their own foreign policy objectives but have also retained the symbolism and institutions through which to conduct bilateral diplomacy amongst themselves. The notion that processes of integration represent a displacement of one structure or set of arrangements by another appears untenable. Rather, institutions have adapted to serve the purposes of both Union membership and the retention of Member States' independence.

NOTES AND REFERENCES

1. Accounts of the health and vitality of the formal integrative project have been offered at different stages of the history of the Union. As indications, see: E. Haas, *The Uniting of Europe: Political, Social and Economical Forces*, 1950–1957 (London, Stevens & Sons, 1958); M. Camps, *European Unification in the Sixties: From the Veto to the Crisis* (New York, McGraw-Hill, 1966); B. Barber and B. Reed (eds), *The European Community: Vision and Reality* (London, Croom Helm, 1973); K. Kaiser et al (eds), *The European Community: Progress of Decline* (London, RIIA, 1983).
2. 'The Transformation of the European Community, 1985–1988', in D. Dinan, *Ever Closer Union: An Introduction to the European Community* (London, Macmillan, 1994), chapter 5; J. Pinder, 'The Single Market: A Step Towards Union', in J. Lodge (ed.), *The European Community and the Challenge of the Future*, 2nd edn (London, Pinter, 1993).
3. The strengthening of any process of integration requires the dissolution of other structures whether political, economic, social or cultural. For an exploration, see: I. Brennan, 'The Concept of Antinomic Process and its Relevance for Integration Theory', in F.R. Pfetsch (ed.), *International Relations and Pan-Europe: Theoretical Approaches and Empirical Findings* (Hamburg, Lit, 1993).
4. For a recent example, see: M. Holland, *European Community Integration* (London, Pinter, 1993).
5. W. Wallace, *The Dynamics of European Integration* (London, Pinter for RIIA, 1992), pp.8–12.
6. *Ibid.*, p.9.
7. The Single European Act codified European Political Co-operation and also provided the European Council with a legal foundation. The TEU established the three-pillar structure to extend foreign policy co-operation to Home and Judicial Affairs. Simultaneous to the Treaty-based new forms of co-operation there was the establishment of the Eureka programme (1985), the Schengen Agreement (1985) and the revitalisation of the Western European Union.
8. Haas, *op. cit.*, Preface, pp.xv–xvi.
9. Haas, *op. cit.*, Preface, p.xiii.
10. Haas, *op. cit.*, p.5.
11. P. Howe, 'A Community of Europeans: The Requisite Underpinnings', *The Journal of Common Market Studies* 33, 1 (March 1995): 27–46.

12. Haas, *op. cit.*, pp.28–9.
13. F. Romero, 'Cross Border Population Movements', in Wallace, *op. cit.*, chapter 10.
14. Haas, *op. cit.*, p.6.
15. Haas, *op. cit.*, p.8.
16. This notion of displacement has been central to the traditional conception of the integrative process: 'Political integration is the process whereby political actors in several distinct national settings are persuaded to shift their loyalties, expectations and political activities toward a new centre, whose institutions possess or demand jurisdiction over the pre-existing national states.' (P. Vujakovic, 'Mapping Europe's Myths', *Geographical* LXIV, 9: 15–17).
17. See EC Treaty, Title IX Culture, as inserted by Article G(37) TEU.
18. See Article 128.3: 'The Community and the Member States shall foster co-operation with third countries and the competent international organisations in the sphere of culture, in particular the Council of Europe'.

    For details on co-operation with countries and organisations outside the Union, see: 'New Prospects for Community Cultural Action', *Background Report*, ISEC/B26/92.
19. The MEDIA Action Programme had a budget of $282 million for the period 1991–1995; *The European*, 8–14 April 1994. For proposed MEDIA II programme, see: 'Television without Frontiers: New Rules and Legal Framework for the Internal Market Information Society Services', *Commission of the European Communities*, IP/95/287.
20. 'US Opts to Bide Time on Audio-visual Battle', *Financial Times*, 15 December 1993, p.6.
21. 'Europe's answer to CNN focuses on second year', *The European*, 14–20 January 1994, p.20. The EU provided a subsidy of $4.7 million for 1994.
22. 'TV News with a European Identity Crisis', *Financial Times*, 13 May 1994, p.2, offers Euronews' claim to reach 13.9 million viewers through cable and 57 million through terrestrial re-broadcasting. In contrast, CNNI claims that it has an audience outside of the US of 55 million counted from the viewers watching TV sets able to receive CNNI. See: 'The Myth of Global News', *New Perspectives Quarterly* 11, 1 (Winter 1994): 39–45, p.42.
23. Haas, *op. cit.*, p.105.
24. L.N. Lindberg, *The Political Dynamics of European Economic Integration* (Oxford, Oxford University Press, 1963).
25. See: C. Grant, *Inside the House that Jacques Built* (London, Nicolas Brealey, 1994); G. Ross, *Jacques Delors and European Integration* (London, Polity Press, 1995).
26. P. Schmitter, 'A Revised Theory of Regional Integration', *International Organisation*, 24, 4 (Autumn 1970): 836–68.
27. M. Pollack, 'Creeping Competence: The Expanding Agenda of the European Community', *Journal of Public Policy* 14, 2: 95–145.
28. F. Laursen, 'Explaining the Intergovernmental Conference on Political Union', in F. Laursen and S. Vanhoonacker, *The Intergovernmental Conference on Political Union* (Dordrecht, Martinus Nijhoff, 1992).
29. For a full account of the roles of the different actors in the process, see *ibid.*
30. A recent survey of the foreign policy-making elite in one Member State illustrates that a shared attitude towards the EU does not translate across all

issue areas. D. Saunders and G. Edwards, 'Consensus and Diversity in Elite Opinion: The Views of the British Foreign Policy Elite in the Early 1990s', *Political Studies* XLII, (1994): 413–40.

31. The sense in which ideology is being used is drawn from Karl Mannheim. That is that thought on the outcome of the European integrative process is characteristic of the period in which it developed and the tendency to conserve that style of thinking has produced an integrative ideology making the context appear more stable than it actually is. K. Mannheim, *Ideology and Utopia: An Introduction to the Sociology of Knowledge* (trans. from the German by L. Wirth) (London, Routledge & Kegan Paul, 1960).
32. E. Wistrich, *The United States of Europe* (London, Routledge, 1994), chapter 8.
33. J. Pinder, *European Community: The Building of a Union* (Oxford, Oxford University Press, 1995), pp.5–6.
34. E. Fursdon, *The European Defence Community: A History* (London, Macmillan, 1980).
35. Andrea Bosco, in A. Bosco (ed.), *The Federal Ideal*, Vol.II, *The History of Federalism since 1945* (London, Lothian Foundation Press, 1992), pp.5–6.
36. In the EC provisions on the institutions, the Presidency is mentioned in two articles (EC Treaty Articles 146 and 147), merely noting that the Presidency is held for six months in turn (and then detailing the order) and that the Council 'shall meet when convened by its President on his own initiative or at the request of one of its members or of the Commission' (Article 147, EC Treaty).
37. The European Council meeting in Brussels on 10–11 December 1993 adopted an amendment to the EC Treaty as part of the Accession Treaties for the three proposed applicants, adding: 'The Office of the President shall be held in turn by each Member State in the Council for a term of six months in the order decided by the Council acting unanimously'.

    An order of rotation was then adopted that takes the Union to 2003:

1995	France, Spain
1996	Italy, Ireland
1997	Netherlands, Luxembourg
1998	United Kingdom, Austria
1999	Germany, Finland
2000	Portugal, France
2001	Sweden, Belgium
2002	Spain, Denmark
2003	Greece

('Presidency Conclusions: European Council in Brussels 10 and 11 December 1993', *Commission of the European Communities*, SN 373/93, Annex III)

38. Tristan Garel-Jones, who was actively involved as a Minister of State, Foreign and Commonwealth Office during the UK Presidency of the last six months of 1992; The Rt. Hon. T. Garel-Jones, MP, 'The UK Presidency: An Inside View', *Journal of Common Market Studies* 31, 2 (June 1993), 261–7, p.264.

39. E.J. Kirchner, *Decision Making in the European Community: The Council Presidency and European Integration* (Manchester, Manchester University Press, 1992), pp.79–87.
40. *Agence Europe*, 22 December 1993, pp.3–4.
41. Pangalos described Germany as 'a bestial giant with a child's brain' and the Turkish government as 'muggers' who were 'dragging bloody boots across the carpets of Europe' in the weeks in the run-up to the commencement of the Presidency; *Financial Times*, 22 December 1993, p.10.

    The UK, Germany, the Netherlands and Denmark recognised Macedonia despite the opposition of Greece.
42. 'EU claims progress on Macedonia dispute', *Financial Times*, 25 February 1994, p.2.
43. *The Week in Europe*, 7 April 1994.
44. *Guardian*, 30 May 1994, p.8.
45. 'Presidency Conclusions: European Council at Corfu 24–25 June 1994', *The European Commission*, Brussels, SN 150/94.
46. 'German Policy on Asia: Ten Points for a Fresh Approach', *Press Release*, Embassy of the Federal Republic of Germany, London, 7 February 1994.
47. *Idem.*
48. See: J. Story, 'Spain in the European Diplomatic System', *Diplomacy and Statecraft* 2, 1 (March 1991): 54–78.
49. *FT Survey*, 3 November 1992, p.III.
50. C. Hill (ed.), *National Foreign Policies and European Political Co-operation* (London, Allen & Unwin, 1983).
51. *Guardian*, 27 May 1994, p.12.
52. 'Political Rivalries Derail Plan to Share Embassies', *The European*, 6–12 May 1994, p.6.
53. *Idem.*
54. *Press Release*, Foreign and Commonwealth Office, London, No. 155, 17 November 1994.
55. See: 'Uncorking the Bottle: Popular Opposition to European Unification in the Wake of Maastricht', *Journal of Common Market Studies* 32, 4 (December 1994): 455–72.

7 The European Parliament: Source and Identity

> Parliament has too little control over CFSP implementation and, despite its right to make recommendations its role in this field is limited. The national parliaments are even more poorly placed for monitoring CFSP implementation, since they are only able to monitor their respective governments. This demonstrates, if there were any need to, that, in order to be effective, democratic controls must be effected at the same level as the source of power.[1]

Legislatures have traditionally had a minimal impact on the formulation and implementation of foreign policy. In most systems of government the executive has guarded its exclusive powers to conduct foreign policy to such an extent that legislatures have been granted little attention in academic study.[2]

This chapter explores the role of the European Parliament (EP) from a number of dimensions. Firstly, consideration is given to the European Parliament as a distinctive facet of the international identity of the Union. Secondly, the chapter details the involvement of the EP and its parliamentarians in the exercise of their formal powers over the international agreements undertaken by the Union. Thirdly, the progressive involvement of the EP within the EPC/CFSP process is detailed. Within each of these examinations the instruments that the EP has deployed to create its own distinctive contribution to the construction and representation of the international identity are detailed. The assertion of this chapter is that through its actions, and its involvement in the policy-making process of the Union, the EP has sought to bring together both the EPC/CFSP and external relations strands of the Union as the means through which the international identity of the Union could be enhanced. The conclusion is that the aspirations and organisational structure of the Parliament outstrip the formal role that the Parliament enjoys in the policy-making process.

THE EUROPEAN PARLIAMENT AS A FACET OF THE INTERNATIONAL IDENTITY

In Chapters Two and Five detailing the decision-making and legal structure of the Union, it was made clear that the institutional arrangements by which the Union governs and organises itself are analogous, but not identical, to the constitutional arrangements of a nation state. One of the notable departures from that of the nation state is where the power to legislate resides. The EP can be considered, at most, to be a partial legislature with powers to veto, rather than to initiate, legislation.

Federalist commentators on the European Union view the EP as a part of a two-chamber parliament consisting of the Council as the representatives of the states and the EP as the representatives of the citizens of the EU.[3] The logic of this view is that the EP should attain equal powers of legislation with the Council and that this would assist in closing the 'democratic deficit' of the Union by providing an equal role for the Parliament, which is directly elected by the citizens of the Union.

The European Parliament supports this position, and in 1984 adopted a Draft Treaty on European Union encompassing such powers for the Parliament. Neither the Single European Act nor the Treaty on European Union that were adopted by the Member States fully extended equality of power to the EP. Indeed, the EP played no formal role in the drafting or the ratification of either Treaty. The assent procedure with which the EP is involved, and detailed in Chapter 5, does not extend to Treaty modifications. However, the EP exerted an influence upon both the SEA and TEU revisions of the founding treaties. The process of negotiating the SEA was itself initiated through an examination of the Parliament's Draft Treaty that President Mitterrand persuaded his counterparts to adopt at the Fontainebleau European Council meeting in June 1984.[4] The ratification of the TEU by the Italian and the Belgian parliaments was made dependent upon the approval of the Treaty by the European Parliament.[5] The Parliament, therefore, has exercised an influence that extends beyond its formal powers.

From an extra-EU perspective, the EP contributes a distinctive facet to the international identity of the European Union. It is a directly elected chamber consisting of 624 members elected at five-yearly intervals in accordance with the electoral systems of the Member States. Therefore, it is distinctly different from the Parliamentary Assemblies of intergovernmental organisations such as NATO, the Council of Europe or the WEU. Aside from its direct election, initiated in 1979, the Parliament is distinctive in that its members are organised into political groups within the Parliament and its five-yearly elections generate the political campaigning and media coverage reminiscent of elections to the legislatures of the Member States.[6] Although the voter turn-out for the EP elections is poor, in contrast to national elections of the Member States, the existence of the opportunity to vote for a supranational Parliament of a Treaty-based organisation is a unique exercise in transnationalism.[7]

The distinction of the EU from other international organisations comes from the legal basis of the Union (as was noted in Chapter 5) and in particular from the ability, and indeed the requirement, to adopt legislation that is binding across all the Member States for the Union to act under the Community pillar. In the original ECSC, EAEC and EEC treaties, the then Assembly was only given a consultative role in the legislation process and the adoption of the EC budget.[8] The primary power that the Assembly was granted in controlling the Commission was the ability to pass a motion of censure on the Commission and thereby force the resignation of the whole Commission.[9] The EP, whose fixed term of office now coincides with that of the Commission, is, under an amendment introduced by the TEU, required to take a vote of confidence in an incoming Commission and has organised public Committee hearings to vet the proposed Commissioners.[10] After a vote of approval of the Commissioners, the Parliament oversees the work of the Commission during its term of office and this entails an oversight of the role of the Commission in external relations, as detailed in Chapter 2.

The powers of the Parliament have been progressively extended through three means: Treaty amendments; rulings of the Court of Justice; and inter-institutional agreements.[11] The role of the Parliament in the legislative process was expanded under the SEA to include a co-operation procedure for the adoption of legislation and the creation of a second reading by the Parliament for legislation adopted under the procedure (Figure 5.2). Under the TEU a new legislative procedure was introduced, co-decision (Figure 7.1). This, as its title suggests, gives the Parliament the ability to co-decide with the Council on legislation proposed under the procedure by the Commission. Each of these three procedures remains in place and the adoption of legislation under any one of the procedures is determined by the Treaty provisions governing the topic under discussion. The existence of the co-decision procedure is significant for the international identity of the Union in that it gives this transnational Parliament the ability effectively to veto legislation passed through the Council, the body that directly represents the Member States. In agreeing to the co-decision procedure through the ratification of the TEU, the Member States were not merely accepting, as was the case under qualified majority voting (QMV), that they might be outvoted in legislation enacted domestically, but that the EP might modify or veto decisions previously passed by Member States in the Council. Furthermore, under Article 138b of the EC Treaty, introduced

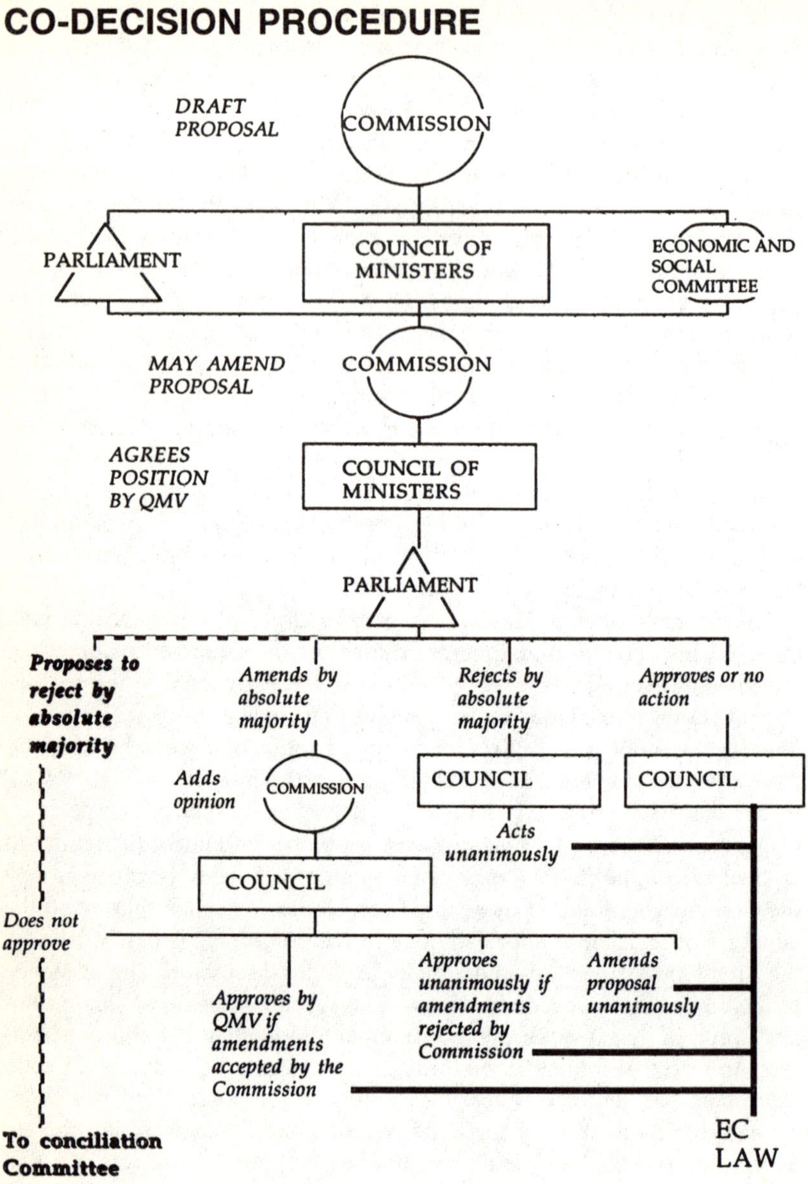

Figure 7.1 The co-decision procedure for legislation
Source: Author

by the TEU, the EP can request the Commission to submit a proposal for a Community act in conformity with the objectives contained within the Treaty. Therefore, although not having a formal right to initiate legislation itself, the EP has a substantive power to pressure the Commission to initiate a process of legislation.

The EP debates and votes on the annual legislative programme proposed by the Commission. The EP debate and resolution on the Commission programme is significant for the international identity for the Union in that the EP, in its resolution, proposes initiatives for action in external relations that are absent from the Commission proposals. In the Resolution of the European Parliament on the 1994 legislative programme the EP proposed the consideration of new relations with South Africa that the Commission subsequently adopted.[12]

The EP's substantive area of power prior to the SEA and the TEU amendments were its powers over the budget of the Union. Under the 1970 Treaty Amending Certain Budgetary Provisions of the Treaties, and the 1975 Treaty Amending Certain Financial Provisions of the Treaties, the EP was granted powers over the EP's budget. The 1970 Treaty initiated a system whereby the EU was given its own financial resources, which were to consist of revenue which, although collected by the Member States, belong to the Union as a right. The Union, therefore, has its own resources at its own disposal that do not derive from the assessed contributions from Member States and are fully at the disposal of the Union. The Union has revenue sources and a budget that are both separate, but not separable from those of the Member States, in that the Members States are involved in both the revenue collection and the process of agreeing the annual budget for the Union. The revenue of the Union comes from four elements: customs duties levied under the Common External Tariff; agricultural levies to bring the price of agricultural imports to the level in the Community and those in surplus supply; a proportion of the VAT levied within the Member States (currently 1.4 per cent); and contributions from the Member States based upon their share of the total GNP of the Union and giving the Union 1.27 per cent of the total Union GNP. The sources of budget revenue are broken down in Table 7.1.

The budget itself is drafted by the Commission annually by 1 September 1994 and considered and amended by the Council. By 5 October, the Council passes the budget to the EP which must state its position on the budget within 45 days. The budget consists of both compulsory and non-compulsory items of expenditure. The EP is free to propose modifications to the compulsory part of the budget and can

Table 7.1 The sources of European Union budget revenue, 1993–1994 (million ecu)

	*1993**	*1994***
Agricultural levies	1,032.1	1,023.4
Sugar and isoglucose levies	1,115.3	1,242.2
Custom duties	12,259.3	14,021.5
Own resources collection costs	–1,440.7	–1,628.7
VAT own resources	35,560.0	35,850.5
GNP-based own resources from previous year	16,555.7	18,988.8
Balance of VAT and GNP-based own resources from previous year	–1,129.6	***
Budget balance from previous year	1,004.0	***
Other revenue	500.0	515.8
Total	65,456.4	70,013.5
	% GNP	
Maximum own resources which may be assigned	1.2	1.20
Own resources actually assigned to the budget	1.11	1.19

* Out-turn
** Estimate
*** Token entry

Source: European Commission

propose amendments to the non-compulsory part up to a maximum rate set by the Council. The compulsory component of the budget encompasses agricultural expenditure and other expenditure arising directly out of the treaties and currently accounts for 55 per cent of the budget. Non-compulsory expenditure covers all the policies adopted by the EU including the external action of the Union. The breakdown of the EU budget illustrates that 5.5 per cent of the budget is allocated for external action (Table 7.2) The total appropriations for 1994 were 73,444 million ecu of which the estimated expenditure was 70,013 million ecu.

The importance of the budget process from the perspective of the international identity is that any amendments that encompass non-compulsory expenditure proposed by the Parliament, and involve external action, require a conciliation procedure if they are rejected by the Council. The Parliament acting in a plenary session then approves the modifications agreed in conciliation or may decline to do so by a two-thirds vote of the majority of votes cast of a majority of all members of the Parliament.

Table 7.2 The General EU budget, 1994 appropriations

Sector	*million ecu*
Common Agricultural Policy (apart from EAGGF – Guidance)	36,465
Structural operations, of which:	23,176
European Regional Development Fund	9,000
European Social Fund	6,500
Internal policies, of which:	4,360
research	2,800
education, etc.	300
trans-European networks	300
External action, of which:	4,296
co-operation:	
Latin American countries	700
Mediterranean countries	500
Central and Eastern European countries and independent states of former USSR	1,500
Administrative expenditure	3,617
Reserves	1,530
Total, of which:	73,444
compulsory expenditure	39,000
non-compulsory expenditure	34,500
Payment appropriations required as % of GNP	1.19
Own resources ceiling as % of GNP	1.20

Some figures are appropriations for commitments.
Some figures have been rounded up where appropriate.

Source: XXVIIth General Report on the Activities of the European Communities, 1993

In the 1994 budget, covering the first full year's operations of the EU, the EP sought to increase the budget by 300 million ecu.[13] The EP's deliberations impacted upon several areas of external relations. MEPs proposed a freeze on half the money spent under the TACIS programme of technical assistance of CIS states, following a report on wastage issued by the Court of Auditors.[14] The EP also sought to increase expenditure for South Africa, Latin America and Eastern and Central Europe and earmarked expenditure on funds to promote human rights and anti-torture campaigns.

The Court of Auditors established in 1977 is granted institutional status in the treaties and is involved in the conduct of the external relations of the Union through its examination of the Union's financial affairs. In successive recent annual reports it has publicly criticised the expenditure and implementation of a number of the external relations programmes, including the PHARE programme.[15]

The budget of the EU is the foundation of the positive transference instruments available to the Union. Approximately 5.5 per cent of the budget for 1994 was allocated for the purposes of external action in 1994 and directed towards Central and Eastern Europe, the CIS states, states in the Mediterranean basin, Asia and Latin America. In addition, the Member States provide financial and technical assistance financed through Member State contributions and loans from the European Investment Bank.

The involvement and powers of the EP in the legislative and budget processes and the role it has sought for itself in promoting the formal integration of the Union all illustrate that the Parliament is a substantive actor in intra-Union process and that a number of these processes are of consequence for the international identity. The Parliament also provides a distinctive dimension to the Union and, again, illustrates the inadequacy of conceiving the EU in the same terms as other forms of inter-governmental organisations. However, the EP goes beyond merely being a source of influence on the international identity and presents a distinctive dimension to the international identity of the Union through its role in the procedural instruments of the Union and the creation of its own overt instruments for action.

THE EP AND THE CONDUCT OF EXTERNAL RELATIONS

In Chapter 5 the assent process detailed the involvement of the EP in the legislation of the legal acts to give effect to international agreements conducted by the Union. In Chapters 3 and 5 we detailed the powers of the Commission and Council in the conduct of the external relations of the EC Treaty. The role of the European Parliament is somewhat different in the process. The description of the EP in the EC Treaty as consisting of 'representatives of the peoples of the States brought together in the Community' provides European parliamentarians with a basis upon which to argue for a central role in the construction and representation of the Union as the only directly elected institution of the Union.[16] However, any consideration of the role of the European Parliament in the foreign policy-making process presents us with a peculiar paradox. The European

Parliament (EP) lacks the formal attributes normally ascribed to a parliament yet it has devoted considerable attention to questions of foreign policy, an area of activity in which legislatures have traditionally enjoyed few formal powers.

The EP has demonstrated over time that it has a deep interest in the development of the Union and, more particularly, sought to gain increased powers and a greater role in the EU decision-making process. However, commentators have suggested that involvement of the EP in actually shaping the foreign policy of the Union is somewhat modest.[17] The primary reason for this lack of substantive involvement is inherent in the nature of foreign policy and recognised by the Parliament itself: 'This stems in part from the nature of foreign policy and security whose characteristics (confidentiality and rapidity) are difficult to reconcile with the functioning of a parliamentary body.'[18]

The form and content of foreign policy create a phenomena common to the national parliaments and the EP with both facing similar problems of oversight due to 'the non legislative nature of foreign policy' implemented by Member States.[19] However, as was noted in Chapter 4 on the external sources of influence, the increasing relative importance of foreign economic policy has eroded distinctions between high and low politics. The European Parliament, particularly from the beginning of direct elections in 1979, has increasingly tried to exercise more influence on both the Treaty-based EC external relations and the inter-governmental EPC/CFSP processes. However, any attempt to assess the role of the EP in comparison to the role of national parliaments in external relations policy-making is complicated by two factors: firstly, the division of executive powers across the Council and the Commission; and secondly, the arrangements that place some dimensions of the international identity under the auspices of the founding treaties and other dimensions outside. The inter-governmental arrangements outside the treaties, European Political Co-operation now succeeded by the Common Foreign and Security Policy, cast the Parliament in a different relationship in the policy-making process. The relationship between the Parliament, the Council of Ministers and the Commission does not reflect the normal arrangements of parliamentary systems of government. The party-political composition of the Parliament does not determine the Council, and indeed the Parliament has no power to dissolve the Council of Ministers. As noted above, the power to dissolve does extend to the Commission but has not been exercised.

A more useful approach is to view the EP as both being both engaged in the process of the construction and representation of the international identity of the Union and in its own foreign policy and the representation of that policy. Chapter 5, dealing with the assent procedure for accession, association and other forms of international agreement, showed that no such agreement can be concluded without the assent of the Parliament. The ratification of the accession of new Member States is a power that also has to be exercised by the parliaments of the Member States. The EP's Rules of Procedure require that two debates in plenary session are held on Accession and Association Agreements. The first debate is intended to be held before the negotiations take place by offering an opinion to the Commission that has been granted the negotiating mandate from the Council. In second plenary debate the EP gives its assent to international agreements. The European Parliament acts by a simple majority of those voting, except that the accession of new states requires an absolute majority of MEPs.

The vote on the Accession Treaties for Austria, Finland, Sweden and Norway (the last of whom rejected membership in a referendum) required a vote of 260 of the then 518 MEPs in favour. The context of the vote, on 4 May 1994, illustrates the extent to which intra-Union developments, and the EP's support for a deepening of the formal integration process, can potentially impact upon the international identity. Two issues dominated the enlargement assent debate: firstly, the vote took place very late in the parliamentary term, with elections due in June 1994 and with one-third of MEPs either standing down, or expected to lose their seats. There were concerns that there would be an insufficient number of MEP's in attendance in Strasbourg for the vote.[20] Secondly, there was the 'Ioannina compromise'. This was an agreement among the Foreign Ministers of the Member States to mitigate the impact of changes in Qualified Majority Voting that would be created by the enlargement of the Union. The enlargement, then envisaging that all four new states would accede, required an increase in the number of votes distributed for the purposes of QMV from 76 pre-enlargement to 90 thereafter. This would require the threshold required to block legislation to be raised from 23 votes to 27. Objections by the United Kingdom and Spain to the relative dilution of their votes led to a compromise whereby, if there were between 23 and 26 votes in the blocking minority, then a delay would be allowed to facilitate the search for a consensus rather than pushing matters to a vote in the Council. More than 100 MEPs signed a motion attempting to block the accession because of objections to the compromise as dilution of supranationalism. Chancellor Kohl, as President of the Union, offered the Parliament a substantial concession to approve the vote: involvement in the 1996 Intergovernmental Conference which had been denied the EP in previous IGCs.[21] All of the accession agreements were subsequently approved.[22]

Parliament has used the assent procedure to demonstrate its displeasure with the domestic policies of third parties since it first exercised the power of assent on international agreements in September 1987.[23] In December 1987 the Parliament postponed voting on two protocols under the Association Agreement with Turkey in protest at the arrest of a number of politicians in Turkey, and in March 1988 the EP refused to assent to three agreements with Israel.[24] More recently, the Parliament has frozen protocols containing aid provisions for Morocco, because of failure to implement UN resolutions on the Western Sahara, and aid to Syria because of human rights concerns.[25]

Although the Parliament has no formal right to participate in the negotiation of Association or Trade Agreements, procedures have been adopted over time to keep the EP informed during the negotiation process. The 'Luns procedure' introduced briefing of the EP by the Commission, through the relevant EP committees during the negotiation process and then a briefing by the Council on the conclusion of the negotiations and prior to EP assent. The Council extended the procedure to encompass trade agreements under the 'Westerterp procedure'; the two procedures are collectively known as the 'Luns-Westerterp procedure'.[26] The lack of a direct role for the EP in the negotiation process is in contrast to the role of the EP in the implementation of Association Agreements.

The Association Agreements that the Union has concluded and that are currently in force have contained provisions for Joint Parliamentary Committees (JPCs). There are currently five JPCs in existence.[27] The EP provides a delegation of between 19 and 23 MEPs for the meetings with their third party counterparts and are described as forums to 'meet and exchange views'.[28]

Seventy MEPs are also members of the Joint Assembly of the Agreement between the African, Caribbean and Pacific States and the European Union (the Lomé Convention) that meets twice yearly. The Joint Assembly meetings are held alternately in the European Union and an ACP member state and are required to deliberate on all matters relating to ACP–EU co-operation. They are attended by the Development Commissioner and by a Minister from the Presidency-in-Office.[29] However, the agenda extends to encompass political matters.[30] The EP has used the Joint Assembly to express displeasure at political developments in ACP member states: the February 1994 Joint Assembly due to be held in Gabon was moved to Strasbourg after pressure from MEPs for its cancellation because of accusations of irregularities in the Gabonese election held in the previous November.[31]

The EP has also unilaterally established a network of Parliamentary delegations which are separate from the international agreements established between the Union and a third party. Twenty delegations are currently in existence, giving the EP a global coverage.[32] The delegations are used both for fact-finding and to discuss the questions of human rights and other political matters.[33] A number of the delegations have met on a sustained and regular basis with their parliamentary counterparts from their region of interest in forums that explore questions of common interest which encompass the content of both the CFSP and external economic relations.[34] The EP also maintains contacts with the organisations such as the UN and the GATT through special delegations. The Commission has accepted members of the European Parliament as members of its Community delegation to the GATT.[35]

The EP creates and maintains direct contacts with governments and Heads of State and makes its plenary sessions available to visiting Heads of State or other eminent persons for an address to MEPs. In recent years a variety of Heads of State have addressed the plenary sessions of the EP, including Presidents Carlos Menem, Vaclav Havel, Nelson Mandela and Virgilio Barco. The division of executive and legislative powers in the Union system and, in particular, the duality of Commission and Council roles in the representation of the Union creates a context in which the EP has a space to act on its own initiative and a set of procedures through which to conduct its own relations.

The EP conducts a great deal of its work through its 20 standing committees.[36] The primary function of these committees is to scrutinise legislation, but they also generate their own reports and question the President-in-Office of the Council. The Committees draw up reports entrusted to a rapporteur, and when passed by the Committee and considered in a plenary session, the rapporteur acts as the Committee's spokesperson. Reports are considered in one of the 11 plenary sessions per year. Three committees are of particular interest for the construction and representation of the international identity: Committee C1, the Committee of Foreign Affairs, Security and Defence Policy, which has two permanent subcommittees, one on security and disarmament and another on human rights; C6, the Committee on External Economic Relations; and Committee C13, the Committee on Development and Co-operation. The work of the Committee on Foreign Affairs and Security is illustrative. The Committee meets for two days each month (excepting August), and its agenda encompasses a variety of activities including a quarterly colloquy, an exchange of views with the Presidency-in-Office on CFSP matters, meetings with the EU representative to the former Yugoslavia;

and meetings with government ministers and representatives of peoples from third countries.[37]

The Committee considers reports produced under its auspices by its own rapporteurs, that are the basis for Resolutions submitted to the plenary session of the Parliament, and exchanges views with its two permanent subcommittees. The Committee also plays a role in the legislative process of the EP for international agreements.

The inter-related work of the Committee structure of the EP in the assent procedure can be illustrated by the Association Agreement signed with Hungary.[38] The Council formally consulted the Parliament through a letter recommending assent. The President of the Parliament referred the recommendation to the Committee on Foreign Affairs as the committee responsible, and additionally referred it to nine other committees that ranged from the Committee on Transport and Tourism to the Committee on Culture, Youth Education and the Media. The wide-ranging content of the Articles of the Association Agreement encompassed all Committees' subject areas. All of these nine committees produced opinions that were conveyed to the Committee on Foreign Affairs and Security, which were then attached to the latter's report and conveyed to the plenary session of Parliament, which then gave its assent to the conclusion of the Agreement.

The Committee on Foreign Affairs and Security of the EP represents the forum in which the role of the Parliament in the legislative process required of international agreements is most extensive. However, the work of the Committee on Foreign Affairs and Security extends to CFSP, and it is the Parliamentary committee that is responsible for the Parliament's role in the Common Foreign and Security Policy. It is to a consideration of the EP's role in the CFSP that we now turn.

THE EUROPEAN PARLIAMENT AND THE COMMON FOREIGN AND SECURITY POLICY

As was noted above, the EP can use its formal powers in the budget and the assent processes to impact upon the construction of the international identity. Furthermore, the EP has created the parliamentary delegation as an instrument with which to conduct its own involvement in international affairs. The investigative processes by the EP committees, and subcommittees, especially in the field of human rights, have been used in an attempt to enforce human rights standards.[39] These measures are often not welcomed by the third country and have been described as unacceptable interferences in the country's internal affairs by their targets.[40] The progressive attempts by the European Parliament to involve itself in the EPC, and now the CFSP process, have on occasion met a similar response from the Member States, as well as their national parliaments, viewing the Parliament's actions as encroaching on their own powers.[41] The assumption is that national sovereignty is exercised through foreign policy, and any shift of power from the national institutions to a European supranational institution threatens that sovereignty and the democratic process within the Member States.[42] The recently expressed view of the European Parliament is that the parliaments of the Member States are unable to give effective oversight to the process because their domain covers only one of the Member State governments.[43] Indeed, even in providing oversight of their own government's foreign policy Member State parliaments may be ill equipped.[44] The European Parliament, by contrast, devotes considerable time and energy to foreign affairs, understood as the contents of the CFSP process, an area in which its formal powers are in fact marginal.

A previous study of the role of the European Parliament in shaping the foreign policy of the EPC process from its initiation until 1990 concluded that the role of the EP, through its questions and resolutions submitted to foreign ministers in their regular meetings, have 'no quantifiable impact in terms of legislation or policy initiatives'.[45]

Since 1990 the role of the EP in EPC, and its successor CFSP, has increased in an incremental fashion. However, the role of the EP remains marginal. The role of the EP within EPC/CFSP follows a similar pattern to that which was charted in the development of EPC in Chapter 3.

The Luxembourg Report on the problems of political unification stated that the EP 'must be associated with the construction of the political union so as to ensure that it is a democratic process' and provided for an annual progress report by the President-in-Office to the EP.[46] In the area of EPC the Report provided for six-monthly informal meetings between the Member State Foreign Ministers and the Political Affairs Committee (the predecessor of the Committee on Foreign Affairs, Security and Defence Policy) of the EP, in order to ensure that both MEPs and Ministers could express their views freely.[47] The Copenhagen Report did not result in any substantial change to the role of Parliament; it only increased the meetings between the EP and Foreign Ministers from two to four. The introduction of a new procedure notifying the Political Affairs Committee in advance of the main subjects for discussions improved communications on foreign policy issues between the Political Affairs Committee and Foreign Ministers. This coincided with the improvement of the role of the Parliament in negotiating international agreements with the introduction of the Luns-Westerterp procedure in 1973.

From the perspective of the EP, the Luxembourg and the Copenhagen Reports had the merit of linking the EP with the EPC process. However, the Luxembourg and the Copenhagen Reports presented obstacles to the Parliament playing a full role in the process. The meetings held with the Political Affairs Committee took place after the topics had been already fully discussed at ministerial level, and therefore limited any influence that the EP might play in the process. Although the main issues were notified in advance, the EP Political Affairs Committee could only report to the session of the European Parliament following the meeting and before the EP meeting in plenary could express its views on a specific subject.[48] Therefore the European Parliament was not genuinely consulted, but rather informed as to the latest developments.

The EP continued to press for an enhanced role in the decision-making process for international agreements as a way of strengthening the democracy of the Community system.[49] At the 1974 meeting of Heads of Government and State in Paris, the Member States agreed to grant the Parliament the right to have questions asked by the Members of the European Parliament on specific EPC matters answered by the President or Foreign Minister of the President-in-Office.[50]

The practice that has evolved from this date and continues into the CFSP process is for the Foreign Minister of the President-in-Office to reply to oral questions for 20 minutes during each of the Parliament's 10 annual plenary sessions. If the 20 minutes expires, then replies may be given in writing and attached as an annex to the report of the debate. The responses to written questions are drafted by the CFSP Secretariat and sent to the Presidency, then cleared through all Member States over the COREU network, before being released to the Parliament.

In June 1979 the first direct elections for the European Parliament enhanced the argument that the EP possessed both a mandate and a legitimisation for playing an active and a deeper role in the Community decision-making process. Furthermore, this was seen to strengthen the arguments of the EP for a greater influence in the development of EPC.[51] The Parliament continued to argue for an enhanced role in EPC both before and after the commencement of direct elections. The EP expressed its view through the passage of several Resolutions, including the Blumenfeld Report of 1978 and the Elles Report of 1981.[52] In the Resolution on the latter report, the Parliament urged that measures should be taken to improve contacts between the Foreign Ministers and the European Parliament by holding regular colloquies and 'improving the quality and speed of answers to Parliament's questions concerning European political co-operation'.[53]

The Solemn Declaration adopted by the Heads of State and Government in Stuttgart on 19 June 1981 in its passage on the European Parliament acknowledged that 'The European Parliament debates all matters relating to European Union, including European Political Co-operation'.[54] The Solemn Declaration then went on to codify the existing practices of the EP in the EPC process that was to be detailed in the London Report of October the same year.

A number of suggestions that the EP had previously made were to be later adopted by the Member States. As was noted in Chapter 4, the London Report of 1981 accepted the view held by the EP that the Commission had to be associated with EPC activities at all levels, and introduced the 48-hour emergency meeting procedure.[55] The London Report of 1981 acknowledged the principles set out in the Solemn Declaration that at the end of every meeting of the European Council, the President of the Council would report to the EP on the meeting and this statement would include the political cooperation topics discussed at the meeting. The role of the European Parliament in EPC was also reinforced with the setting up of informal meetings between ministers and leaders of the political groupings of the European Parliament for an informal exchange of ideas.

The Report also confirmed that the speeches given by each Presidency at the end of its term of office to the Plenary session of the Parliament usually contained EPC matters and operated, alongside the annual report on political co-operation to the Plenary, and the four annual colloquies with the Political Committee, to keep the EP associated with EPC.[56] From their perspective, the Foreign Ministers acknowledged:

> Taking account of the need to further strengthen ties with the directly-elected Parliament, the Ten envisaged the possibility of more frequent reference to resolutions adopted by Parliament in the deliberations, communiqués and declarations of the Ten, and in ministers opening statements at colloquies with the Political Affairs Committee of Parliament.[57]

The 1984 Draft Treaty on European Union passed by the Parliament encouraged the Member States to make some further progress towards European integration. The eventual outcome of the Member States' deliberations, the Single European Act, enhanced the EP's powers in the areas of assent and formally institutionalised EPC and the EP's role within the process.

As was outlined in Chapter 3, the SEA essentially codified existing EPC practice. The SEA reconfirmed the role of the EP in EPC but did not extend its involvement, and merely stated that the Member States shall ensure that the European Parliament is closely associated with European Political Cooperation. To that end the Presidency shall regularly inform the European Parliament of the foreign policy issues which are being examined within the framework of Political Co-operation and shall ensure that the views of the European Parliament are duly taken into consideration.[58]

The establishment of a EPC Secretariat also greatly contributed to improved communication between Parliament and the Foreign Ministers through a structure for handling written questions noted above. However, as one participant in the process has noted, the quality of the rotating six-monthly Presidency is crucial to the involvement that the Parliament had in the EPC process, and enjoys under the CFSP:

Parliament cannot oblige the Foreign Minister of the Presidency to be present at topical debates on foreign policy questions. The resolutions on EPC matters passed by Parliament only rarely have a direct influence on EPC, the value of the three monthly *colloque* with the Political Affairs Committee of Parliament depends on the approach and personal commitment of the Presidency who is the Committee's interlocutor.[59]

Unsurprisingly, the EP continued to push in its Resolutions for the unification of the EPC and the Community structures.[60] The TEU confirmed the rights of the EP to be regularly informed by the Presidency on foreign policy and to have its views taken note of:

The Presidency shall consult the European Parliament on the main aspects and the basic choices of the common foreign and security policy and shall ensure that the views of the European Parliament are duly taken into consideration. The European Parliament shall be kept regularly informed by the Presidency and the Commission of the development of the Union's foreign and security policy.[61]

The Parliament retains the structures and the provisions that have previously existed for EPC but these have not provided effective means of oversight of the process in the past.[62] The TEU included a provision that the EP should 'hold an annual debate on progress in implementing the common foreign and security policy'.[63] The Committee on Foreign Affairs, Security and Defence Policy produced a report as the basis for the Plenary debate that details the current view of the Parliament on its role in the CFSP.[64] The Committee itself had pressed for greater contact than the two existing quarterly colloquies with the Presidency.[65]

The Committee report noted that the EP had been kept informed by the Council and the Commission on developments in the CFSP but received this information too late.[66] The Committee went on to note that, contrary to the requirements of the CFSP, the EP had not been consulted on the main aspects or basic choices of the CFSP or on any proposals for joint action and therefore had little control over CFSP implementation.

The EP has sought to involve itself in the implementation of the CFSP since its foundation. In one of the first Joint Actions, the despatch of monitors to the Russian elections, the EP asked to be associated and was involved.[67] The Committee on Foreign Affairs was informed of the Joint Action after it had been agreed by the Council and the urged the involvement of the EP on the Council.[68] The EP itself had actually pre-empted the instruments first used under the CFSP with the despatch of its own election observers to over 30 countries during its last session before the TEU came into force.[69]

CONCLUSION

The scope of this chapter was not to provide a fully comprehensive historical and institutional analysis of the development of the powers of the European Parliament (EP), but rather the focus was upon the relevance of the Parliament as a one of the sources that contribute to the international identity of the European Union.

The future role of the European Parliament in foreign policy may well depend upon the results of Treaty revision which was to take place in 1996. As has been charted below, during the past 10 years the Parliament has fought to increase its involvement in both the external relations and the EPC/CFSP structures. The EP has sought to create its own diplomacy through the creation of parliamentary delegations but has also given these measures a particular tenor since May 1986 with an intensified commitment to the respect of human rights in the world. It has thereby contributed to the formulation of joint policies of the Member States in this area. Through an increase in the amount of written and oral questions submitted to the Presidency-in-Office the impact of the EP in foreign policy has been, at best, indirect. However, the EP has been both more aware and more willing than the Member States to use the economic significance of the Union to help achieve policy objectives.

NOTES AND REFERENCES

1. 'Report on progress made in implementing the common foreign and security policy (November 1993–December 1994) of the Committee on Foreign Affairs, Security and Defence Policy', *European Parliament Session Documents*, 24 April 1995, DOC EN\RR\272\27340.
2. The literature on comparative roles of Parliaments in recent years is minimal; see: C. Carstairs and R. Ware (eds), *Parliament and International Relations* (Buckingham, Open University Press, 1991).

   The involvement of individual legislatures in the making of their state's foreign policy abound and are to be found in a single-state case studies; see, for example, the literature on American foreign policy making; C.W. Kegley and E.R. Wittkopf, *American Foreign Policy: Pattern and Process*, 4th edn (New York, St Martin's Press, 1991).
3. See, for example: J. Pinder, *European Community: The Building of a Union* (Oxford, Oxford University Press, 1995), chapter 2.
4. E. Wistrich, *The United States of Europe* (London, Routledge, 1994), p.42.
5. S. Mengelberg, 'The European Parliament and the Ratification of the Maastricht Treaty', in F. Laursen and S. Vanhoonacker, *The Ratification of the Maastricht Treaty* (Dordrecht, Martinus Nijhoff, 1994), p.279.
6. See, for example, the coverage of the *Financial Times*, 10 May 1994–14 June 1994. As illustrative, see: 'Right Makes Strong Gains on Continent', *Financial Times*, 13 June 1994, p.1; 'European Elections 1994', Supplement, *Financial Times*, 14 June 1994.
7. The average turn-out for the elections was 56.4% down on the previous elections in 1989. For a full breakdown of results by Member State, including contrasting figures with national elections, see: *The Economist*, 18 June 1994, pp.43–7.
8. The process is illustrated in Chapter 5 by Figure 5.3.
9. Now Article 144, *EC Treaty*.
10. Article 158, *EC Treaty*, as amended by the TEU, Article G(48).
11. A. Duff, J. Pinder and R. Pryce, *Maastricht and Beyond: Building the Union* (London, Routledge, 1994), p.207.
12. 'Resolution of the European Parliament on the 1994 Legislative Programme' and 'Joint Declaration of the European Parliament and the Commission on the 1994 Legislative Programme', *Bulletin of the European Union*, Supplement 1/94.
13. 'Euro-MPs Scrutinise Annual Share-out', *The European*, 10–16 December 1993, p.7.
14. *European Parliament News*, 14–18 November 1994, p.1.
15. 'Brussels Misjudgments have Cost Millions, Watchdog says', *Financial Times*, 27 November 1992, p.20; 'Auditors Count the Cost of Fraud', *The European*, 19–25 November 1993, p.7.
16. Article 137. For an illustration of this argument, see: R. Bieber, 'Democratic Control of European Foreign Policy', *European Journal of International Law* 1, 1/2 (1990): 148–173.

17. J. Elles, 'The Foreign Policy Role of the European Parliament', *The Washington Quarterly* 13, 4 (1990): 69–78.
18. 'Opinion of the Committee on Foreign Affairs and Security for the Committee on Institutional Affairs on the Treaty on European Union, 21 January 1992 in European Parliament', *Maastricht*, Luxembourg, 1992, p.23.
19. *Idem.*
20. 'May be delayed', *The Economist*, 23 April 1994, pp.32–7.
21. 'Kohl Seeks to Smooth Vote on Enlargement', *Financial Times*, 4 May 1994, p.2.
22. The Accession Agreements were approved as follows:
Norway: 374 For, 24 Against, 58 Abstentions
Austria: 374 For, 24 Against, 61 Abstentions
Finland: 377 For, 21 Against, 61 Abstentions
Sweden: 380 For, 21 Against, 60 Abstentions
23. *Official Journal of the European Communities* (1987), C281/92. The EP gave its assent to 10 protocols.
24. Bieber, *op. cit.:* 160.
25. *European Parliament News*, 10–14 February 1992, p.1.
26. Named after two Dutch Ministers of Foreign Affairs: M. Palmer, *The European Parliament: What it Is, What it Does, How it Works* (Oxford, Pergamon Press, 1981), p.49.
27. The JPC's are as follows:
EU – Turkey Joint Parliamentary Committee
EU – Cyprus Joint Parliamentary Committee
EU – Malta Joint Parliamentary Committee
EU – Poland Joint Parliamentary Committee
EU – Hungary Joint Parliamentary Committee
(European Parliament *List of Members* 13.3.1995).
28. Article 107 (Hungary) and Article 9 (Poland) European Agreements.
29. Article 32 of the Lomé IV Convention.
30. At the most recent Joint Assembly held in Dakar from 30 January to 3 February 1995 Resolutions were adopted on Angola, Gambia, Haiti, Mozambique, Rwanda, Sierra Leone, Somalia and Western Sahara; *The Courier*, No. 150 (March–April 1995), p.10.
31. *Agence Europe*, No. 6142 (6 January 1994), p.9, and No. 6143 (7 January 1994), p.6.
32. European Parliament, *List of Members*, 13 March 1995.
33. See, for example, the visit of the delegation for relations with China that met the Chinese Foreign Minister, Ministers of Agriculture and Trade and Chinese parliamentarians to discuss a range of issues including human rights, the resumption of nuclear testing and Tibet; *Agence Europe*, No. 6102 (6 November 1993), p.5.
34. See, for example, the European Parliament US Congress parliamentary meeting, the 42nd such gathering, held in Athens 13–15 January 1995, that discussed Partnership for Peace, peace process in the Middle East and former Yugoslavia, and EU-US trade relations on the audio-visual sector, civil aviation and NAFTA; *Agence Europe*, No. 6147 (13 January 1994).

35. At the GATT Conference of Ministers 5–7 December 1988 in Montreal. See Bieber, *op. cit.*: 169.
36. Detailed in European Parliament, *List of Members*, 13 March 1995.
37. See Committee on Foreign Affairs and Security, *Draft Agenda*, 2 July 1992, DOC EN\OJ\209\209004.
38. See Committee on Foreign Affairs and Security, 'Draft Report on the Conclusion of an Association Agreement between the European Economic Community and the Republic of Hungary', 13 July 1992, *European Parliament*, DOC EN\PR\210\210781.
39. Elles, *op. cit.*, p.72.
40. Abdellatif Filali, Morocco's Minister of European Affairs, quoted in *European Parliament News*, 10–14 February 1992, p.1.
41. J. Monar, 'The European Parliament as an Actor in the Sphere of EPC/CFSP', paper delivered to the conference *The Community, the Member States, Foreign Policy, Coming Together or Drifting Apart?* European Policy Unit, European University Institute, Badia Fiesolana, 1–3 July 1993.
42. A. Cassese (ed.), *Parliamentary Control over Foreign Policy* (Alphen aan den Rijn, Sijhoff & Noorhoff, 1980), p.158.
43. See note 1.
44. A recent case study of the foreign policy-making process of the United Kingdom has suggested that those parliamentarians who are devoted to, and indeed equipped to, oversee foreign policy are minimal; M. Clarke, *British External Policy-making in the 1990s* (London, Macmillan, 1992), chapter 5.
45. Elles, *op. cit.*, p.72.
46. *Bulletin of the European Communities* 11 (1970): 9–14 (hereafter *Bulletin*).
47. *Ibid.*, Part Two.
48. *Bulletin* 9 (1973): 14–21.
49. See, for example, the Vedel Report, *Bulletin, Supplement* 4/1972, para. 38.
50. S. Nuttall, 'The Institutional Network and the Instruments of Action', in R. Rummel (ed.), *Toward Political Union: Planning a Common Foreign and Security Policy in the European Community* (Boulder, Col., Westview Press, 1992), pp.55–76, p.57.
51. D. Millar, 'European Political Co-operation' in C. Carstairs, R. Ware (eds) *Parliament and International Relations* (Buckingham, Open University Press, 1991), pp.140–59.
52. EP resolution of 19 January 1978, OJEC No. C36/1978 of 13 February 1978, p.32, based on the Blumenfeld Report on European Political Co-operation; EP Resolution of 9 July 1981, OJEC No. C234 of 14 September 1981, p.67, based on Lady Elles – Report on European Political Co-operation and the Role of the European Parliament.
53. EP Resolution of 9 July 1981, *op. cit.*, pp.67–9.
54. *Bulletin* 6 (1983) pp.24–5, Point 2.3.2.
55. *Bulletin*, Supplement 3/81, pp.14–17.
56. *Ibid.*, Point 11.
57. *Ibid.*, Point 11, para 3.
58. Title III, Article 30.3(c), *SEA*.
59. Nuttall, *op. cit.*, p.57.
60. EP Resolution on the Intergovernmental Conference in the context of Parliament's strategy for European Union, 11 July 1990, Doc. A3-166/90.

61. TEU, Article J.7.
62. S. Nuttall, in A. Duff, J. Pinder and R. Pryce, *Maastricht and Beyond: Building the European Union* (London, Routledge, 1994).
63. TEU, Article J.7, para 2.
64. *European Parliament Session Documents*, op. cit.
65. *Agence Europe*, No. 6145 (10–11 January 1994), p.5.
66. *Ibid.*, Point 29.
67. *Agence Europe*, (24 November 1993), p.4. For details, see Chapter 3.
68. *Agence Europe*, No. 6121, (4 December 1993).
69. *Agence Europe*, No. 6189, (12 March 1994), p.6.

8 Conclusion

The main proposition of this text is that a new, distinctive and significant actor has entered the international arena. In charting the construction and representation of the international identity of the European Union the study has asserted the significance of the EU for contemporary international relations.

The European Union has become a significant international actor *without* transforming itself into a nation state. The reason for this state of affairs is that the international context within which the Union now operates, and the instruments available at its disposal, have undergone a convergence to create circumstances in which the relative significance of the Union has been enhanced. Furthermore, in asserting its international identity the Union has not supplanted the foreign policy or the instruments of diplomacy of the Member States. The instruments that are available to the European Union that were detailed in this text are common instruments, not single instruments. The EU instruments are supranational in that they are the outcome of a supranational decision-making and implementation process. The Member States contribute to this process rather than being supplanted by the process.

The use of the term 'international identity' required clarification and encompasses the operations of the European Union that are explicitly directed outwards from the Union. The international identity was conceived both in terms of those instruments that are available to the Union to give expression to policy, and furthermore, how elements of the Union that define its *sui generis* nature also contribute distinctive facets to its international identity.

The concept of international identity takes us beyond existing categorisations in the literature. The international identity is not a synonym for 'foreign policy' or 'external relations'. The broad agreement that foreign policy is a function of the nation state creates a circumstance in which the European Union can only be considered significant for international relations if it resembles the form and functions of a nation state. The text demonstrates the international significance of the Union without asserting that it has created the accoutrements of a nation state.

The use of the term 'international identity' also represents a departure from the conventions, within the literature, on maintaining a distinction between the Community's external competencies as governed by the founding treaties, in contrast to the Common Foreign and Security Policy, and its predecessor EPC, conducted among the Fifteen on an inter-governmental basis. In exploring the international identity of the European Union the analysis has been primarily empirical. The theoretical dimension of the study was explicitly outlined in Chapter 1. The focus upon the theoretical approaches demonstrated that the literature on the European Union could be broken down into two dimensions: firstly, against existing preconceived concepts of what are considered to constitute the significant actors for an understanding of international relations; and secondly, new conceptual categorisations to fit the case of the EU and as an attempt to measure the capability of the EU as an international actor.

A NEW, DISTINCTIVE ACTOR

The existing literature was found to be inadequate for considering the contemporary international significance of the Union. The context of the post-Cold War era and the tentative exploration of questions of defence have rendered the civilian power hypothesis obsolete as a comprehensive explanation for the international role of the Union. However, it was of utility in drawing attention to the wider European context as crucial for an understanding of the Union's contemporary significance. The Union's pursuit of integrative diplomacy would appear to be a legacy of a distinctive conception of the appropriate role for the Union in international affairs. The idea that the EU might be a superpower in the making was dismissed. Although the Member States of the Union collectively have considerable capabilities, the resource power of the Union, relative to the other putative superpowers, is rendered less significant by the nature of contemporary international relations. The relative decline of questions of 'high politics', the rise of economic diplomacy and a wider definition of the pre-requisites for security all enhance the international significance of the Union.

The difficulty of locating the Union within the confines of the literature on international relations provided a basis from which a distinctive approach was proposed whilst drawing upon existing insights gained from the literature. Instead of measuring the Union against pre-existent categories, its *sui generis* nature was accepted as a starting point, and, from that basis, it was proposed to explore the international significance of the Union through the instruments that the Union has at its disposal.

The introduction to this text stated that three inter-related assertions formed the substance of this study. Firstly, it was asserted that the operations of the European Union that are explicitly directed outwards from the

Union can be characterised as the 'international identity' of the Union and that the international identity was conceived in terms of those instruments that are available to the Union to give expression to policy. The second assertion was that the notion of the international identity of the Union requires the development of a framework to facilitate analysis, and a framework was offered, drawing upon the literature of international relations that provided a method for a unified consideration of all facets of the external policy of the Union. Finally, a consideration of the process, by which this international identity is both constructed and represented, required an assessment of the nature of that process and the identification of sources of influence that impact upon the process.

The approach adopted in this study was to treat the construction and representation of the international identity of the European Union as a problematic that was amenable to the application of systems thinking. The organisational framework was garnered from a theme within the literature of IR on foreign-policy decision-making. The systems approach did not attempt to explain the Union in its totality. Rather, by approaching a particular problem – the international role of the Union – it provided a method to organise a study to enhance understanding of the Union applicable in both the disciplines of international relations and European studies. The primary advantage of the methodology adopted was that it has offered the opportunity both to isolate, and to consider in totality, the sources of influence that impact upon the Union in its attempt to construct and represent its identity on the international scene.

The text explored the elements of the system; the operational environment, decision-making structure and the means of implementing the international identity. The instruments and sources of influence of the international identity of the European Union designated what factors are considered to be significant in accounting for the contemporary international identity of the Union. However, the main claim to original knowledge contained within this study is not methodological but empirical. The systems methodology was utilised to explore the initial assertion of this text that the European Union is a new and significant actor in the international system.

The centrepiece of this text was the exploration of the distinctive nature of the EU, which is the decision-making structure through which the Union asserts its international identity. The decision-making structure has not displaced the foreign ministries of the Member States of the Union, and throughout the supranational decision-making structure has been detailed stressing, not how the decision-making structures are replicating or duplicating traditional methods of diplomacy, but rather, how the EU decision-making structure contributes to the uniqueness of the EU as an international actor.

The outcome of the supranational decision-making process was the utilisation of an instrument and the manifestation of a decision to upgrade common interests through use of the Union. Chapter 3 charted how the EPC/CFSP process has been drawn progressively closer to the Community pillar. Throughout it has been demonstrated that it is possible to retain a conceptual and analytical distinctiveness of the Union from its Member States.

From the foundation of the European Coal and Steel Community (ECSC) in 1951 to the codification of European Union in 1993, the progressive development of instruments under the Community structure have given the Union the ability to operate internationally (and predate the development of EPC). By detailing the development and instruments for implementation within the EPC and the CFSP framework, the study has challenged the existent literature on EPC/CFSP which judges the process as a 'success' or 'failure' on the basis of those occasions on which the Member States co-ordinate their actions. It was demonstrated that the CFSP is actually a supranational decision-making process. More importantly, the process requires an understanding of a variety of sources of influence rather than reliance upon the characterising the CFSP as intergovernmental. Furthermore, it was demonstrated that in the implementation of joint actions the Union has acquired new and innovative instruments during the limited duration of its operation.

However, the Member States' perception of foreign policy as an area of 'high' politics continues and is exemplified by the Treaty on European Union. CFSP essentially operates via the existing structure of foreign ministries and embassies operated by the Member States. As signatories to the Treaty of Rome, the Member States of the EC ceded representation of economic issues in an international context to the EC but they have retained tight control over the Commission in this area and exercise the power of decision. The CFSP process represents a departure by moving beyond the economic strength of the EU to back up its foreign policy decisions and through the joint actions that were detailed. These measures have not displaced the actions and efforts of Member States but rather are reliant upon the Members as a primary source of influence and implementation.

A NEW AND SIGNIFICANT ACTOR

The changing international context has created a situation in which the instruments available to the Union have become increasingly significant in the post-Cold War era. The contention is that changes to the international context, within which the Union has operated, have blurred the distinctions within the Union between the integrative and inter-governmental dimensions of the international identity. Despite the co-existence of dual systems of decision-making, the Union has become a significant international actor without transforming itself into a nation state. The reason for this state of affairs is that the international context within which the Union now operates, and the instruments available at its disposal, have undergone a convergence to create circumstances in which the relative significance of the Union has been enhanced. The Union is in a curious circumstance in that it is the collective capabilities of the fifteen Member States of the Union that contribute to the international significance of the Union, yet the Union lacks the ability to fully transform, and to utilise, the capabilities of the Member States and thereby to put them fully at the disposal of the Union.

The international significance of the EU is not that it should be measured as a nation state writ large. The geographical, demographic, economic and diplomatic resources of the fifteen Member States of the Union contrast favourably with those of the other significant powers in the international system. The Union has also created a network of relations with third states that encompass both trade and political relations. Alongside the rise of the integrative diplomacy of the Union there has been the rise of regionalism and globalisation that have raised questions about the viability of the nation state as an appropriate form of political organisation. The rise of the international significance of the Union is therefore dependent upon both the measures that it has undertaken to enhance its own international identity but also the changed international context within which the Union operates.

In particular, within the European sub-system of the international system, the EU is undoubtedly the most significant actor. The Union is enmeshed within an institutionalisation in Europe, and is part of a wider informal integrative process, yet stands apart from the other institutions of the European sub-system. This is for two substantive reasons: firstly, because of the unique legal arrangements that the Union is both founded upon and has progressively developed; and secondly, because of the processes of integration that have taken place within the Union itself.

In considering the legal sources of influence that impact upon the construction and representation of the international identity of the Union there was a wider consideration than a purely institutional focus upon the European Court of Justice. It was demonstrated that the legal order of the Union has contributed a distinctive facet to its international identity and that the legal order of the European Union represents the single most important factor for the inadequacy of classifying the European Union as an international organisation. The treaties and other legal arrangements have created a distinctive legal order that governs and facilitates the conduct of the international relations of the Union. In pursuing policy under the Articles of the treaties, legislative acts are required to give effect to Union international agreements.

The focus upon Community law demonstrated that it must not be conceived of as a mere collection of international agreements, nor can it be viewed as a part or appendage of national legal systems. On the contrary, through the establishment of the Community, the Member States have limited their legislative sovereignty and in so doing have created a self-sufficient body of law that is binding on them and on their subjects. Yet at the same time the Community legal order and the national legal orders are interlocked and mutually dependent on one another. The legal dimension of the identity of the Union is separable, but not separate, from the Member States.

The intimate involvement of the Member States in the construction and representation of the international identity of the Union was demonstrated through the decision-making process. It was also outlined how the Member States represent substantive sources of influence through holding the office of the Presidency and through the foreign policy traditions that they bring to the Union. Of particular note was when the behaviour of these states is seen to be at variance with the other Member States and thereby both restraining the Union in its actions and enforcing an impression of disunity amongst the Member States to third-party observers. It was also demonstrated how the Member States themselves have used the Union as an instrument through which to pursue their own foreign policy objectives. This reinforced the argument that the processes of integration do not represent the displacement of one structure or set of arrangements by another but, rather, that institutions have undergone adaptation to serve the purposes of both Union membership and the retention of Member States' independence.

The distinctiveness of the EU as an international actor is also demonstrated through the role of the European Parliament. The European Parliament and its parliamentarians also illustrate the EU's distinctiveness from other international organisations. The European Parliament contributes a distinctive facet to the Union since it differs in important ways from the assemblies that exist in other international organisations. Furthermore, the aspirations and organisational structure of the Parliament outstrip the formal role that the Parliament enjoys in the policy-making process.

The future role of the European Parliament in foreign policy may well depend upon the results of Treaty revision which was to take place in 1996. The Member States of the Union may make further decisions about how to utilise or to project all of these capabilities to further the interests of the Union directly. The stand-point of this book has been that the Union has developed a set of instruments that are both distinctive and distinguishable from those deployed by the Member States.

The process of integration is only one contributing factor, among others, in comprehending the Union's international role. The idea that a comprehensive account of the international identity of the Union can be written from a purely integrationist standpoint is rejected. The point made was not that the logic of integration, or the methods of conceptualising integration, are flawed but rather, from the stand-point of seeking to assess the international presence of the Union, a focus upon a *process* of integration can only provide a partial account of the Union's international significance.

The contemporary reality is that the Union possesses a decision-making structure, instruments available at its disposal, and a set of sources that impact upon the construction and representation of the Union's interests in the international system. It has not been suggested that the Union has developed all the accoutrements of diplomacy. The Union has not displaced the arrangements of the Member States by creating a single permanently unified foreign ministry, or a single network of embassies, or permanent diplomats. There is the existence of a framework that is composed of elements specific to the Union and elements drawn from the Member States operating as facilitators and manifestations of the international identity of the European Union.

THE INSTRUMENTS OF THE INTERNATIONAL IDENTITY

The 'system of implementation' identified as necessary for actor capability has been characterised as a set of instruments that are available to the European Union. These instruments are not formally identified by the Union as its 'system of implementation', but provide a typology by which we might establish a framework to consider the extent to which the EU is fulfilling its aspiration to assert its international identity. A five-fold set of instruments available to the Union which provide manifestations of the international identity was identified – informational, procedural, declaratory, transference and overt. The examples cited to clarify the instruments at the disposal of the Union are intended to be indicative rather than exhaustive and simultaneously provide the opportunity for reflection upon the

Union's attempt to realise its aspiration to assert its identity on the international scene.

The 'decision-making system' of the two component parts of the EU's external relations remain separate but not separable. In the instance of the foreign economic policy of the EU the treaties demarcate areas of external competence for the Communities, expanding as the common policies of the Community themselves expand, and to which Member States subscribe as signatories of the treaties. In these areas of competence powers are formally granted by the Member States to be exercised on their behalf by the institutions and instruments of the Union as laid down in the treaties. The contemporary conduct of the external relations of the Community is marked by a number of factors. Firstly, under the auspices of various articles of the treaties the Community has created a network of relations of association, partnership and co-operation, or co-operation – the procedural dimension of the international identity of the Community. These relationships extend a variety of forms of privilege or preferential trading relationships together with different forms of institutionalised relations. Secondly, the Commission has created a number of instruments through which to conduct the competencies of the Union of both a financial and an overt nature. For example, the financial and technical assistance relationships that the Union has created with third countries or the incremental spread of Commission delegations in third countries. Thirdly, the Member States of the Union have sought to maintain a close control over the conduct of external relations of the Community through, for example, the operation of the Article 113 Committee and appeals to the European Court of Justice.

The other dimension of the international activities of the Union, the CFSP, is also notable for a number of reasons. Firstly, the Commission has been progressively permitted to participate in the work of EPC and shares rights of initiation under the CFSP. Secondly, the creation of common positions and joint actions provided for under the CFSP would appear to suggest that the Member States intend to go beyond the over-reliance upon the declaratory instrument that was the hallmark of EPC. Thirdly, the CFSP represents a rite-of-passage for the Union, in the breaking of the 'defence-as-security' taboo.

The breaking of this security taboo has also coincided with a major reconsideration of the notion of security which might to be said to place civilian forms of power in a more favourable terrain. The military, political, economic, societal and environmental sectors of security now all jostle for attention in the crowded market place of security.[1] In the light of such a transformation, it would appear that the separate consideration of the external relations and CFSP processes, both empirically and conceptually, would be at the cost of neglecting study of the factors, that are common to both sets of policies, and can lead to a failure in exploring conceptual frameworks that may accommodate both sets of processes and their contribution to the security of the Union. However, it is fully accepted that by retaining a distinction between these two sets of processes the Union does not use its influence to the greatest effect.

ASSERTING THE INTERNATIONAL IDENTITY?

The starting point of this study was to chart the birth of the European Union. The Treaty on European Union that came into force on 1 November 1993 established a three-pillar structure of the European Union that provided the new Union with a set of goals that included the 'assertion of its identity on the international scene'.[2]

The self-proclaimed aspirations of the Union have been measured against the reality of their realisation. The conflict in the territories of the former Yugoslavia has been used to demonstrate both the inability of the Union to cope with a conflict of such magnitude through its own efforts and also problems of decision-making in a system in which the Member States are a substantive source of influence. The EU can take little comfort from its involvement in the region and has been a secondary actor in the attempts at conflict resolution since the UN involvement at the end of 1991. A paradox exists in which the EU is the political actor of greatest significance in Europe yet is effectively marginalised in the resolution or the management of the conflict. The Yugoslav crisis has proved a salutary lesson in the development of the international identity of the Union and has contributed to the closure of the gap between the realisation of the capabilities of the Union and expectations made of it. The innovative instruments identified in this study that the European Union has utilised in the Yugoslav crisis have not mitigated the criticism of inaction and ineffectiveness that has been levelled at the Union. In short, there remains a gap between the expectations made of the Union and its capabilities.[3] The capabilities that are expected of the Union is that it can replicate the actions and instruments of the nation state as an actor in international relations.

It is not asserted that the Union is becoming a more significant actor in international relations through the adoption of state-as-actor characteristics. The typology of instruments that has been identified represent the output of a decision-making process, a process that is subject to a variety of sources of influence, and requires a framework of analysis capable of accommodating such complexity.

The attempts by the Union to assert its international identity have not required the construction of a single foreign policy infrastructure. The international significance of the Union is, in part, a consequence of its heterogeneous composition. Whether this makes for the most efficient projection of the international identity of the Union is a matter of no small significance. The thrust of this study is that what is needed is to clarify the framework and set of instruments available to the Union and then to make an assessment of its effectiveness.

With the debate on the future of the European Union already under way in the context of the 1996 Inter-governmental Conference of the Union any attempts that the Member States may undertake to add to the instruments at the disposal of the Union, provide an on-going programme of further research and assessment.[4] The enhancement of the CFSP is a primary consideration of these deliberations. As this study has demonstrated, under the CFSP the Union has tentatively gone beyond drawing upon existing Community strengths in the Joint Actions that it has undertaken thus far by seeking to create specific instruments to serve particular Joint Actions. Although these draw upon the resources of the Community and the Member States, they are explicitly for furthering the CFSP and, in turn, enhancing the international identity and represent an operationally tentative, but profoundly symbolic advance on EPC.

The work of the Group of Reflection that considered the appropriate agenda for the Inter-governmental Conference launched in 1996 asserted that the enhancement of 'External Union Action' should be a priority.[5] In considering the implementation of the CFSP, the Group of Reflection argued that the word 'implementation' in describing the external aspects of CFSP should be replaced by the descriptor 'administration'.[6] In seeking to provide a typology of instruments of implementation it is to be hoped that this study has contributed to the future study of administration.

NOTES AND REFERENCES

1. B. Buzan, *People, States and Fear*, 2nd edn (London, Harvester Wheatsheaf, 1991).
2. TEU, Title I Common Provisions, Article B.
3. C. Hill, 'The Capability-Expectations Gap, or Conceptualising Europe's International Role', *Journal of Common Market Studies* 31, 3 (September 1993): 305–28.

4. Article N.2 of the Treaty on European Union stated that 'a conference of representatives of the governments of the Member States shall be convened in 1996 to examine those provisions of this Treaty for which revision is provided'.
5. *Reflection Group's Report*, Brussels, 5 December 1995, SN 520/95 (REFLEX 21).
6. *Ibid.*, Point 154.

Index